> **RESTRICTED**
> The information given in this document is not to be communicated either directly or indirectly to the Press or to any person not authorised to receive it.

BRITISH ARMY OF THE RHINE

BATTLEFIELD TOUR

FIRST DAY

8 CORPS OPERATIONS EAST of CAEN, 18=21 JULY 1944
(OPERATION GOODWOOD)

The Naval & Military Press Ltd

JUNE 1947   Prepared under the direction of
G (Trg) HQ BRITISH ARMY of the RHINE

Published by

The Naval & Military Press Ltd
Unit 5 Riverside, Brambleside
Bellbrook Industrial Estate
Uckfield, East Sussex
TN22 1QQ England

Tel: +44 (0)1825 749494

www.naval-military-press.com
www.nmarchive.com

In reprinting in facsimile from the original, any imperfections are inevitably reproduced and the quality may fall short of modern type and cartographic standards.

THE OBJECT OF THE BOOK

This book describes the operations of the British Second Army, East of the River ORNE between 18 and 21 July 1944. It is especially concerned with the part played by 8 Corps in those operations. The aspects covered in the greatest detail are :—

(a) The plan for the concentration of 8 Corps before the Battle.

(b) The fire plan.

(c) The air plan.

(d) The operations of 11 Armd Div.

It forms the necessary background to a detailed study of the battle carried out on the ground.

Owing to discrepancies in the records from which the book was compiled some errors are inevitable. A final edition is being printed after the 1947 Tour and will incorporate such amendments or additions as are brought to light by officers who took part in the action.

CONTENTS

PART I. PLANNING THE OPERATION

		Page
Section I	Introduction	1
Section II	Topography	3
Section III	The Enemy	5
Section IV	Planning the Operation	9
A	The Object of the Operation	9
B	The Army Plan	9
C	The Corps Commander's Problems	11
D	The Corps Plan	11
E	The outline plans of the armoured divisions	13
Section V	Concentration before the Battle	15
Section VI	The RE Plan	19
Section VII	The Fire Plan	23
Section VIII	The Air Plan	27

PART II. ACCOUNT OF THE BATTLE

Section I	Events prior to the start of the Operation	33
Section II	Operations during the morning of 18 July	35
Section III	Operations during the afternoon of 18 July	41
Section IV	Operations during 19 July	49
Section V	Operations during 20 July	57
Section VI	Operations during 21 July	61
Section VII	Summary of Operation GOODWOOD	65

APPENDICES

A. Order of Battle	71
B. 8 Corps Operation Instruction No. 4 (less Appendices)	75
C. 11 Armd Div Operation Order No. 3 (less Appendices)	83
D. RA 8 Corps Operation Order No. 2 (including Appendix A showing RA Order of Battle)	87

MAPS

Part I

	Facing Page
No. 1. General situation in NORMANDY first light 18 July 1944	1
No. 2. Enemy dispositions East of the River ORNE before Operation GOODWOOD	5
No. 3. Operation GOODWOOD (planning map)	9
No. 4. Routes for concentration for the operation	15
No. 5. Concentration area East of the River ORNE	17
No. 6. The Fire Plan	23
No. 7. The Air Plan	27

Part II

No. 8. Opening of Operation GOODWOOD. Advance during the morning of 18 July 1944	35
No. 9. The advance continued—situation at 1200 hours 18 July 1944	37
No. 10. Situation at 2359 hours 18 July 1944	41
No. 11. Situation at 2359 hours 19 July 1944	49
No. 12. Situation at 2359 hours 20 July 1944	57
No. 13. Situation at 2359 hours 21 July 1944	61

Operation Goodwood 18–21 July 1944	Map at end

PART I

Planning the Operation

SECTION I

INTRODUCTION

The circumstances in which operation GOODWOOD was mounted and the objects which it was hoped that it would achieve are set out clearly in Field Marshall Viscount Montgomery's book "NORMANDY to the BALTIC." He writes :—

"The Situation, 18 July

"We were now on the threshold of great events. We were ready to break out of the bridgehead.

"We still firmly retained the initiative. We had prevented the enemy from switching further reinforcements to the Western flank and had forced him to commit again the armoured forces he had sought to withdraw into reserve. We had continued to punish the enemy severely and force him into what I call 'wet hen' tactics—rushing to and fro to stem our thrusts and plug the holes in his line.

"The sooner we got going on the Western flank the better, while the setting for the break-out remained favourable. Apart from the local conditions in NORMANDY, it seemed impossible that the enemy should continue much longer to anticipate an invasion in the PAS DE CALAIS; however great his anxiety for the safety of the flying bomb sites, he must surely soon give overriding priority to the NORMANDY battlefield, and when he took that decision substantial reinforcements would become available from Fifteenth Army.

"I have said how important it was to my plans that, once started, the break-out operation should maintain its momentum. It was therefore essential to ensure that the assault would make a clean break through the enemy defences facing the Americans, and that a corridor would be speedily opened through which armoured forces could be passed into the open country. To make sure of this, it was decided to seek heavy bomber assistance ; but because of the weather, the operation had to be progressively postponed until 25 July in order to obtain favourable flying conditions.

"Meanwhile, on the Eastern flank, offensive operations were sustained ; by 17 July 8 Corps was ready to begin the offensive East of the ORNE.

"The operations of 8 Corps between 18 and 21 July gave rise to a number of misunderstandings at the time. It was a battle for position, which was designed first to bring into play the full effect on the enemy of a direct and powerful threat to FALAISE and the open country to the East of the town, and secondly to secure ground on which major forces could be poised ready to strike out to the South and South-East, when the American break-out forces thrust Eastwards to meet them. I now believe that the misconception concerning this operation arose primarily because the forthcoming battle for position was in fact the prelude to operations of wider scope, which, when the time came, were to form part of the Allied drive to the SEINE. Added to this, the break-out operation by First United States Army was, for obvious reasons, being kept a close secret, and, since it was clearly time we broke the enemy cordon surrounding us, it was understandable that a major operation of this kind should suggest wider implications than in fact it had."

The attached map shows the situation in NORMANDY when the operation began on 18 July and the ground gained as a result of Operation GOODWOOD.

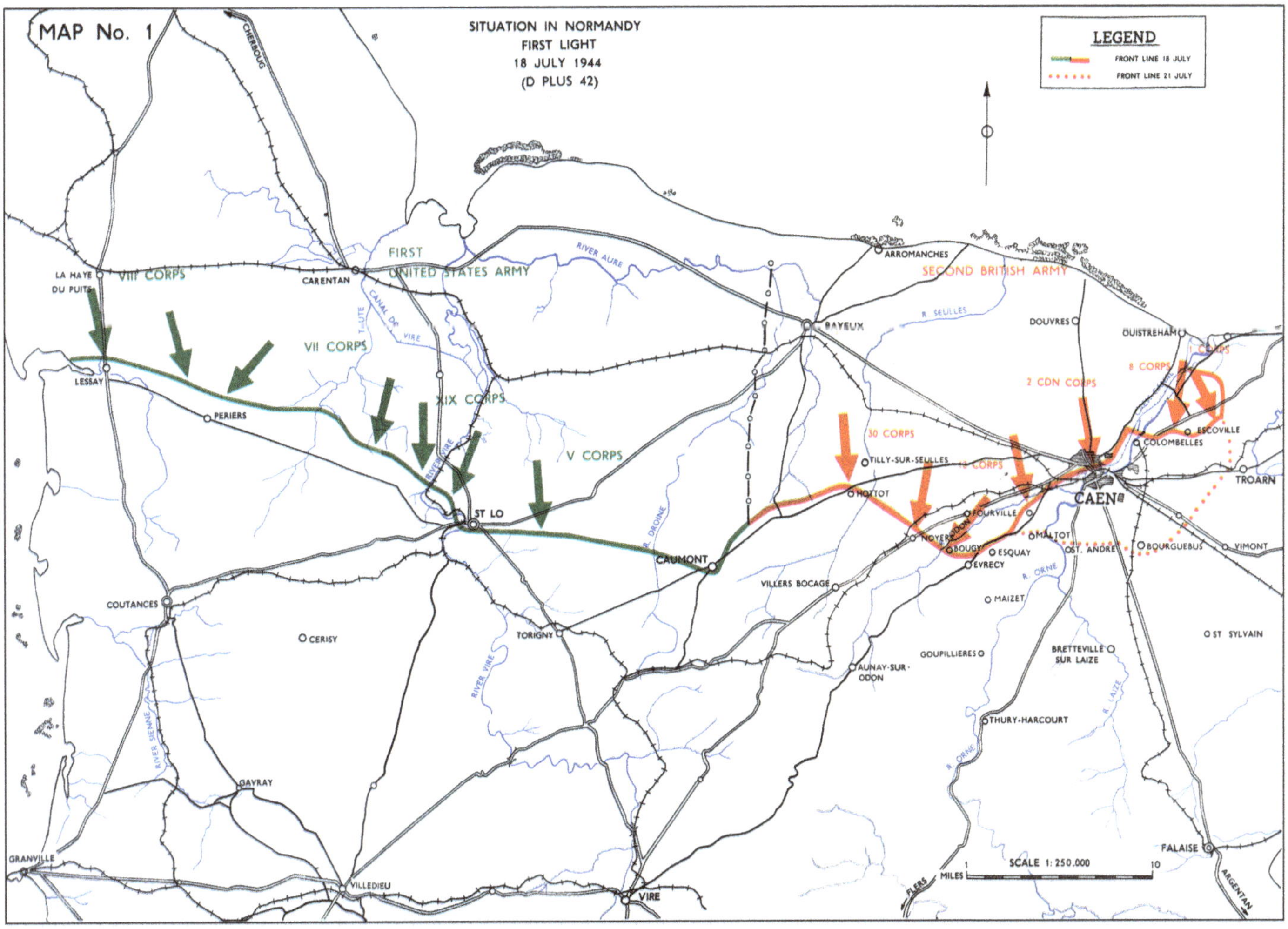
MAP No. 1
SITUATION IN NORMANDY
FIRST LIGHT
18 JULY 1944
(D PLUS 42)
LEGEND
FRONT LINE 18 JULY
FRONT LINE 21 JULY
CHERBOURG
FIRST UNITED STATES ARMY
SECOND BRITISH ARMY
VIII CORPS
VII CORPS
XIX CORPS
V CORPS
30 CORPS
12 CORPS
2 CDN CORPS
8 CORPS
1 CORPS
LA HAYE DU PUITS
CARENTAN
LESSAY
PERIERS
ST LO
CAUMONT
BAYEUX
ARROMANCHES
DOUVRES
OUISTREHAM
TILLY-SUR-SEULLES
HOTTOT
NOYERS
FOURVILLE
MALTOT
BOUGY
ESQUAY
EVRECY
CAEN
COLOMBELLES
ESCOVILLE
TROARN
BOURGUEBUS
VIMONT
ST. ANDRE
VILLERS BOCAGE
MAIZET
COUTANCES
CERISY
TORIGNY
AUNAY-SUR-ODON
GOUPILLIERES
BRETTEVILLE SUR LAIZE
ST SYLVAIN
THURY-HARCOURT
GAVRAY
GRANVILLE
VILLEDIEU
VIRE
FALAISE
ARGENTAN
FLERS
RIVER AURE
R. SEULLES
CANAL DE VIRE
RIVER VIRE
R. DROME
R. ORNE
R. LAIZE
RIVER SIENNE
MILES
SCALE 1: 250.000
10

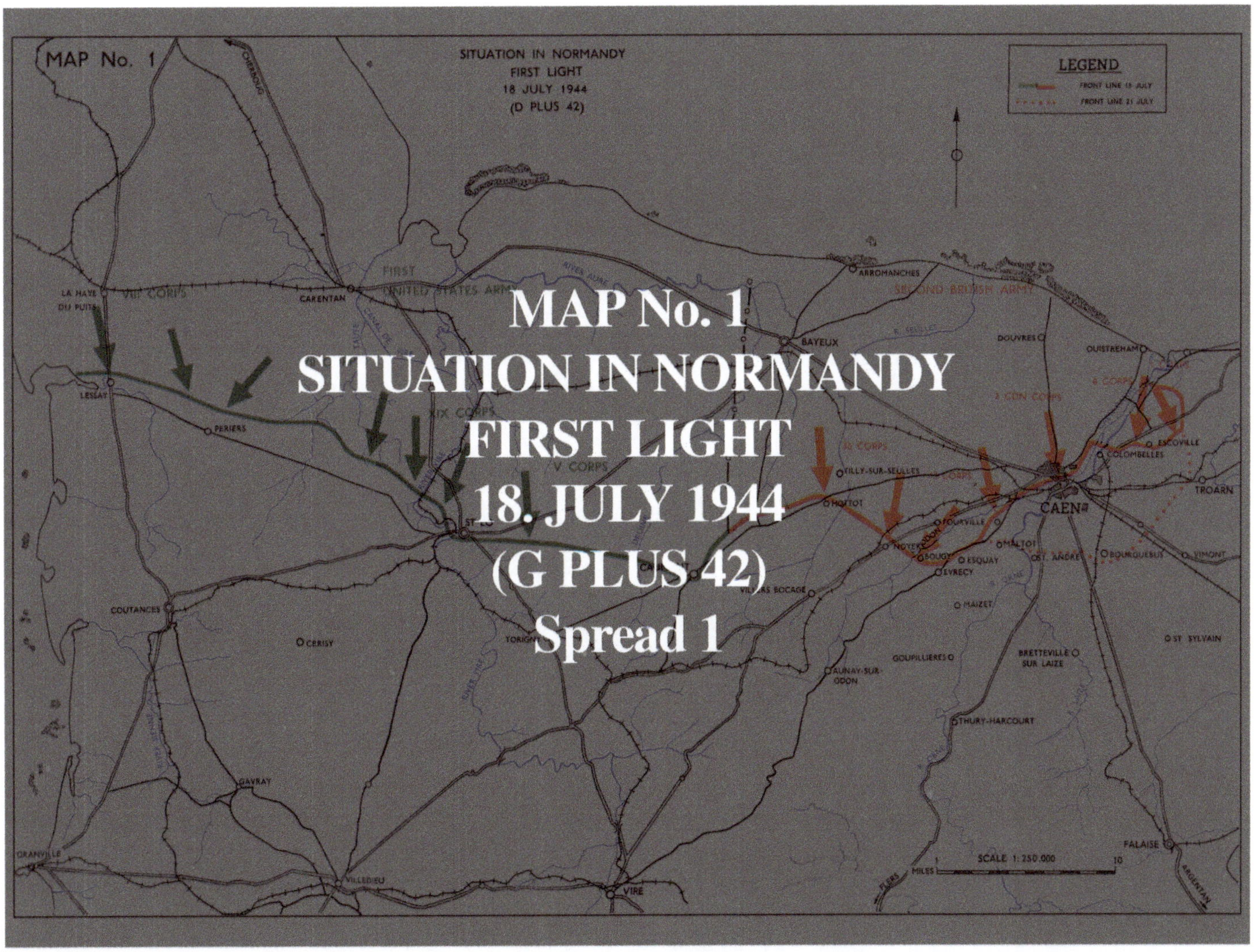
MAP No. 1
SITUATION IN NORMANDY
FIRST LIGHT
18. JULY 1944
(G PLUS 42)
Spread 1

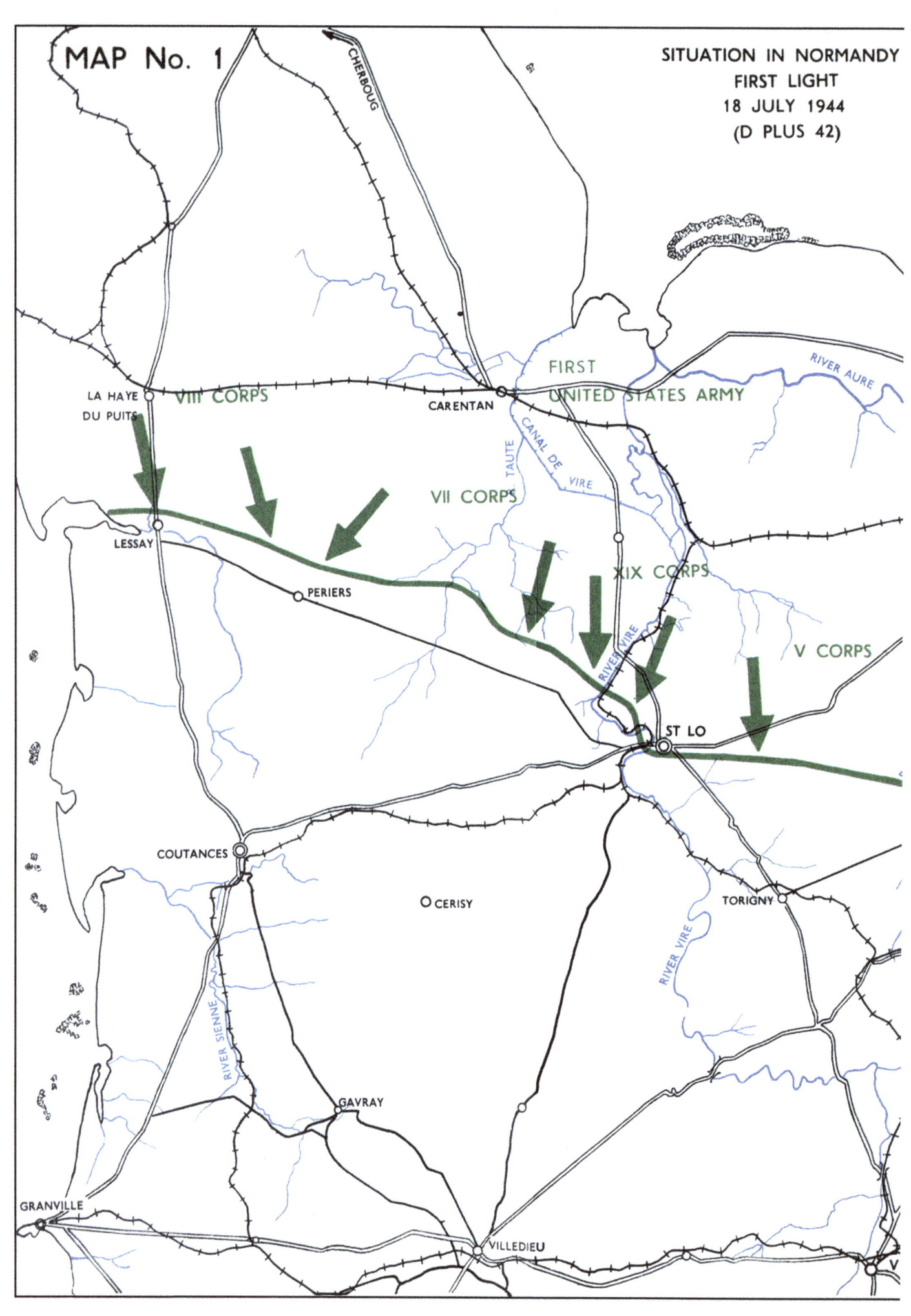

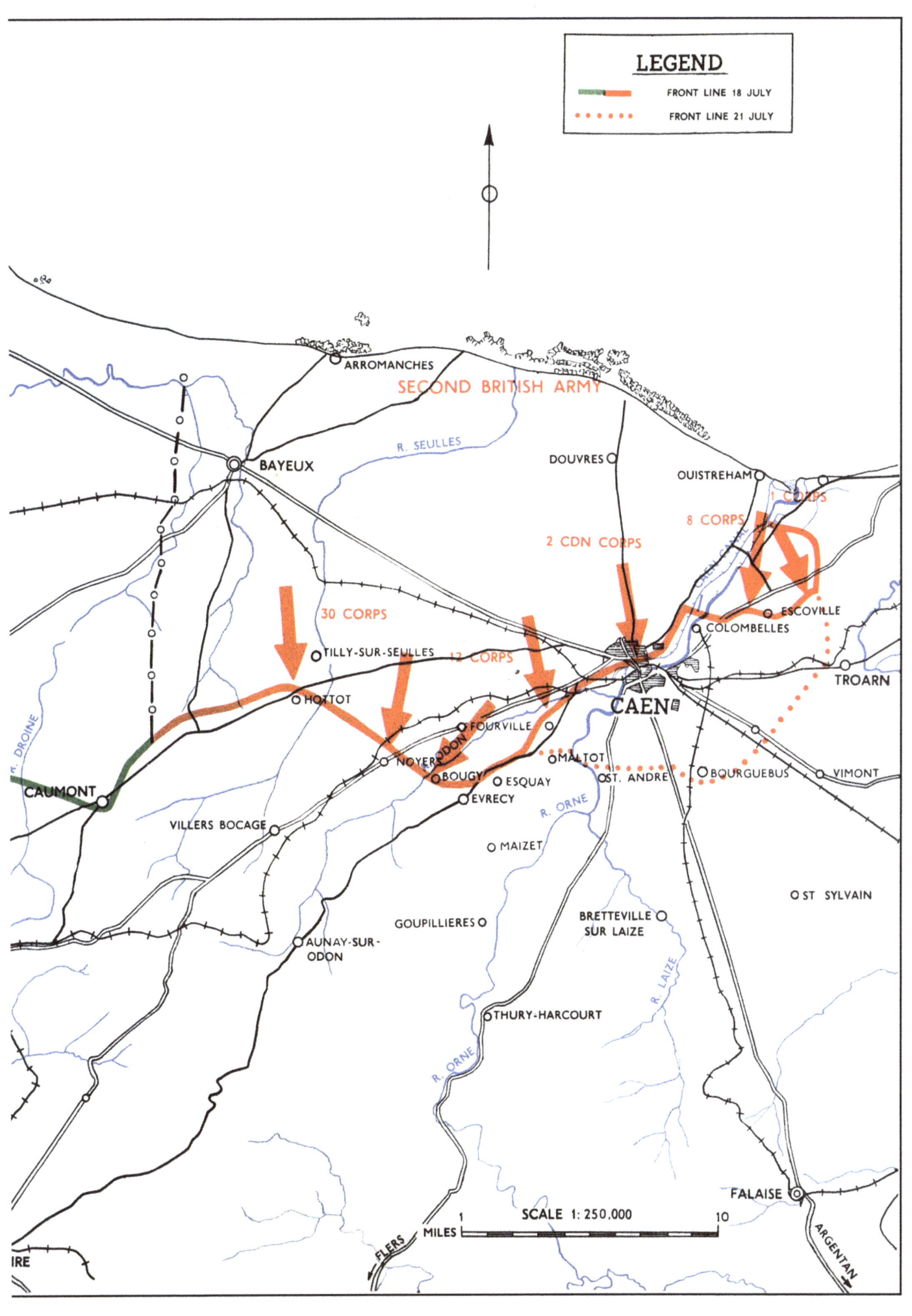

SECTION II

TOPOGRAPHY

On the main axis of the British advance the ground is agricultural and fairly open, and was studded at this time with a number of compact, well built stone villages, with their surrounding orchards, most of which were enclosed with stout fences or lines of large trees. Between the villages the ground is completely open with no banks or hedges and very few fences.

Crossing the line of advance at right angles are the roads CAEN-TROARN and CAEN-VIMONT. Both are main roads and, in a few places, are lined with trees: these do not present any obstacle to an advance.

Two railways also cross the front and run close, respectively, to these two roads. The first, CAEN-TROARN, is a single line and, for a large part of the distance, has six feet high embankments on both sides, which, during the battle, were found to be impassable to wheeled vehicles. The second railway, CAEN-VIMONT, runs alternatively along an embankment or through a deep cutting. In both cases the banks are ten feet or more high and, except in a few places, were considerable obstacles to tanks.

The ground rises slightly from the Start Line and then falls gently to the road and railway CAEN-TROARN. It then rises again in a series of slight undulations to the road BRAS-BOURGUEBUS-LA HOGUE and then again to the woods and villages TILLY LA CAMPAGNE-GARCELLES SECQUEVILLE-SECQUEVILLE LA CAMPAGNE. This high ground affords complete observation over almost the entire area of the advance, and, for the defender, permits long fields of fire, while the woods and villages give facilities for concealed movement.

The villages of BRAS, HUBERT FOLIE, BOURGUEBUS, LA HOGUE, SOLIERS GRENTHEVILLE and FOUR give a series of natural, mutually-supporting strong points, not more than 1,500 yards apart. In between, the country consists mainly of open cornfields: during the battle, the crops were shoulder high and it was hard to locate such field defences as were sited in the intervening ground.

The advance was made through a narrow corridor, bounded on the Right by the built up and factory areas of GIBERVILLE, MONDEVILLE and CORMELLES and, on the Left, by the BOIS DE BAVENT and the bocage country in the neighbourhood of TOUFFREVILLE, SANNERVILLE and BANNEVILLE LA CAMPAGNE. These areas command the country over which the advance was made, provide good observation and, for the attacker, restrict manoeuvre.

The setting for Operation GOODWOOD thus favoured the defence.

SECTION III

THE ENEMY

GENERAL

Since the capture on the 9 July of that part of CAEN which lies West of the River ORNE, the enemy had been sensitive about his Right flank. His position on this flank was the pivot for his whole NORMANDY front : if it gave way, his front would collapse and a break through by Second Army towards FALAISE would cut off his forces further West.

He therefore had reason to suppose that Second Army might launch an attack on this front, with a view to a break-out to the South and that this attack might be either East or West of the ORNE. He was able to observe from his own positions part of the bridgehead East of the river and would doubtless expect some warning of any large scale British concentration.

Since D Day the enemy had been given little respite anywhere on the front and had found it difficult to disengage his Panzer Divisions to form an adequate reserve of armour. On the Second Army front he had managed, however, by 15 July, to withdraw from the line both 1 SS Pz Div (ADOLF HITLER) and 12 SS Pz Div (HITLER JUGEND). 9 and 10 SS Pz Divs were committed West of the River ORNE.

When, on 15 and 16 July, 12 and 30 Corps attacked West of the ORNE, the enemy's attention was naturally focussed there, but, after 48 hours, neither 1 nor 12 SS Pz Divs had put in an appearance.

ENEMY DISPOSITIONS EAST OF THE RIVER ORNE

According to our Intelligence, at the start of Operation GOODWOOD, the enemy dispositions were as follows :—

On the Left with its Left boundary resting on the river was 16 GAF Div. This division was deployed with two regiments in the line, 32 and 46 GAF Regts. It had been involved in the battle for CAEN some two weeks earlier, had fought hard and had suffered some casualties. The strength of the two regiments in the line was estimated at 900 men each : 31 GAF Regt in reserve was thought to be 300 strong, and the reserve probably also included 16 GAF Fus Bn.

It was believed that elements of another division were helping to hold FAUBOURG DE VAUCELLES. There had been no reliable identifications to indicate which division this might be, but it was variously forecast as 192 PGR or Battle Group LUCK, both of 21 Pz Div, or, less likely, as part of a Panzer Grenadier Regiment of 12 SS Pz Div. In the event, it was found to be part of 272 Inf Div, a new arrival on the NORMANDY front which had been expected for some days.

On the Right of 16 GAF Div and with its Left boundary probably along the road ESCOVILLE–TROARN, was thought to be 346 Inf Div, with five out of the eight battalions in the line. The two infantry regiments of this division, 857 and 858, had been in the area since D Day, had suffered heavy losses but had been reinforced. They were now said to be about 1,400 men strong each, and to be supported by 346 Fus Bn with about 400 men. Artillery resources of this division included two 75 mm anti-tank companies and one Flak company.

On the Right of 346 Div and covering the sector to the coast was said to be 711 Inf Div. This formation had originally been employed on coastal defence between the rivers DIVES and SEINE. Most of the division was believed to be East of the DIVES with probably only two battalions of 744 GR (combined strength of 500 men) on the West side of the river.

The immediate armoured reserve was provided by 21 Pz Div, which was believed to be concentrated mainly in the area of ARGENCES and VIMONT with elements possibly as far West as CAGNY, and a likelihood of Battle Group LUCK being in FAUBOURG DE VAUCELLES. The two Panzer Grenadier Regiments of this division, 125 and 192, were thought to have a combined strength of about twelve to thirteen hundred men. 22 Pz Regt could contribute up to fifty Pz Kw IVs. In the way of artillery, figures quoted included thirty to forty anti-aircraft and anti-tank guns (between 50 mm and 88 mm), twenty-five field or medium guns and thirty-five assault guns. Generally, this division might be expected to be a fairly formidable opponent. The Commander of 21 Pz Div (General EDGAR FEUCHTINGER) when interrogated by Canadian Historical Officers in August 1945, stated :—

MAP 2
APPRECIATED ENEMY DISPOSITIONS
EAST OF THE RIVER ORNE
FIRST LIGHT 18 JULY
LEGEND
ENEMY GUN AREAS
OTHER ENEMY POSITIONS
FIGURES IN SQUARE BRACKETS SHOW ESTIMATED NUMBER OF GUNS
HERMANVILLE-SUR-MER
OUISTREHAM
CABOURG
COASTAL GUNS
FRANCEVILLE-PLAGE
COASTAL GUNS
711 DIV
DIVES-SUR-MER
III/744
WEST OF R. DIVES
SALLENELLES
[12 - 24]
BRUCOURT
BENOUVILLE
BEUVILLE
346 FUS BN
BREVILLE
BAVENT
RANVILLE
HEROUVILLETTE
III/858 GR
CAEN CANAL
[12 . 24]
LONGUEVAL
346 DIV
ESCOVILLE
III/857 GR
BOIS DE BAVENT
COLOMBELLES
PRE BARON
ST. HONORINE
I AND II 857
II/858
1/32 GAFR
CUVERVILLE
1/46 GAFR
P6420 BN UNLOCATED IN RES
16 GAF DIV
REMNANTS 31 GAFR
II/46 GAFR
16 GAF FUS BN
UNLOCATED IN RES
CARPIQUET
GIBERVILLE
DEMOUVILLE
LIROSE
SANNERVILLE
BANNEVILLE LA CAMPAGNE
TROARN
86 CORPS
CAEN
[40]
MONDEVILLE
FAUBOURG DE VAUCELLES
EMIEVILLE
LE QUAI
JAUVILLE
LOUVIGNY
FACTORY
LE MESNIL-FREMENTEL
CUILLERVILLE
PONT DE JANVILLE
ETERVILLE
FLEURY SUR ORNE
CORMELLES
ELTS 12 SS PZ DIV OR BATTLE GP LUCK
GRENTHEVILLE
CAGNY
PONTS DE LA RAMEE
[12 - 24]
1 SS PZ DIV
BASSE
IFS
BRAS
SOLIERS
21 PZ DIV
[20]
FOUR
HUBERT-FOLIE
FRENOUVILLE
ST ANDRE-SUR-ORNE
BEAUVOIR FE
PT. 72
ARGENCES
VIMONT
BOURGEBUS
VERRIERES
TILLY-LA-CAMPAGNE
LA HOGUE
BELLENGREVILLE
9 AND 10 SS PZ DIVS
MAY-SUR-ORNE
SECQUEVILLE
I SS PZ CORPS
CHICHEBOVILLE
LA CAMPAGNE
ROCQUANCOURT
[100]
GARCELLES SECQUEVILLE
FONTENAY-LE-MARMION
CRAMESNIL
PT. 122
ST. AIGNAN DE CRAMESNIL
12 SS PZ DIV FURTHER SOUTH
CLINCHAMPS SUR-ORNE
[10 HEAVY]
R. MUANCE
MEZIDON
CINTHEAUX
ST. SYLVAIN
FORET DE GRIMBOSQ
BRETTEVILLE SUR LAIZE
FORET DE CINGLAIS
THURY-HARCOURT 3 MILES
FALAISE 7 MILES
R. LAISON
Scale 1:101,000

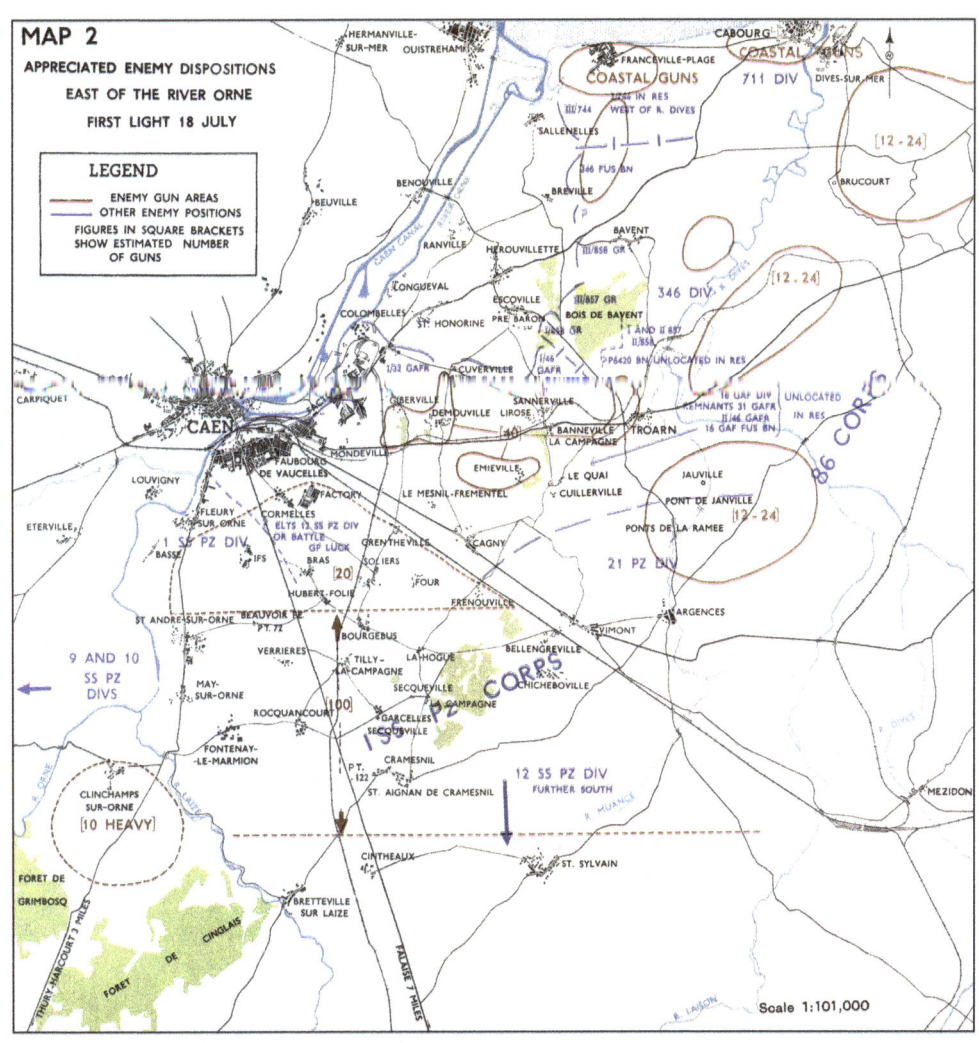

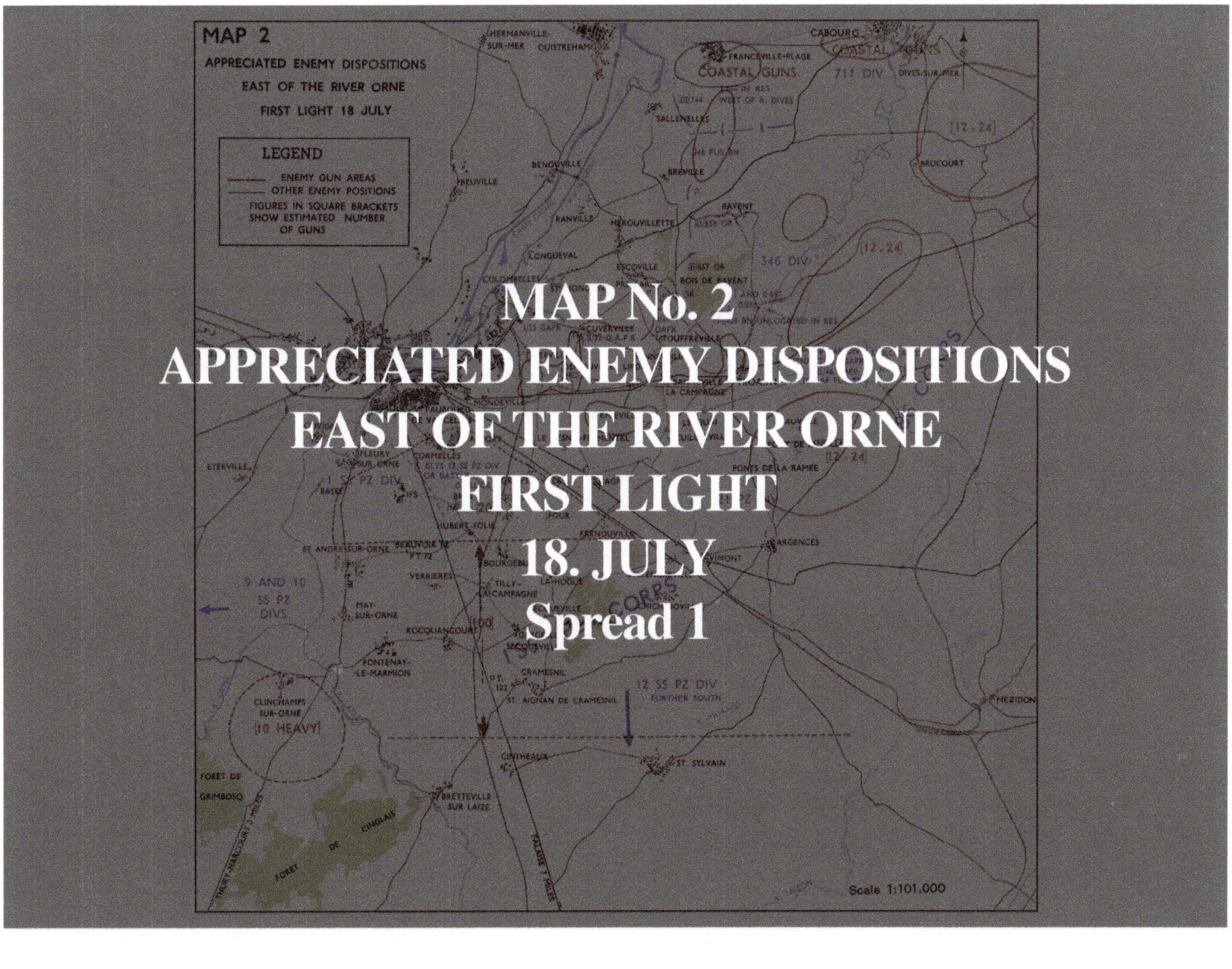

MAP No. 2
APPRECIATED ENEMY DISPOSITIONS
EAST OF THE RIVER ORNE
FIRST LIGHT
18. JULY
Spread 1

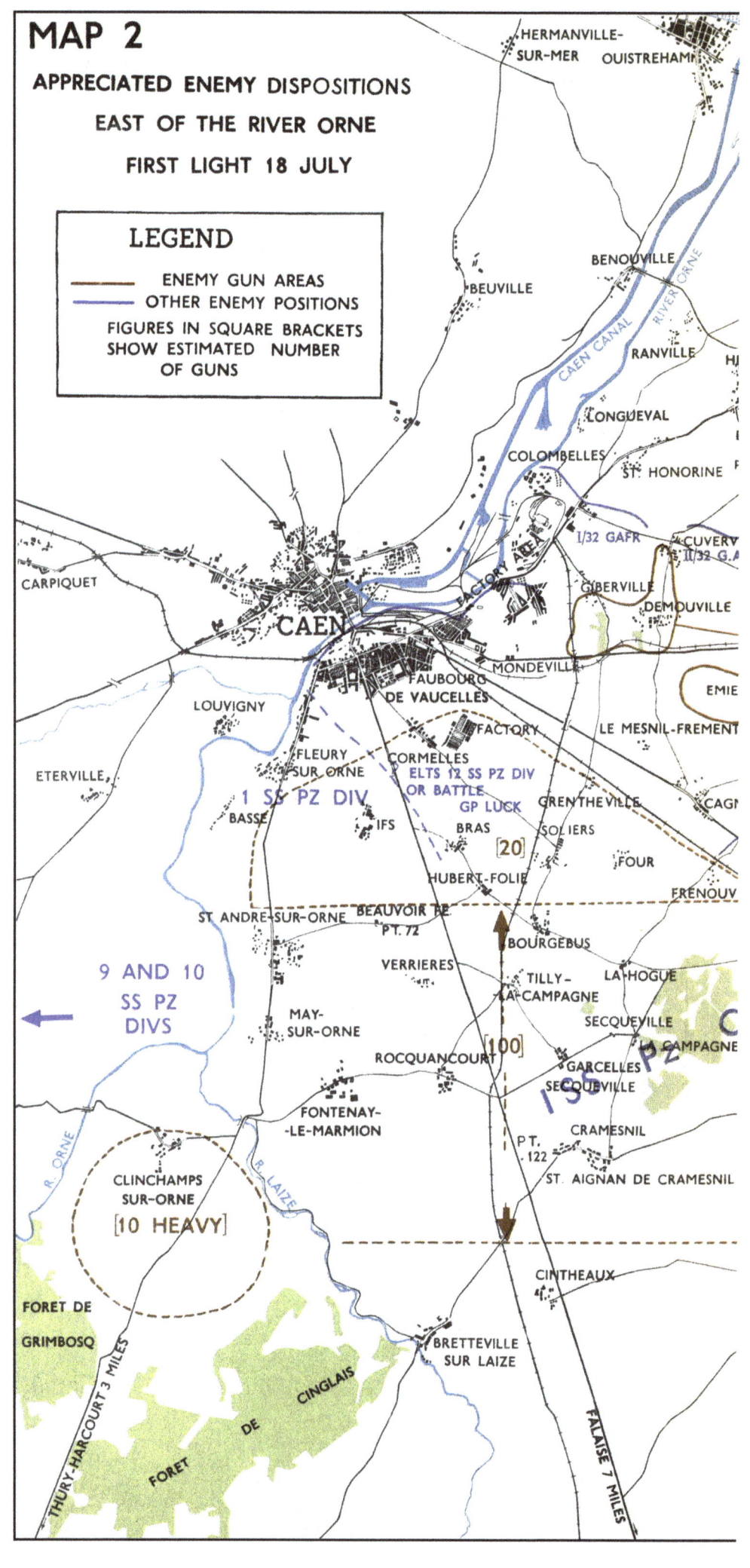

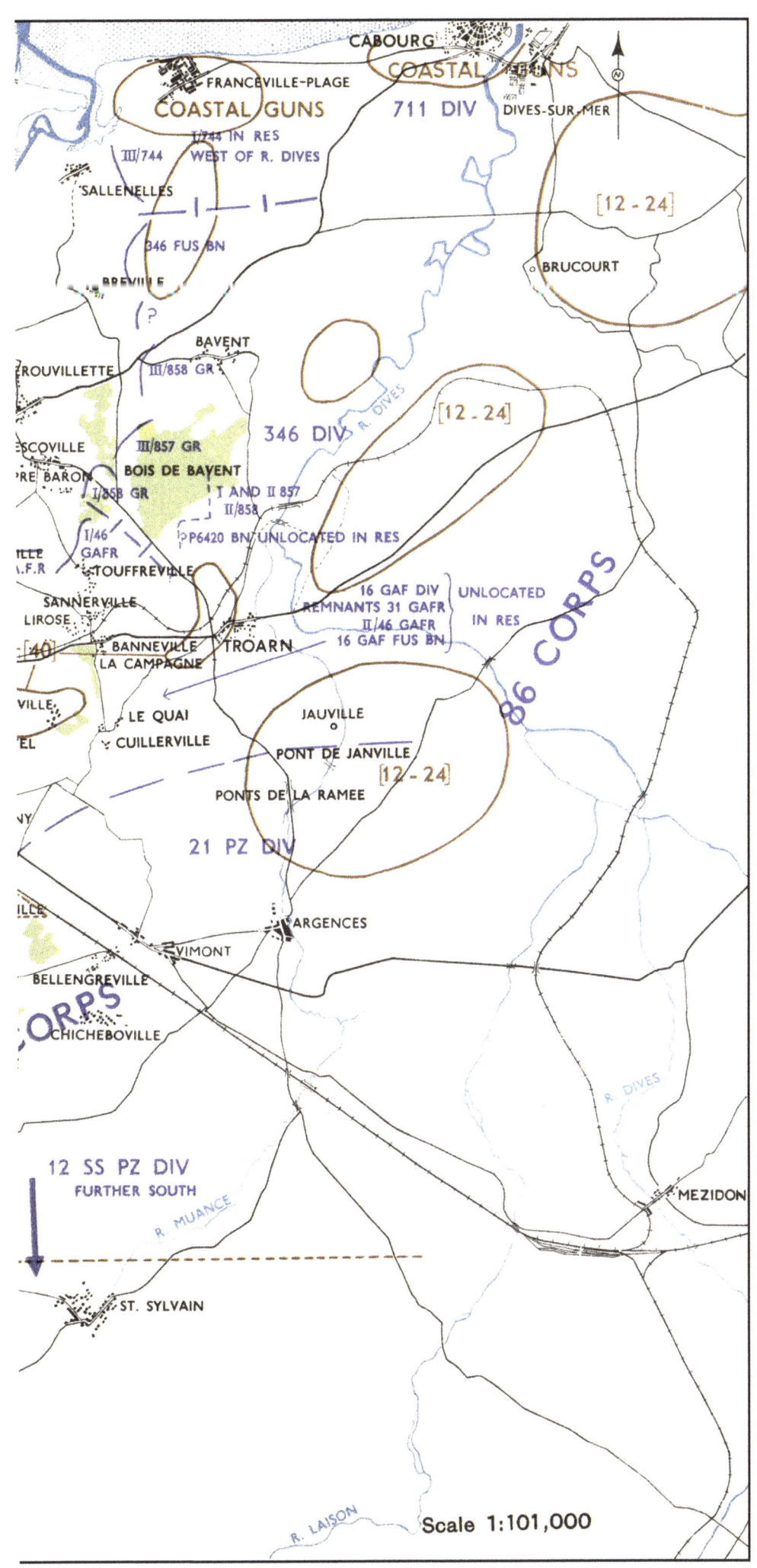

"I realised that the ORNE bridgehead had been considerably strengthened, and that an attack from this direction was to be expected. 125 PGR was used to back up the remaining two regiments of 16 GAF Div, while 192 PGR was deployed on the division's Left flank."

This statement indicates that 21 Pz Div was rather further West than anticipated: this was found to be the case.

As already stated 1 and 12 SS Pz Divs formed the remaining armoured reserves.

The British Intelligence staffs were not clear about the exact location of 1 SS Pz Div. It was thought, however, that the infantry less one Panzer Grenadier Regiment was East of the River ORNE, probably in the area due South of CAEN, that the artillery was deployed between FLEURY-SUR-ORNE and ST ANDRE-SUR-ORNE, and the tanks were at any rate East of the river. The resources of this division were thought to include a total strength of up to 15,000 men, 100 tanks (sixty Mk IIIs or IVs and forty Mk Vs (Panthers)), seventy-five guns of calibre between 50 mm and 88 mm, forty to fifty field or medium guns, and some unspecified number of assault guns.

In any event, the division was likely to resist strongly wherever it was encountered. The Commander of 1 SS Pz Div (Brigadefuehrer WISCH) in his interrogation, supports the above appreciation in some respects only :—

"The concentration area for the division at the time when Operation GOODWOOD opened on 18 July was mainly the LAISON valley with a Right boundary through MAIZIERES over to the road CAEN-FALAISE on the Left. They had suffered great losses of infantry during the short time they had been in the line, mainly from artillery fire. Unfortunately, WISCH could give no precise details. When asked his attitude to the campaign at this time, he said that he still felt fairly confident as he had not suffered so heavily as other divisions. His tank strength was still high, having about 100 to 120 runners."

12 SS Pz Div, again, was not definitely located. It was thought possible that it was concentrated just South of the junction of the rivers ORNE and LAIZE. This division had done much hard fighting and was estimated to consist of 7,000 men and up to 50 tanks. Its artillery resources amounted to fifty guns of 50 to 88 mm calibre, and twenty field or medium guns. The Commander of 12 SS Pz Div (Brigadefuehrer KURT MEYER) supports these tank strength estimates, but says he had only 2,000 men and does not give the location of his division. The Commander of 1 SS Pz Corps (Colonel-General JOSEPH "SEPP" DIETRICH) said later that the division was in the area of ST SYLVAIN from the time the battle of CAEN ended.

The sector East of the River ORNE was under 1 SS Pz Corps. To the East of this and probably controlling 346 and 711 Divs was 86 Corps and to the West 2 SS Pz Corps. The Corps troops of the two SS Corps included two heavy tank battalions which together could probably muster 5 Panthers and 30 Tigers. In addition there were two heavy artillery battalions of twelve guns each and a number of Nebelwerfers (15 and 21 cms).

It was thought that the boundary between 1 SS Pz Corps and 86 Corps was along the line of the road ESCOVILLE–TROARN, but once again the Commander of the former has stated that 21 Pz Div was under command of 86 Corps, which would put the boundary much further West. DIETRICH went on to say :—

"About the 12 July, 272 Inf Div came up from its sector in the South of FRANCE and slowly began to take over part of the sector held by 1 SS Pz Div. They assumed responsibility for the area between the CAEN-FALAISE and CAEN-VIMONT roads. A company of tanks of 1 SS Pz Div was left with 272 Div for support. When the balance of 272 Inf Div arrived about 16 July it took over the sector held by 9 SS Pz Div between the ODON and ORNE rivers. Thus, when Operation GOODWOOD began on 18 July, designed to capture FALAISE, 1 SS Pz Corps had 272 Inf Div in the line and both 1 SS and 12 SS Pz Divs in reserve."

This version confirms the general British appreciations.

ENEMY ARTILLERY RESOURCES

The estimated gun strengths of each division have been given in the above account. Their dispositions were believed to include a number of large coastal guns in the FRANCEVILLE and CABOURG areas, which although they were normally sited to fire North or North-West, could be turned round. Three areas, each containing between twelve and twenty-four guns were centred on BRUCOURT and GOUSTRANVILLE, East of the River DIVES, and JAUVILLE, South-East of TROARN.

Between the rivers ORNE and DIVES and North of the railway CAEN–VIMONT, there were probably up to 130 guns of various types : South of the railway and down to Northing 55, there were about another 120, whilst between the rivers ORNE and LAIZE another 10 heavy guns might be firing West of the River ORNE, but could be turned round if necessary.

It was anticipated that our armour would meet its greatest opposition from enemy artillery as it approached the rising ground about BOURGUEBUS and LA HOGUE.

SUMMARY

The enemy layout, as considered, immediately prior to the battle is shown on Map No. 2. The appreciation was in most respects accurate. It was anticipated that opposition would be strong and that it would include in the neighbourhood of 250 tanks. It is doubtful, however, if the enemy's very considerable gun strength was fully appreciated by all Commanders and whether or not it had been sufficiently emphasised. In the event, his reaction to our attacks, after recovering from the effect of the air bombardment, was very quick.

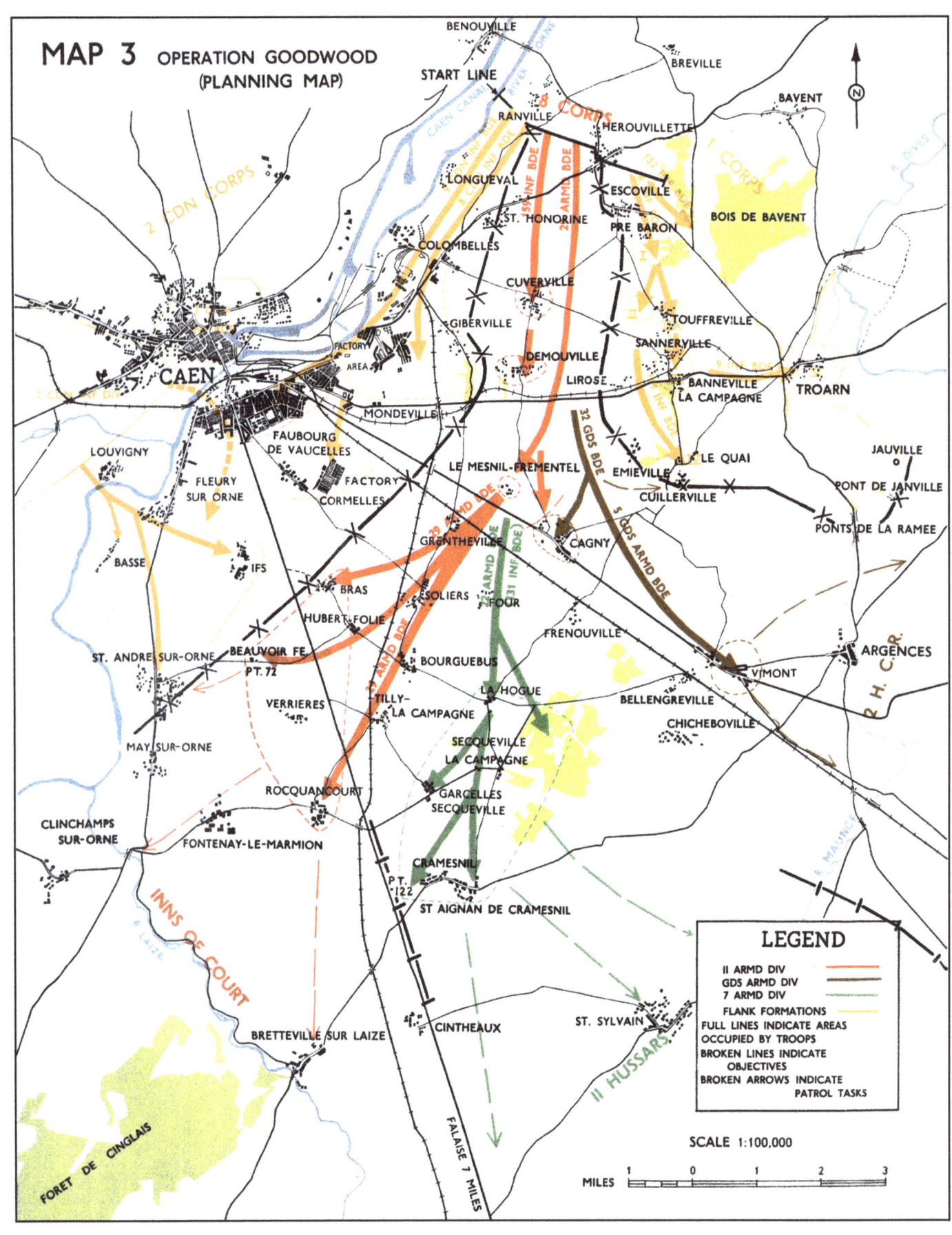

SECTION IV

PLANNING THE OPERATION

A. THE OBJECT OF THE OPERATION

Operation GOODWOOD was the name given to the operations of 2 Canadian, 8 and 1 Corps East of the River ORNE starting on 18 July 1944. The objects of Operation GOODWOOD, which was closely bound up with the operations of 12 and 30 Corps due to start to the West of the river two or three days earlier, were :—

(a) To break out of the Southern flank of the ORNE bridgehead with a view to occupying the high ground South and South-West of CAEN, thereby enabling 2 Canadian Corps to capture the portion of the town of CAEN that lies South of the River ORNE.

(b) Subsequently to break through into the CAEN–FALAISE plain, with a view to an armoured thrust in the direction of FALAISE.

(c) As a result of the above operations, to draw the maximum number of enemy armoured formations into the CAEN sector, to relieve the pressure on the American front.

B. THE ARMY PLAN

Starting on 15 July, Second British Army with five corps under command was to carry out a series of attacks at the Eastern end of the NORMANDY front, astride the River ORNE. The order of battle for this task was as follows :—

30 Corps	*12 Corps*	*2 Cdn Corps*	*8 Corps*	*1 Corps*
49 Div	15 (S) Div	2 Cdn Div	Gds Armd Div	3 Brit Div
50 Div	43 (W) Div	3 Cdn Div	7 Armd Div	51 (H) Div
59 Div	53 (W) Div	2 Cdn Armd Bde	11 Armd Div	6 Airborne Div
8 Armd Bde	4 Armd Bde		2 HCR	27 Armd Bde
33 Armd Bde	31 Tk Bde		11 H	One regt 33 Armd Bde
56 Inf Bde	34 Tk Bde		INNS OF COURT	

12 Corps (Operation GREENLINE)

12 Corps attack was due to start on 15 July. On the night 15/16 July 15 (S) Div was to attack EVRECY and the following morning to attack up the ODON valley from the area of TOURVILLE directed on BOUGY ; the next night (16/17 July) it was to launch an attack on MAIZET. Thereafter, 12 Corps was to exploit as opportunity arose to the general line VACOGNES–GOUPILLIERES.

By the time Operation GOODWOOD started EVRECY had not fallen and was still being attacked.

30 Corps (Operation POMEGRANATE)

The 30 Corps attack on the Right of 12 Corps was to go in on the morning of 16 July and was to be carried out in two phases. In Phase I, 59 Div was to advance and secure the area of NOYERS by 1800 hours 16 July : Phase II involved exploitation to the high ground North-East of VILLERS BOCAGE, also to be done by 59 Div.

By the time that Operation GOODWOOD started 30 Corps had not occupied NOYERS which was strongly held by the enemy and the attack was continuing from the North.

2 Cdn Corps (Operation ATLANTIC)

2 Cdn, 8 and 1 Corps were all to operate East of the River ORNE and the plans for their preliminary movements, fire support and air support were completely co-ordinated. The attack by 2 Cdn Corps was primarily designed to support the Right flank of the main armoured break out by 8 Corps.

The Corps task was to capture FAUBOURG DE VAUCELLES and the village of GIBERVILLE, and then to exploit Southwards to the area of ST ANDRE-SUR-ORNE. At the same time CAEN was to be held as a firm base and the river was to be bridged between CAEN and FAUBOURG DE VAUCELLES by midnight 18 July with one class 40 and one class 9 bridge.

To carry out the above tasks, two divisions were to be employed—2 and 3 Cdn Inf Divs.

3 Cdn Inf Div was to cross the River ORNE in the area of BENOUVILLE on the night D-1/D and attack Southwards the following morning at the same time as 8 Corps. 8 Cdn Inf Bde, supported by one armoured regiment, was to advance on the Left and establish itself in the factory area South of COLOMBELLES–GIBERVILLE—North of MONDEVILLE. 9 Cdn Inf Bde, supported by two armoured squadrons, was to advance on the Right of 8 Cdn Inf Bde and establish itself in FAUBOURG DE VAUCELLES. 7 Cdn Inf Bde, in reserve, was to remain holding the firm base in CAEN. 8 and 9 Bdes were ordered to leave their assembly areas at H Hour and cross the Start Line behind a rolling barrage at H plus 45 minutes. 2 Cdn Inf Div was to remain West of the river in the area CARPIQUET—ST OUEN–ETERVILLE (where it was to concentrate on night 17/18 July) and be prepared to operate on orders of Commander 2 Cdn Corps. Its task would be to exploit Southwards, and secure the area BASSE–IFS–point 72, ST ANDRE-SUR-ORNE, and the area of VERRIERES, if the latter had not already been captured by 8 Corps.

This operation was to be carried out in three phases.

In Phase I, 4 Cdn Inf Bde was to reconnoitre the river South of LOUVIGNY for suitable places to ford it, and, if the ST ANDRE feature was not already held, cross the river and occupy that feature on the orders of the Divisional Commander.

If 4 Cdn Inf Bde had not occupied ST ANDRE-SUR-ORNE in Phase I, 5 Cdn Inf Bde was to do so in Phase II. To do this, 5 Cdn Inf Bde was to assemble South-West of FAUBOURG DE VAUCELLES, and, supported by one armoured squadron, advance on the village from the North. During this Phase, 4 Cdn Inf Bde with the help of one armoured regiment was to capture LOUVIGNY.

Phase III was the capture of the VERRIERES feature if this had not already been done by 8 Corps. One of three methods would be employed :—

If 4 Cdn Inf Bde was in ST ANDRE-SUR-ORNE

    either,   6 Cdn Inf Bde was to cross the river and pass through 4 Cdn Inf Bde from the West on to the VERRIERES feature,

    or,   4 Cdn Inf Bde itself was to capture the VERRIERES feature.

If 5 Cdn Inf Bde was in ST ANDRE-SUR-ORNE

    6 Cdn Inf Bde was to cross the river and pass through 5 Cdn Inf Bde from the North on to the VERRIERES feature.

8 Corps

The outline tasks were as follows:—

8 Corps, consisting of three armoured divisions was, on 18 July, to debouch from the existing bridge head East of the River ORNE with a view to :—

    (a) Dominating the area BOURGUEBUS–VIMONT–BRETTEVILLE SUR LAIZE ;

    (b) Destroying any enemy armour or other forces encountered on the way to or in this area, and

    (c) if conditions were favourable, exploiting to the South in the direction of FALAISE.

This plan is dealt with in detail later in the book.

1 Corps

As in the case of 2 Cdn Corps, the attack by 1 Corps was closely co-ordinated with the 8 Corps operation. H Hour was the same : the fire support and air support plans were combined. 1 Corps task was to protect the Left flank of 8 Corps by occupying the general area TOUFFREVILLE–SANNERVILLE–BANNEVILLE LA CAMPAGNE–EMIEVILLE–LE QUAI, and subsequently TROARN. It was also to maintain a firm base for 8 Corps in its existing area.

The main flank protection task was to be carried out by 3 Brit Inf Div with 152 Inf Bde (51 (H) Div) under command and supported by 27 Armd Bde. The method to be employed was as follows :— 8 Inf Bde supported by 13th/18th Ryoal Hussars (Queen Mary's Own) (13/18 H) and one squadron Staffordshire Yeomanry (STAFFS YEO) was to :—

(I) Neutralise the area between PRE BARON and TOUFFREVILLE ;

(II) Neutralise enemy positions 800 yards North-West of TOUFFREVILLE ;

(IIA) Mop up TOUFFREVILLE ;

(III) Mop up SANNERVILLE.

The tasks of 152 Inf Bde were to maintain a firm base facing East towards LE BOIS DE BAVENT and support 8 Inf Bde by engaging enemy in area West of the road triangle 1,200 yards South-East of ESCOVILLE, occupying the road triangle if possible.

If the enemy were to withdraw, 152 Inf Bde was to exploit up to 1,000 yards down the road to TROARN beyond the triangle : in this event, a brigade of 6 Airborne Div might be available to relieve 152 Inf Bde of its task facing East. 152 Inf Bde would be supported by 141st Regiment Royal Armoured Corps (141 RAC).

185 Inf Bde was to hold a firm base to the West of 152 Inf Bde in the area RANVILLE-HEROUVILLETTE and ESCOVILLE. One battalion of this brigade was to be prepared to move forward riding on the tanks of the STAFFS YEO to the railway near LIROSE and from there, supported by STAFFS YEO, mop up the area of LE QUAI. Later, the whole brigade was to move forward to the LE QUAI area and protect the Southern flank while 9 Inf Bde was in action.

9 Inf Bde, supported by the East Riding Yeomanry (E RIDING YEO) was to pass through 8 Inf Bde, when the latter had reached their objectives, and capture TROARN and the bridges over the rivers MUANCE and DIVES immediately to the East.

They were then to send patrols to seize the bridges at PONT DE LA RAMEE, PONTS DE JANVILLE and JAUVILLE, and also to patrol vigorously North and North-East of TROARN. The bridge North-East of BURES was, if possible, to be destroyed. The other bridges were to be prepared for demolition, and blown only if there was any danger of the enemy occupying them.

Of the other brigades of 51 (H) Inf Div, 153 Inf Bde was to remain concentrated West of the River ORNE and to be prepared to cross on the evening of D Day. 154 Inf Bde was to concentrate in the area between STE HONORINE LA CHARDONERETTE and RANVILLE as soon as possible after H Hour (taking care not to interfere with the forward moves of 2 Cdn and 8 Corps), and be prepared to occupy CUVERVILLE and DEMOUVILLE as soon as they had been mopped up by 159 Inf Bde (11 Armd Div).

C. THE CORPS COMMANDER'S PROBLEMS

There were three major factors which affected the planning by the Commander of 8 Corps : firstly, how the large force required was to be assembled : secondly, the ground over which the attack was to be made : and thirdly, the weather.

(a) Three armoured divisions had to be moved across the crowded bridgehead from West to East without being detected by the enemy, and without interfering with the operations and maintenance of the rest of the Army. The area available East of the River ORNE was only large enough to hold one of these divisions at a time. Since the enemy had observation of part of this area, the arrival of the armour had to be delayed until as late as possible:

(b) A real break-out could only be achieved after a long advance on a narrow front through country which was very much in favour of the defence and ideal for the siting of the enemy's artillery, both field and anti-tank.

(c) The operation was dependent on air support, and that was dependent on the weather. a final decision on whether the Royal Air Force could operate or not could only be made a few hours before the battle was due to start. It was not possible to delay the concentration of the armour until this decision was given, and this meant that plans had to be made to conceal the large troop concentrations, so that the element of surprise, upon which the success of the operation so largely depended, would not be sacrified in the event of postponement.

D. THE CORPS PLAN

Planning began on 13 July when the Corps Commander received his orders from the Commander Second Army.

8 Corps, with its Left and Right flanks protected by 1 Brit and 2 Cdn Corps respectively, was to debouch from the bridge head East of the River ORNE with a view to dominating the area BOURGUEBUS-VIMONT-BRETTEVILLE SUR LAIZE, destroying any enemy armour encountered in the process, and, if conditions were favourable, subsequently exploiting to the South. The three

armoured divisions in the Corps were to cross the Start Line in the order 11, Gds and 7 Armd Divs. Owing to the bottleneck between DEMOUVILLE and SANNERVILLE and the small number of gaps which could be made in our own defensive minefield, the Corps could only advance on a one brigade front : 29 Armd Bde, which was to lead, could only advance one regiment up for the first two or three thousand yards, thereafter opening out to two regiments up. 11 Armd Div tasks were:—

(a) To occupy CUVERVILLE and DEMOUVILLE.

(b) To continue the advance across the railway between GRENTHEVILLE and CAGNY, leaving one armoured regiment to contain CAGNY until Gds Armd Div arrived, and

(c) To establish itself firmly in the area of BRAS-ROQUANCOURT—exclusive FONTENAY LE MARMION–BEAUVOIR FERME. All enemy encountered were to be destroyed.

Gds Armd Div was to follow 11 Armd Div across the Start Line with the tasks of :—

(a) Relieving the armoured regiment of 11 Armd Div opposite CAGNY, and

(b) Establishing a firm base in VIMONT.

All enemy encountered were to be destroyed, and the Left flank of the Corps protected.

7 Armd Div was to follow the Guards, cross the railway West of CAGNY and be prepared to support 11 Armd Div if required. It was then to move to and occupy the area LA HOGUE–woods North-East of SECQUEVILLE LA CAMPAGNE–ST AIGNAN DE CRAMESNIL–Point 122–GARCELLES SECQUEVILLE.

On arrival on their objectives, all three Divisions were given patrolling tasks which are shown on Map No. 3.

Concentration before the Operation

The problems involved in the Corps concentration are given in detail in Section V.

11 Armd Div was to concentrate in the bridge head East of the River ORNE before H Hour, the infantry brigade group arriving on the night of D-2/D-1 and the armour crossing during the night of D-1/D.

There was not room in the bridge head for the other two divisions to cross the river until after the battle had started. Gds Armd Div was to be formed up ready to cross the river at H Hour, and thence to move straight over the Start Line. 7 Armd Div, who had moved to a forward assembly area about 10 miles West of the river, was to start crossing at H+60.

A most careful traffic plan had to be made to co-ordinate these moves with movement essential for the maintenance of troops already on the ground, and to ensure that the armour moved freely and rapidly across the Start Line and into the battle.

RE Tasks

11 Armd Div and Gds Armd Div were each allotted one squadron less a troop of AVsRE : 7 Armd Div was allotted one troop.

Maintenance of routes up to the Start Line was the responsibliity of 1 Corps, while South of the Start Line route development was to be undertaken by 8 Corps as the operation progressed.

South of the Start Line and extending across the front of all three Corps East of the river was a defensive minefield. The original plan was that the whole of this minefield should be lifted, but when this was attempted on the night of 15/16 July, it was found impracticable. CRE 51 (H) Div who was responsible for clearing the minefield suggested that it should be gapped and this was agreed to. Gaps were to be made, on the flanks as required by 3 Brit and 3 Cdn Divs, and on 8 Corps front for each Corps route or track (of which there were three) and wherever there were any other routes or tracks already in existence.

Details of the RE plan are given in Section VI.

Fire Support

A comprehensive fire plan in support of the attack was arranged and was to be carried out by over 700 guns of all calibres, assisted by ships of the Royal Navy anchored off the beaches. Up to an hour and a half before H Hour, the guns were available to fire an anti-flak counter battery programme on located enemy positions. For an hour and a half before H Hour all guns were to fire a counter battery programme which was to be organised by 1 Corps. At H Hour, 11 Armd Div was to advance as far as the railway CAEN-VIMONT behind a rolling barrage, and barrages and concentrations were to precede the advance of 3 Brit and 3 Cdn Divs on the flanks. Counter battery fire was to be continued as long as required while the armour was advancing, and, in addition to two field regiments in direct support of each armoured division, a number of regiments was available to bring down concentrations on various targets as the leading troops called for them.

Owing to the very small area of the bridgehead East of the River ORNE most of the guns had to be sited to the West of the river. This had the effect of reducing very appreciably the distance over which they could support the advance, and of increasing the length of time before they could again be in action, since they had to be phased in to the continuous stream of traffic across the bridges.

Further details of the fire plan are given in Section VII.

Air Support

The advance was to be preceded by an air effort, on a larger scale than anything ever before staged in direct support of ground forces. The main features of this air plan which was made on an Army/RAF Tactical Group level, were as follows :—

(a) Heavy bombing of enemy positions on the flanks of the Corps advance.

(b) Fragmentation bombing of the enemy in the path of the armoured divisions.

(c) Neutralisation of certain located enemy gun areas, out of range of our own guns.

It was firmly laid down that if for any reason the air plan could not be put into effect, the attack was to be postponed.

Details of the air plan are given in Section VIII.

Deception Plan

A deception plan was organised by Second Army to give the impression that the armour would be passed through a gap on the 12 Corps sector to the West of the river. 8 Corps and all troops under command were therefore to observe wireless silence until H-30. All troops already in position East of the river were to carry on with normal wireless traffic, reducing to a minimum at H Hour unless they were actually taking part in the operation.

Timings

The leading elements of 11 Armd Div were to cross the Start Line at H Hour, and the operations of 2 Cdn and 1 Corps were to start at the same time. H Hour was the time at which the last fragmentation bomb was dropped by the medium bombers and was 0745 hours 18 July.

E. THE OUTLINE PLANS of the ARMOURED DIVISIONS

11 Armoured Division

PHASE I

The advance was to be led by 29 Armd Bde, moving one regiment up (3rd Royal Tank Regiment (3 R Tks)) for the first 2,500 yards and then opening out to two regiments up (Right 3 R Tks : Left 2nd Fife and Forfar Yeomanry (2 FF YEO)). The leading regiment was to cross the Start Line behind the barrage at H Hour, and advance to occupy the first objective, LE MESNIL FREMENTEL. After capture, this village was to be occupied by the Motor Battalion (8th Battalion The Rifle Brigade (8 RB)) and held until relieved by another formation. 29 Armd Bde had no responsibilities on the Left flank, apart from its own protection, but CAGNY, if occupied by the enemy, was to be watched and neutralised until the arrival of Gds Armd Div.

159 Inf Bde, supported by the Div Armd Recce Regt (2nd Northamptonshire Yeomanry (2 N YEO)) were to cross the Start Line at H Hour on the West of 29 Armd Bde and capture and clear CUVERVILLE and DEMOUVILLE.

The Inns of Court Regiment (INNS OF COURT) less two squadrons (Armoured cars) was to advance behind 29 Armd Bde, and when the latter had reached LE MESNIL FREMENTEL, infiltrate forward and patrol up to the general line ST ANDRE SUR ORNE–BRETTEVILLE SUR LAIZE—ST SYLVAIN, and South-East towards VIMONT.

PHASE II

For this phase, 2 N YEO, if it had finished its supporting role in Phase I, was to come under command of 29 Armd Bde. The latter was then to advance to the final objective BRAS–VERRIERES–ROQUANCOURT, at the same time leaving a containing force opposite CAGNY. It was also to occupy the high ground North of CRAMESNIL until relieved by 7 Armd Div. 159 Inf Bde meanwhile was to complete the clearing of CUVERVILLE and DEMOUVILLE. The second of these two villages was to be held until GIBERVILLE had been cleared by 2 Cdn Corps.

PHASE III

Phase III involved the move forward of 159 Inf Bde to establish a firm base in the area VERRIERES–ROQUANCOURT.

Guards Armoured Division

This division was to follow 11 Armd Div over the Start Line : its plan was in four phases.

PHASE I

5 Gds Armd Bde was to advance as fast as possible to the area of the main road South-East of CAGNY and also relieve the armoured regiment of 29 Armd Bde already containing that village.

One squadron of the 2nd Armoured Reconnaissance Battalion The Welsh Guards (2 Armd Recce WG) was to mask EMIEVILLE and protect the Left flank of the advance.

PHASE II

One armoured battalion of 5 Gds Armd Bde was to push on and secure VIMONT with one squadron of 2 Armd Recce WG protecting its Right flank from a position North-West of CHICHEBOVILLE.

PHASE III

32 Gds Bde was to follow 5 Gds Armd Bde down the axis. As soon as the leading infantry battalion arrived in the CAGNY area, the whole of the armoured brigade was to close up on VIMONT, leaving the infantry brigade to capture the village of CAGNY itself.

PHASE IV

32 Gds Bde supported by one armoured battalion was to take over VIMONT as a firm base. and the rest of the armoured brigade was to withdraw to an area astride the road CAEN-VIMONT,

7 Armoured Division

The action of 7 Armd Div depended largely on the progress of the two divisions in front of it.

22 Armd Bde with one squadron of 11th Hussars (Prince Albert's Own) (11 H) (Armoured Cars) under command was to deploy in the area of LE MESNIL FREMENTEL as soon as the traffic situation allowed, and advance on the axis FOUR–LA HOGUE to capture SECQUEVILLE LA CAMPAGNE.

Subsequently it was to capture the high ground about CRAMESNIL: or, relieve 11 Armd Div, if the latter had already captured it.

The squadron of armoured cars was to establish a patrol line within the divisional patrol boundaries, and maintain contact with the divisions on the flanks, reconnoitring and harassing the enemy as opportunities arose. 131 Inf Bde was to follow 22 Armd Bde down the centre line, take over SECQUEVILLE LA CAMPAGNE, and establish a firm base. This brigade had under command 8th King's Royal Irish Hussars (8 H) (Armoured Reconnaissance Regiment), whose task was to maintain contact with the firm bases on both flanks.

SECTION V

CONCENTRATION BEFORE THE BATTLE

The Object

When the concentration for Operation GOODWOOD was ordered, the armoured divisions of 8 Corps were widely dispersed. 11 Armd Div was about half way between CAEN and BAYEUX : Gds Armd Div was two miles East of BAYEUX : and 7 Armd Div was in the area North of TILLY-SUR-SEULLES.

All three divisions had to be in action East of the ORNE on 18 July, having moved undetected by the enemy and with as little inconvenience as possible to our own troops.

The Problems

The following were the main problems to be overcome :—

(a) Traffic congestion throughout the bridge head was very great and only a limited number of West to East tracks existed.

(b) Only a small number of bridges was available over the CAEN Canal and the River ORNE.

(c) All three armoured divisions had to cross the maintenance routes of 2 Cdn and 1 Corps.

(d) The move of the tanks had to be concealed from the enemy's air reconnaissance.

(e) The bridgehead East of the river was very small and there was not room to concentrate any large part of 8 Corps in that area before the battle started. Parts of the bridgehead were, in addition, overlooked by the enemy. The flow of traffic up to and across the Start Line once the battle started had, therefore, to be carefully controlled and as rapid as possible.

All movement in connection with the concentration was co-ordinated by Second Army, who were to inform Corps when certain routes were to be sealed for the movement of the armoured divisions.

Routes and Bridges

Three routes for wheeled vehicles with affiliated routes for tracks were used for the move of 8 Corps. Parts of these routes are shown on Map Number 4, but they extended several miles further West.

From 2100 hours 16 July until 7 Armd Div arrived East of the river, which was expected to be sometime on the 19 July, these routes were reserved for 8 Corps West to East traffic only.

Three bridges over the CAEN Canal and the River ORNE were similarly available.

The corresponding routes and bridges were as follows :—

West of River ORNE		Bridge	East of River ORNE
WHEELS	TRACKS		(WHEELS & TRACKS)
A	RAT	YORK	PALM
B	CAT	EUSTON	HOLLY
C	CALF	LONDON	BRIAR

Traffic Control

8 Corps was to allot formation block timings on each route and only exercise the control necessary to co-ordinate the moves of formations which followed one another along the same route, or had to be switched from one route to another owing to bridge damage or other causes.

The Corps Traffic Office, working directly under the orders of the BGS, was to be established on Route B about 4,000 yards West of the river.

2 Cdn Corps and 1 Corps were to be responsible for recovery, signing, policing, sealing of routes and minimum movement of North to South traffic within their own areas except for the Bridge Area itself, the boundaries of which are shown on the map. West of 2 Cdn Corps area the armoured divisions were responsible for their own policing of routes etc.

MAP No. 4
ROUTES FOR CONCENTRATION FOR OP. "GOODWOOD"
LEGEND
FDLs
MINEFIELDS
ROUTES FOR WHEELED VEHICLES
ROUTES FOR TRACKED VEHICLES
LINE ON WHICH HEADS OF GUARDS ARMD DIV COLUMNS WERE TO HALT DURING NIGHT 17 / 18 JULY
8 CORPS TRAFFIC OFFICE
T.C.P.
HEROUVILLE
ST. AUBIN-D'ARQUENAY
OUISTREHAM
FRANCEVILLE
SALLENELLES
TOWER BRIDGES
WESTERN BOUNDARY OF BRIDGE AREA
EASTERN BOUNDARY OF BRIDGE AREA
RAT
CAT
CALF
BEUVILLE
BIEVILLE
BLAINVILLE
EUSTON BRIDGES
LONDON BRIDGES
"PALM" WHEELS
"PALM" TRACKS
"BRIAR" TRACKS
BRIAR WHEELS
"HOLLY" WHEELS
"HOLLY" TRACKS
LE BAS DE RANVILLE
RANVILLE
BREVILLE
HEROUVILLETTE
LE MESNIL
LONGUEVAL
ST. HONORINE LA CHARDONERETTE
ESCOVILLE
BOIS DE BAVENT
PRE BARON
COLOMBELLES
FACTORY AREA
BUTTE DE LA HOGUE
CUVERVILLE
TOUFFREVILLE
CAEN
Scale 1:29,500

MAP No. 4
ROUTES FOR CONCENTRATION
FOR OP. "GOODWOOD"
Spread 1

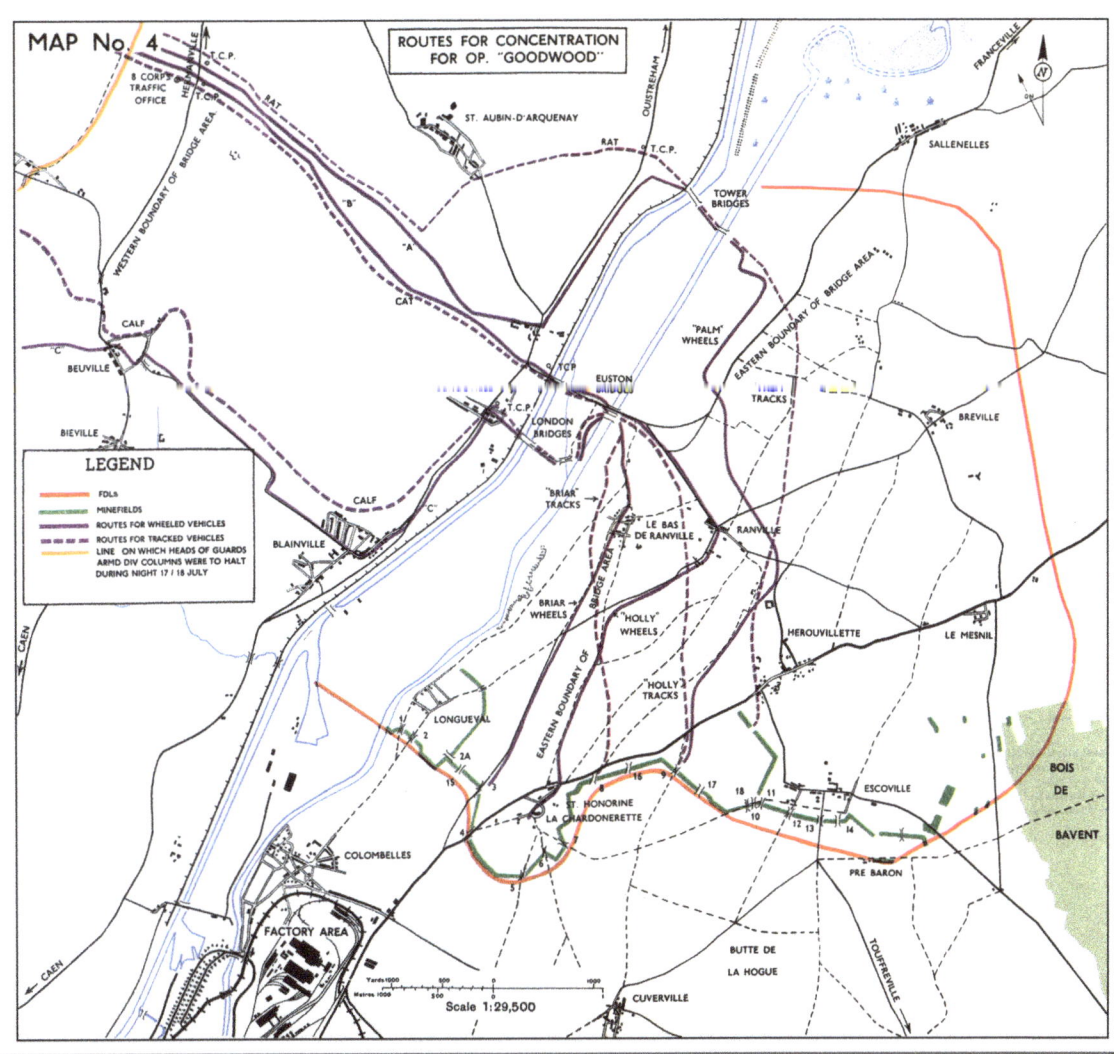

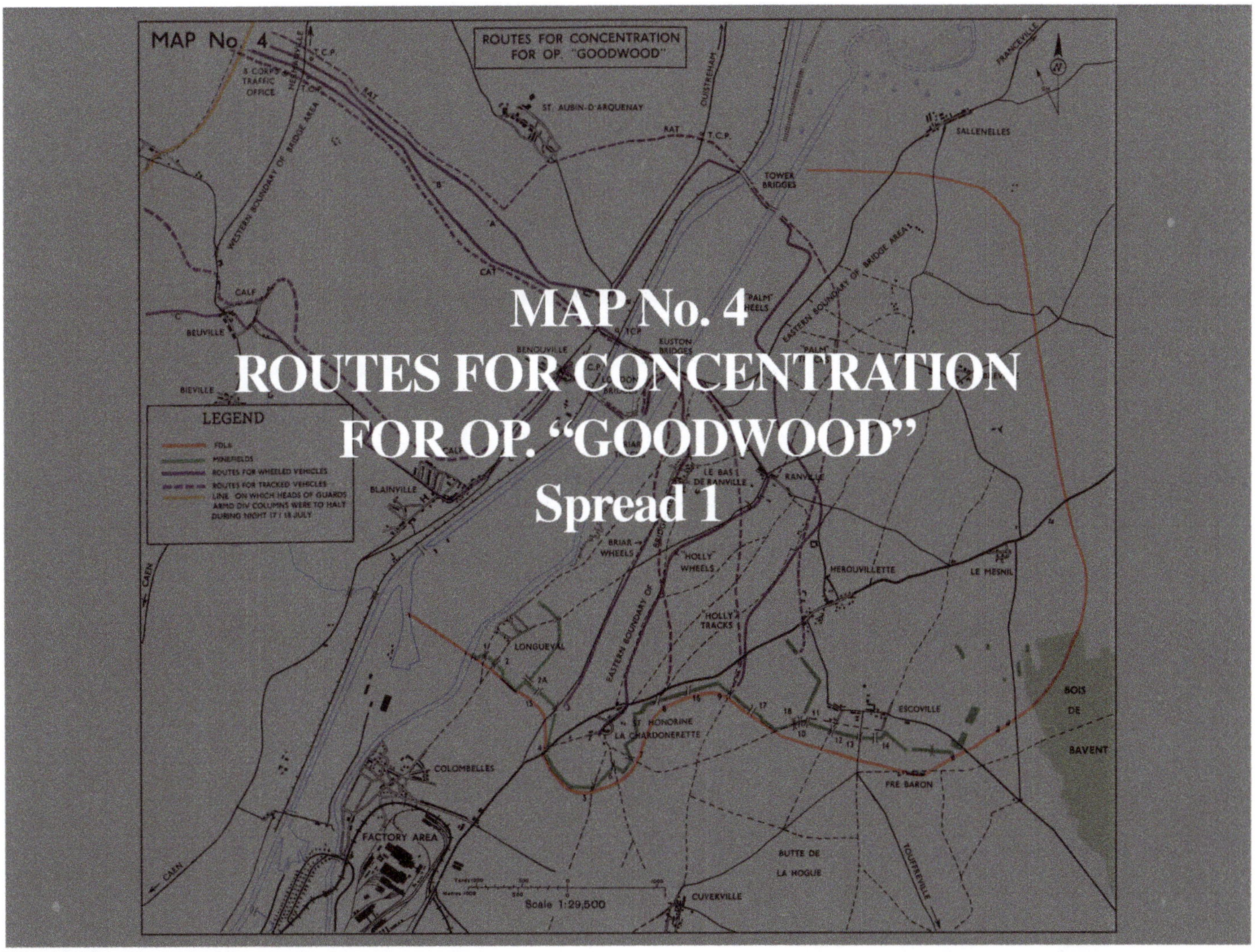

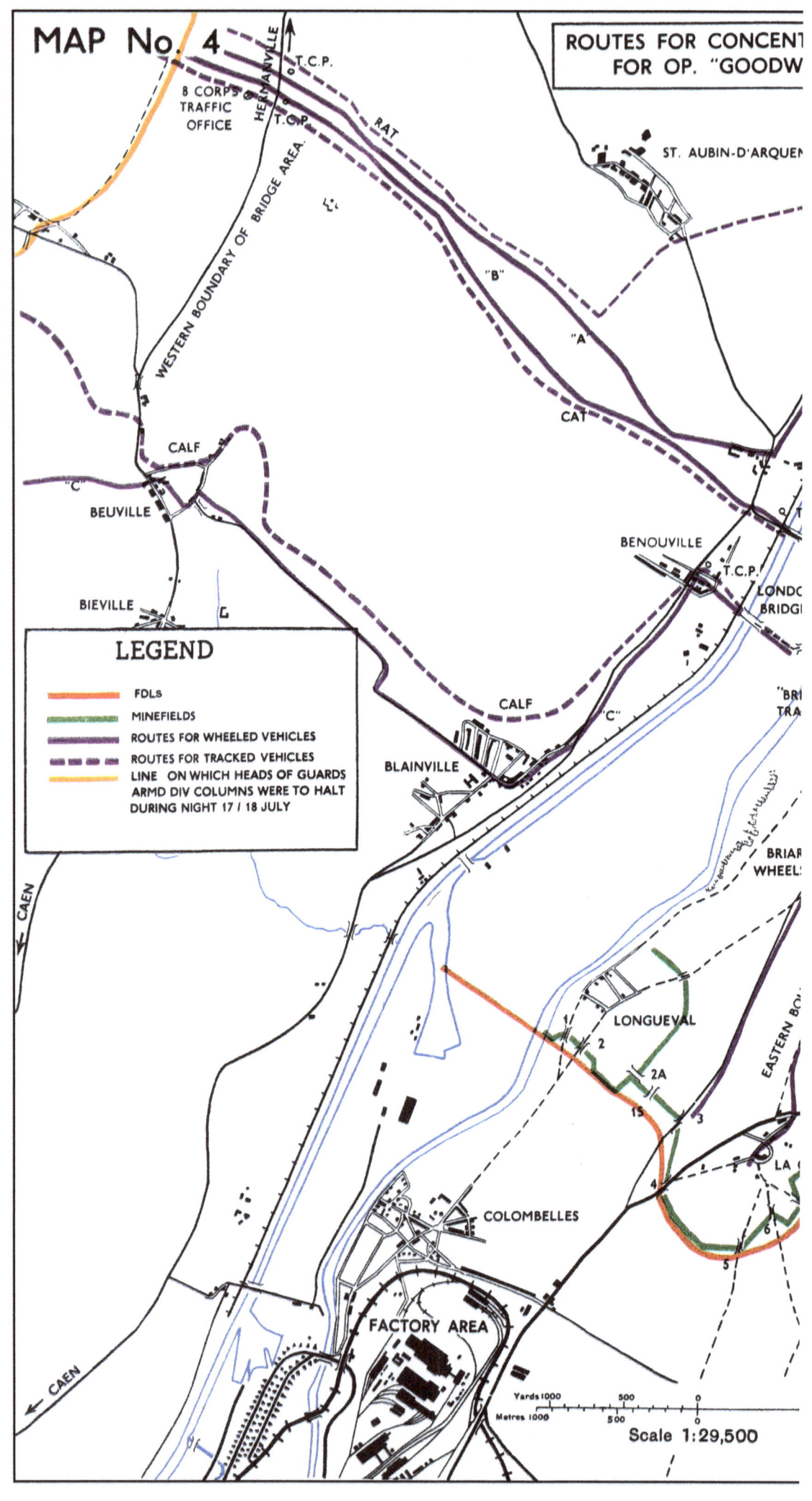

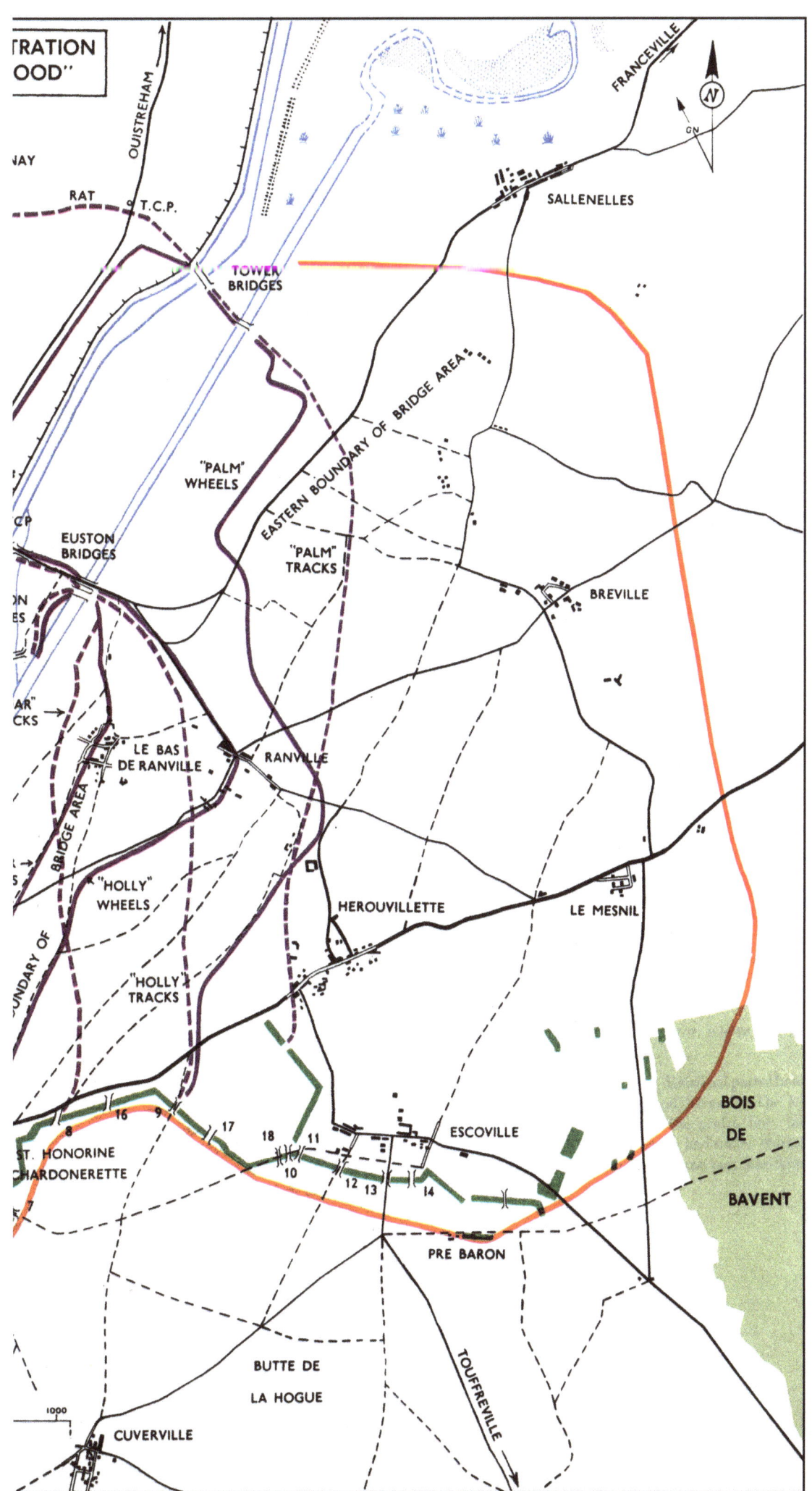

Organisation of Bridge Area

The Bridge area was to be organised by APM 8 Corps. A traffic officer was to be stationed at each pair of bridges and at control points on the line of the road HERMANVILLE–BEUVILLE. The Traffic Office was to be in touch, both by line and wireless, with all these officers, with the BGS at the Corps Command Post and with G(Ops) Gds and 7 Armd Divs.

Each traffic officer was to organise sidings in which down traffic could be held on the East side of each bridge, and sidings were to be provided on the West side into which units could be shunted to allow a last minute change in the order of march or for other reasons.

Signing in the bridge area was to be the responsibility of APM 8 Corps.

1 Corps was to provide recovery vehicles for each pair of bridges, and was also responsible for bridge maintenance.

The Bridge Area Organisation was to start operating at 1800 hours 16 July.

Moves of the Armoured Divisions

11 ARMOURED DIVISION

The move of 11 Armd Div was to be in four parts as under, the tracks, "F" Echelon wheels and the "A" Echelons being kept separate.

(a) During the night 16/17 July the "F" Echelon wheels of Div HQ and HQ 29 Armd Bde and the whole of 159 Inf Bde Group were to move by Routes B and C from their present area, cross the River ORNE and concentrate in the area shown on Map 5. The speed of this move was to be 10 mi2h and vehicles were to cross the bridges at the rate of 120 vehicles per hour.

(b) Also during the night 16/17 July, the Motor Battalion and three armoured regiments of 29 Armd Bde were to move by all three track routes (RAT, CAT and CALF) to an assembly area due West of BEUVILLE and about 7,000 yards West of the river. They were to conceal themselves in this area and remain there until the next night. The speed of this move was to be 10 mi2h and density visual.

(c) During the night D-1/D (17/18 July) all the vehicles in the assembly area were to cross to the East of the river, again using all three routes, and concentrate there. The Armoured Recce Regiment (2 N YEO) and elements of RA and RE were to move up from the original divisional area and also cross the river. One squadron of the 22nd Dragoons (22 DGNS) (Flails) and part of the INNS of COURT (Armoured Cars) were also to cross the river, the latter joining 29 Armd Bde in its concentration area. Density and speed for these moves were the same as on the night before, but vehicles were only to cross the bridges at the rate of 60 vehicles per hour.

(d) "A" Echelons of the division were to cross the river by Route C on 18 July moving at 16 mi2h and 40 vtm.

On the morning of D Day (18 July) before H Hour, the moves up to the Start Line from the concentration areas were to be by PALM Route for 29 Armd Bde Group and by HOLLY Route for 159 Inf Bde Group.

GUARDS ARMOURED DIVISION

Gds Armd Div which was concentrated in the BAYEUX area was not to start moving forward until the evening of 17 July (D-1).

The division was to use Routes RAT and CAT for tracks, and the corresponding routes for wheels, A and B. The order of march was to be as foolows :—

Route RAT   Part of 5 Gds Armd Bde Group (tracks).
                Part of tracked vehicles under command 32 Gds Bde Group.

Route CAT   Remainder of 5 Gds Armd Bde Group (tracks).
                2 Armd Recce WG less one squadron.
                Remainder of tracked vehicles under command 32 Gds Bde Group.

Route A   Two squadrons armoured cars (2nd Household Cavalry Regiment (2 HCR)).
                Part of 32 Gds Bde Group (wheels).
                "A" Echelon 5 Gds Armd Bde Group.

Route B   Remainder of 32 Gds Bde Group (wheels).

The speed on all routes was to be 6 mih and the density 60 vtm.

Each column was to halt when its head reached the line of the track running North and South about 600 yards West of the road HERMANVILLE–BEUVILLE, and all vehicles were to remain in position on the tracks. All AFVs were to top up with POL at this halt.

The march was to be resumed on the morning of D Day so that each column began to cross the ORNE bridges at H Hour.

7 ARMOURED DIVISION

The move of 7 Armd Div was to be in two phases.

In Phase I, it was to move from its area North of TILLY-SUR-SEULLES to a Forward Assembly Area North of the road BAYEUX–CAEN and about 12 miles due West of the ORNE bridges. This phase was to be completed during the night 16/17 July.

Phase II involved the move of the division across the river and into the battle.

CALF track was to be used, and the order of march was to be :—

        22 Armd Bde Group

        11 H less two squadrons (Armoured Cars)

        4 Fd Sqn less one troop

        131 Inf Bde Group

        Two squadrons 11 H.

The density was to be 40 vtm and the speed "the maximum necessary to ensure no delay in following through."

22 Armd Bde was to emerge from the assembly area so as to arrive with its head in BEUVILLE at H-60. It was to follow part of a Canadian Brigade along CALF and was due to start crossing LONDON bridge at H+60, using BRIAR Route East of the river.

Flank Formations

The concentration of the divisions of 1 Brit and 2 Cdn Corps is not considered in detail. It should be noted, however, that 1 Corps had to pass one infantry brigade group and two field regiments across the river during the night 16/17 July : and two infantry brigade groups of 2 Cdn Corps had to cross between 2300 hours 17 July and 0100 hours 18 July and from H Hour to H+60 on 18 July.

These moves had to be carefully co-ordinated with the moves of 8 Corps.

Withdrawal from FDLs during air bombardment

The problem of concentrating troops East of the ORNE was further complicated by the enforced withdrawal from the FDLs during the air bombardment. The whole of 154 Inf Bde and part of 185 Inf Bde had to be withdrawn behind the line shown on Map No. 5. Only the minimum number of troops essential to deny the area South of this line to enemy patrols remained.

154 Inf Bde had to be fitted into the area of HEROUVILLETTE.

Certain armoured elements of 11 Armd Div were allowed to move up to their Start Line just before the bombing came to an end, so as to begin the advance punctually at H Hour.

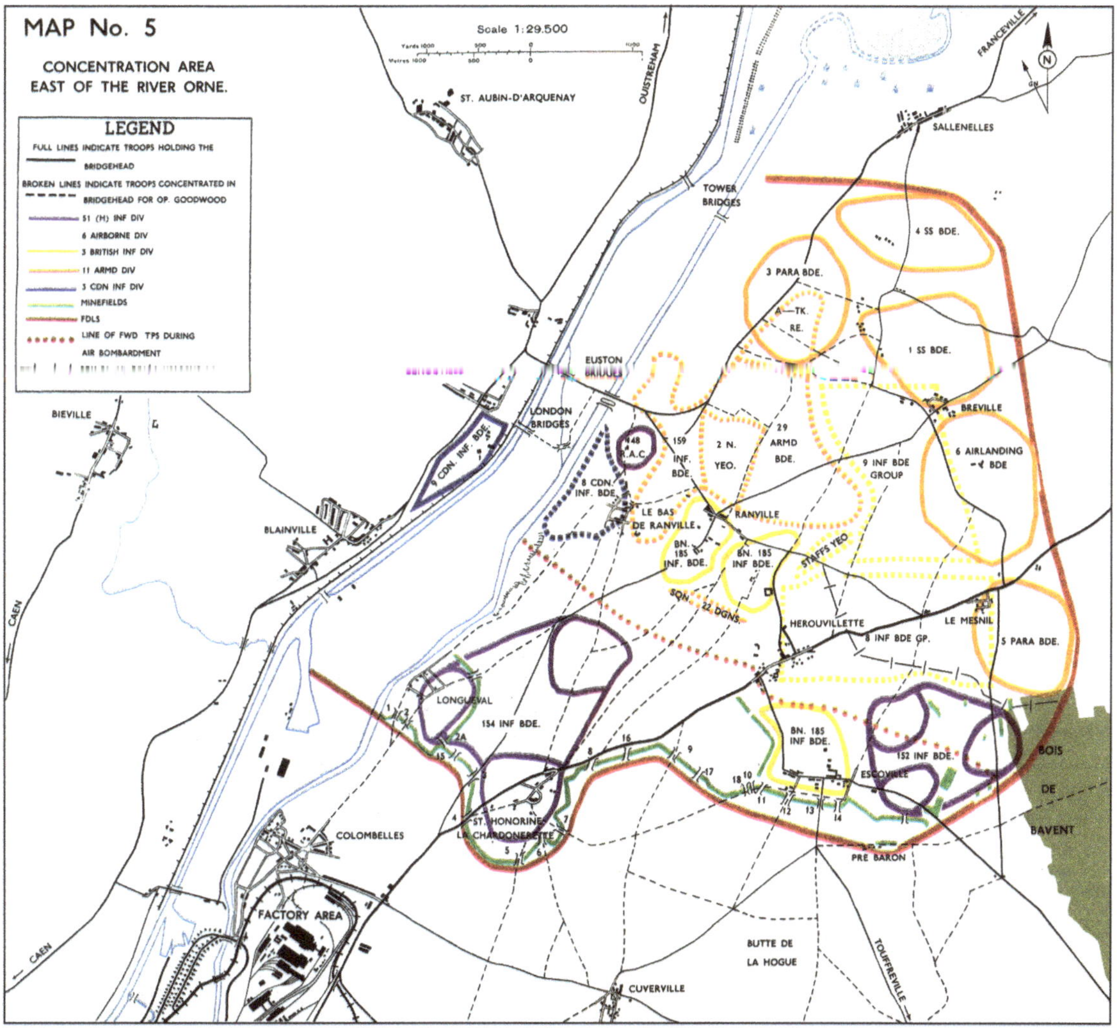
MAP No. 5
CONCENTRATION AREA
EAST OF THE RIVER ORNE.
Scale 1:29.500
LEGEND
FULL LINES INDICATE TROOPS HOLDING THE BRIDGEHEAD
BROKEN LINES INDICATE TROOPS CONCENTRATED IN BRIDGEHEAD FOR OP. GOODWOOD
51 (H) INF DIV
6 AIRBORNE DIV
3 BRITISH INF DIV
11 ARMD DIV
3 CDN INF DIV
MINEFIELDS
FDLS
LINE OF FWD TPS DURING AIR BOMBARDMENT
ST. AUBIN-D'ARQUENAY
OUISTREHAM
FRANCEVILLE
SALLENELLES
TOWER BRIDGES
4 SS BDE.
3 PARA BDE.
A—TK. RE.
1 SS BDE.
EUSTON BRIDGES
LONDON BRIDGES
BIEVILLE
9 CDN. INF. BDE.
148 R.A.C.
159 INF. BDE.
2 N. YEO.
29 ARMD BDE.
9 INF BDE GROUP
BREVILLE
6 AIRLANDING BDE
8 CDN. INF. BDE.
LE BAS DE RANVILLE
RANVILLE
BLAINVILLE
BN. 185 INF. BDE.
BN. 185 INF. BDE.
STAFFS YEO
SQN. 22 DGNS.
HEROUVILLETTE
LE MESNIL
8 INF BDE GP.
5 PARA BDE.
CAEN
LONGUEVAL
154 INF BDE.
BN. 185 INF BDE.
152 INF BDE.
BOIS DE BAVENT
ESCOVILLE
ST. HONORINE LA CHARDONERETTE
COLOMBELLES
PRE BARON
FACTORY AREA
BUTTE DE LA HOGUE
TOUFFREVILLE
CUVERVILLE
CAEN

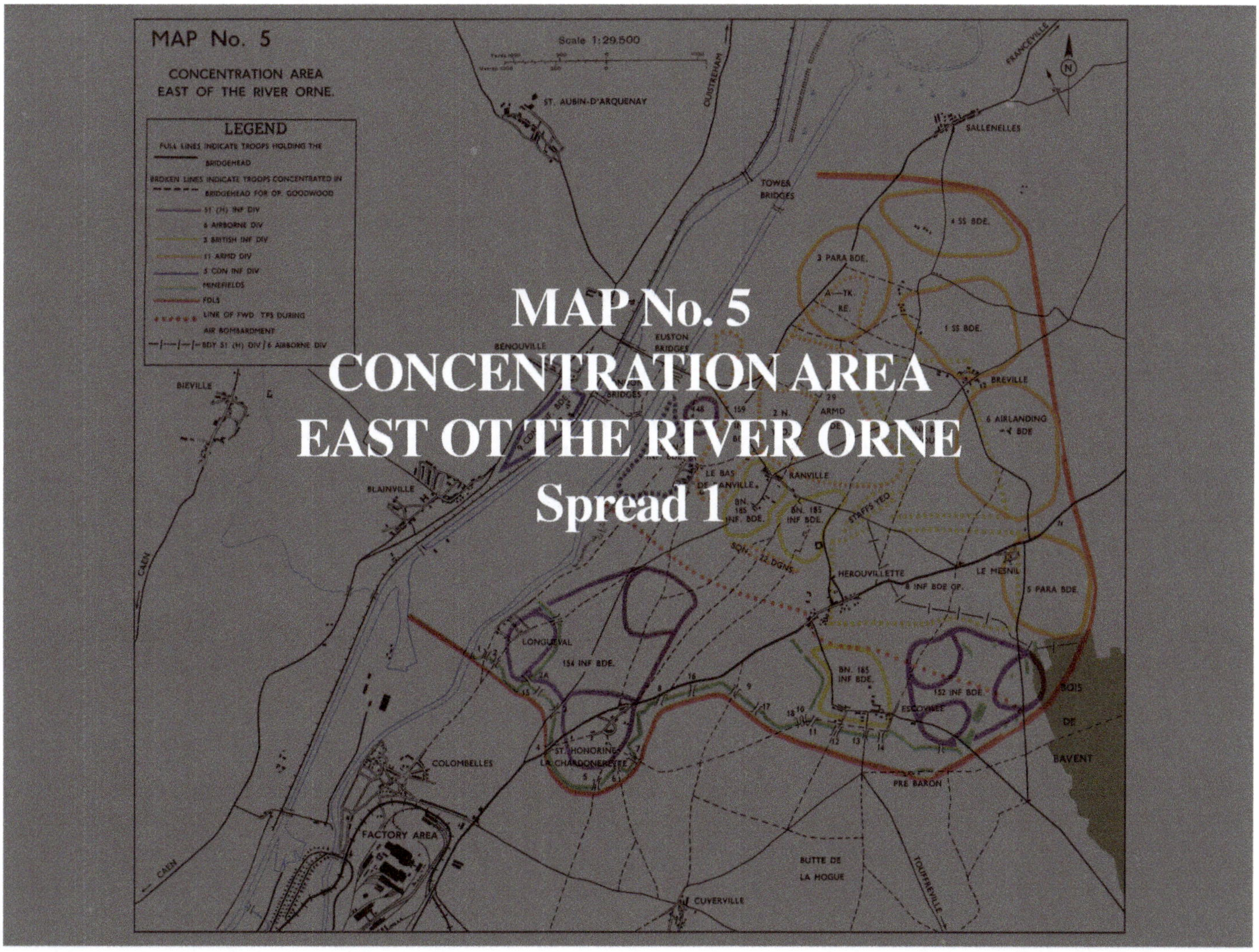
MAP No. 5
CONCENTRATION AREA
EAST OT THE RIVER ORNE
Spread 1

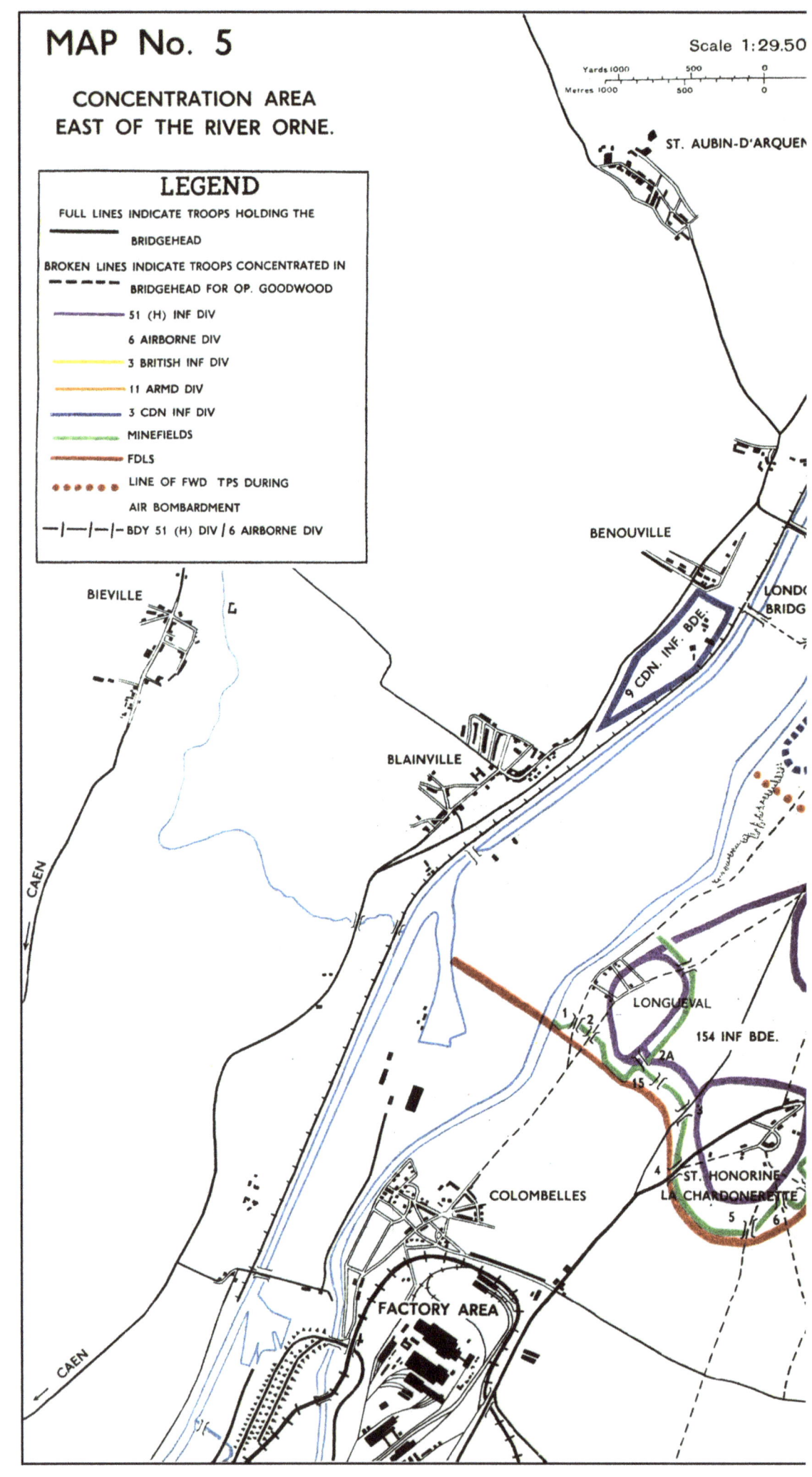

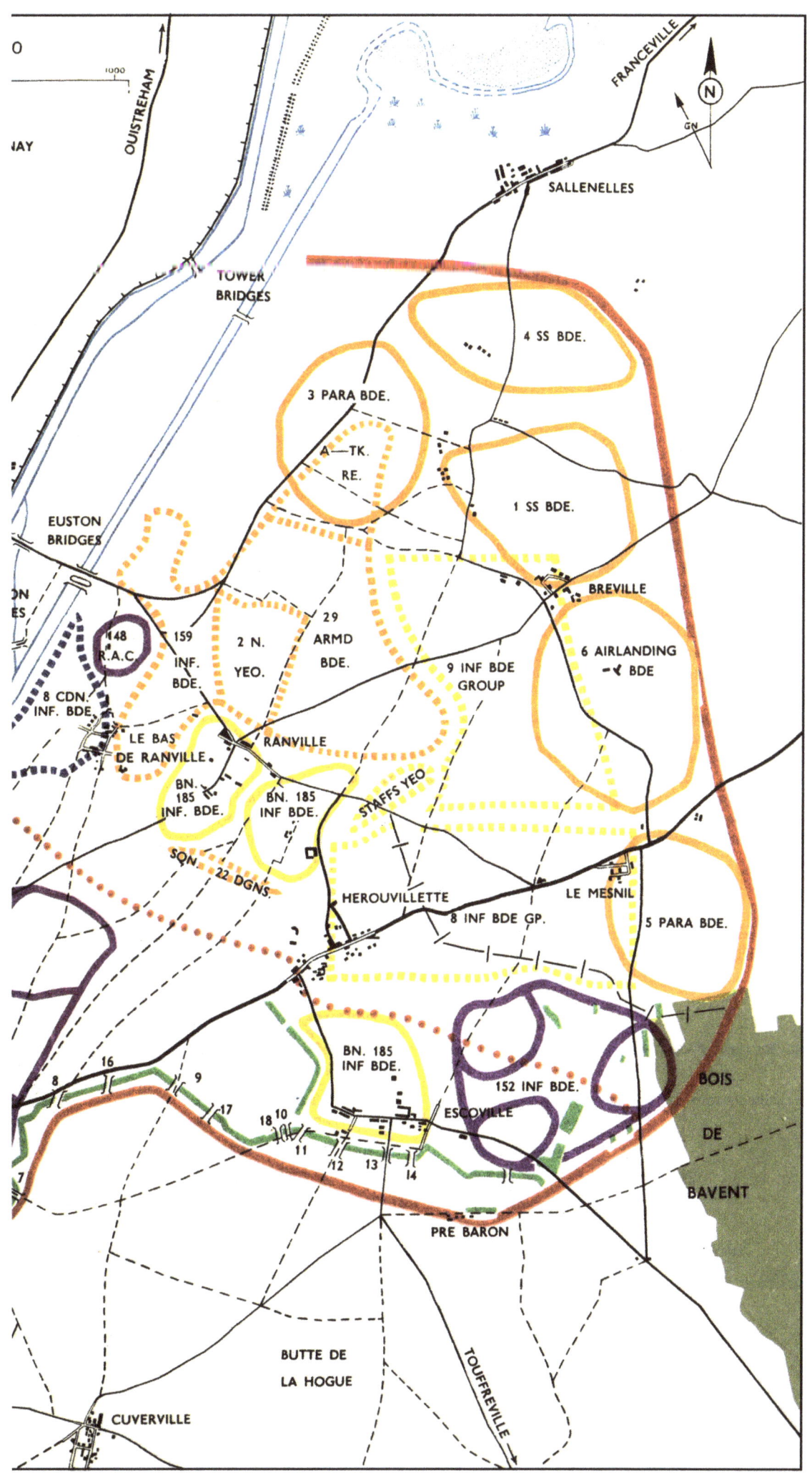

SECTION VI

RE PLAN

The RE tasks in connection with the mounting of Operation GOODWOOD and the operation itself, fall under four main headings.

(a) Development of routes for concentration, and for the subsequent build up during the battle, both up to the Start Lines and beyond, and the maintenance of these routes.

(b) Maintenance of existing bridges over the canal and River ORNE against enemy attacks, and the construction of additional bridges in order to assist the build up and maintenance of the formations operating East of the ORNE.

(c) Clearance of the defensive minefields round the FDLs of the bridgehead East of the ORNE to allow unrestricted movement of all vehicles particularly across the Start Lines.

(d) Unforeseen tasks during the battle, particularly the quick passage of armour across the potential obstacles in the line of the advance.

Route Development

It has already been shewn that three routes were considered necessary for the passage Eastwards of the armoured divisions, and each route had to be duplicated for tracked vehicles. Although in some places suitable routes existed already, a great deal of high speed RE work was required from 13 July onwards to complete all six by last light 16 July, when the concentration of 8 Corps East of the ORNE was due to begin. The sapper resources of Army and Corps could not cope with this demand and the engineer units of at least one armoured division were employed to assist in the construction of the tracked routes.

East of the ORNE it was also considered necessary to prepare three wheeled and three tracked routes from the bridges to the Start Line, and to carry them forward as far as possible as soon as the battle allowed this. 1 Corps was made responsible for the routes to the Start Line and had them completed by 17 July. Forward of the Start Line the responsibility for constructing the necessary routes was given to the attacking formations using their own divisional engineers, and backed up by the Corps troops engineers where necessary.

Maintenance of the above routes, after the battle started, was allotted as follows :—

Routes from the bridges to the line of the road STE HONORINE-ESCOVILLE were to be maintained by 1 Corps. Forward of this road, each Corps was responsible for the maintenance of the routes within its own boundaries.

In the case of 8 Corps, the rapid development of one wheeled route forward for early use by "F" Echelon wheeled vehicles was made the responsibility of 11 Armd Div. The most direct route lay through the villages of CUVERVILLE and DEMOUVILLE, both of which were targets for medium bombers in the air support programme. Although it was intended to use fragmentation and not HE bombs on these two targets, it was uncertain how much resultant damage to buildings would occur, with the consequent blocking of the narrow streets by rubble. A study of air photographs revealed a track, which ran down the East side of CUVERVILLE, skirted the orchards to the South-East, passed the Eastern outskirts of DEMOUVILLE, crossed the railway by an existing level crossing and joined the road CAEN-TROARN about 500 yards East of the main route. It appeared from the photograph as though this track was in use by the Germans for wheeled traffic. It was therefore decided to prepare this track as a temporary diversion as first priority, and to clear the road through CUVERVILLE and DEMOUVILLE as second priority, after which, the diversion would become a tank track only. 13 Fd Sqn (11 Armd Div) was therefore detailed to carry out this task, commencing as soon as 159 Inf Bde had cleared CUVERVILLE.

Bridging

In addition to the road bridges over the canal and the River ORNE between BENOUVILLE and RANVILLE captured intact by 6 Airborne Div on D Day, two extra pairs of bridges were constructed over both obstacles (see Map 5), while the road bridges themselves were strengthened to take class 40 loads. A small additional bridge over a stream between the two Southern bridges

19

was also necessary. Thus by the time the concentration began there were three separate Class 40 routes over the canal and river, and each bridge served one pair wheeled and track routes, approaching from the West and had a similar pair leading away towards the Start Line. Although there were only these three bridges available for the preliminary concentration and the start of the operation, it was strongly felt that additional bridges should be provided at the earliest opportunity. Plans were therefore made for 1 Corps to construct two additional crossings, one further North and one South of the existing ones to be completed by 2359 hours on D Day. 2 Cdn Corps also planned to construct two or three bridges over the River ORNE between CAEN and FAUBOURG DE VAUCELLES, as soon as the situation permitted, which would then leave the other bridges for the use of 1 Corps and 8 Corps.

Maintenance of the original three bridges over both the canal and the river, in the case of damage by enemy action, was the responsibility of 1 Corps.

Minefield Clearance

Prior to Operation GOODWOOD, the policy had been to hold the bridgehead East of the River ORNE against an armoured attack with the maximum use of wire and mines. As a result, there was a defensive minefield across the whole of our own front East of the river, which was thickly sewn. Arrangements therefore had to be made for our attacking troops to get through this minefield. This problem was discussed between CE 8 Corps and CE 1 Corps and it was agreed that 1 Corps would accept the responsibility for the clearance of the minefield, as the engineer units of 8 Corps were, at the time, fully committed, and it was not known when they would be moved into the area East of the ORNE. This task was delegated to CRE 51 (H) Div and his engineer resources were increased to deal with it by one field company from 3 Brit Div being placed under his command.

The orders from 1 Corps about the minefields clearance were as follows :—

(a) From inclusive STE HONORINE North-Westward and from inclusive ESCOVILLE East ward as many gaps as are required by 3 Cdn and 3 Brit Divs respectively.

(b) Between exclusive STE HONORINE and exclusive ESCOVILLE a forty foot gap will be made to carry forward each Corps route and tank track, and in addition, a similar gap will be made for any other existing route or track.

(c) Then, if there is time, all mines will be cleared between exclusive STE HONORINE and exclusive ESCOVILLE.

On the night 15/16 July (D—3/D—2) attempts were made to pick up all the mines in portions of the minefield from the pattern and records. This proved to be a failure for the following reasons :—

(a) Mines had been laid hastily in front of FDLs by various units in bad weather and subject to enemy interference. Minefield records were therefore found to be completely unreliable.

(b) The minefield had been heavily shelled and a number of mines were detonated, displaced or buried.

(c) Mines were laid for the most part in standing corn, in hay, or potato patches, making subsequent location difficult.

(d) Anti-personnel mines were added to the anti-tank minefield at a later date, thus making the task of clearing slower and more difficult.

As a result of this it was decided that gaps would have to be made using the normal gapping drill, without any reference to records. On the night of D—2/D—1 (16/17 July) this was done and fourteen gaps were made. These gaps were wired off with cattle fences, but not clearly marked with white tape. On 3 Brit Div front agreement was reached in detail about the requirements between the two CsRE. CRE 11 Armd Div sent over an officer to HQRE 51 (H) Div who also agreed to the proposed gaps on this front.

On 17 July, Commander 11 Armd Div visited HQ 51 (H) Div. He agreed to the gaps which had been made, but asked for three additional ones at specific places, to assist 29 Armd Bde and 159 Inf Bde to deploy on to their Start Lines. He also requested that the whole of the rear edge of the minefield should be clearly marked with a high wire fence draped with white tape. Accordingly, on the night D—1/D (17/18 July) four extra gaps were made, the rear fence was put up, the "going" up to several of the gaps was improved, white tape was put on the gap boundary and funnel fences, and the routes leading up to the minefield were signed.

It is of interest to note that, after the operation was over and clearance could be tackled by day, it took three field companies five days to lift all the mines on the front of 51 (H) Div.

Unforeseen Tasks during the Battle

For these tasks all divisions taking part in the attack had the full use of their divisional engineers, and in addition, units of 5 Aslt Regt (AVsRE) were allotted to the armoured divisions as follows :—

Gds Armd Div	79 Aslt Sqn less one tp (6 AVsRE with 4 fascines)
7 Armd Div	One tp 26 Aslt Sqn (6 AVsRE)
11 Armd Div	26 Aslt Sqn less one tp (10 AVsRE).

It was thought that the leading armoured division, in particular, would require engineer work on the two railway lines which crossed the front, as it appeared from air photographs that in some places these were potential obstacles to tanks and certain obstacles to wheeled vehicles. In order to ensure that there were enough sappers available well forward for these tasks, one troop 612 Fd Sqn, which was specially mounted in half-tracked vehicles for this operation with two armoured bulldozers, and the Assault Squadron moved immediately in rear of the leading armoured regiment, where they were suitably placed to deal very quickly with any obstacle which the tanks could not negotiate.

SECTION VII

THE FIRE PLAN

Planning and Control

The fire plan for the support of 8 Corps and the allotment of AGRA resources to 2 Cdn Corps and 1 Corps was the responsibility of CCRA 8 Corps.

The detailed fire plans in support of 3 Cdn and 3 Brit Divs were made by RA 2 Cdn Corps and RA 1 Corps respectively.

Counter Battery tasks, including co-ordination of fighter bomber and Royal Navy support were organised by CCRA 1 Corps.

Concentrations were to be fired by regiments grouped under control of 8 AGRA and counter battery shoots were under the control of 4 AGRA. Regiments shooting opening barrages were controlled by RA 51 (H) Div, RA 7 Armd Div and RA 3 Cdn Div on the 1 Corps, 8 Corps and 2 Cdn Corps fronts respectively.

Outline Tasks in each Phase

For RA purposes, the battle was to be divided into five phases.

The tasks in each phase were as follows, excluding CB which is dealt with separately in the next paragraph :—

PHASE I   (Before H—100 and during heavy bombing)

Anti-flak counter battery only ("APPLEPIE").

PHASE II   (H—100 to H—10)

Counter battery only.

PHASE III   (H Hour to H+80)

11 Armd Div was to advance to the line of the railway CAEN–CAGNY–VIMONT behind a barrage fired at Rate 3 by eight field regiments. The barrage was on a front of 2,000 yards, and advanced at a speed of 150 yards per minute to a depth of 4,300 yards. It then switched and advanced at the same rate for another 2,000 yards. Four optional pause lines for the barrage were provided.

3 Brit and 3 Cdn Divs were also to advance behind rolling barrages.

Concentrations were to be fired on a timed programme in support of all three Corps by the following :—

8 Corps	two field regiments,
	six medium regiments,
	three heavy regiments,
	one HAA regiment ;
2 Cdn Corps	two medium regiments,
1 Corps	one field regiment,
	three medium regiments.

PHASE IV   (H+80 to H+200)

During this phase, 11 Armd Div would be advancing beyond the railway CAEN–VIMONT and Gds Armd Div would have crossed the Start Line behind it, and both divisions were to have their own field regiments under command. 11 Armd Div was also to have one field regiment, two medium regiments and one heavy regiment, grouped under 8 AGRA, to fire pre-arranged concentrations at call.

The two armoured divisions were each to have one more medium regiment at call also.

3 Brit and 3 Cdn Divs were to have the same regiments in support as in Phase III available to fire concentrations.

PHASE V   (H+200 onwards)

While 11 and Gds Armd Divs were advancing to their first objectives, each of the three armoured divisions was to have its own two field regiments under command, and one medium regiment at call, and Gds Armd Div was to be supported by two batteries of 155 mms.

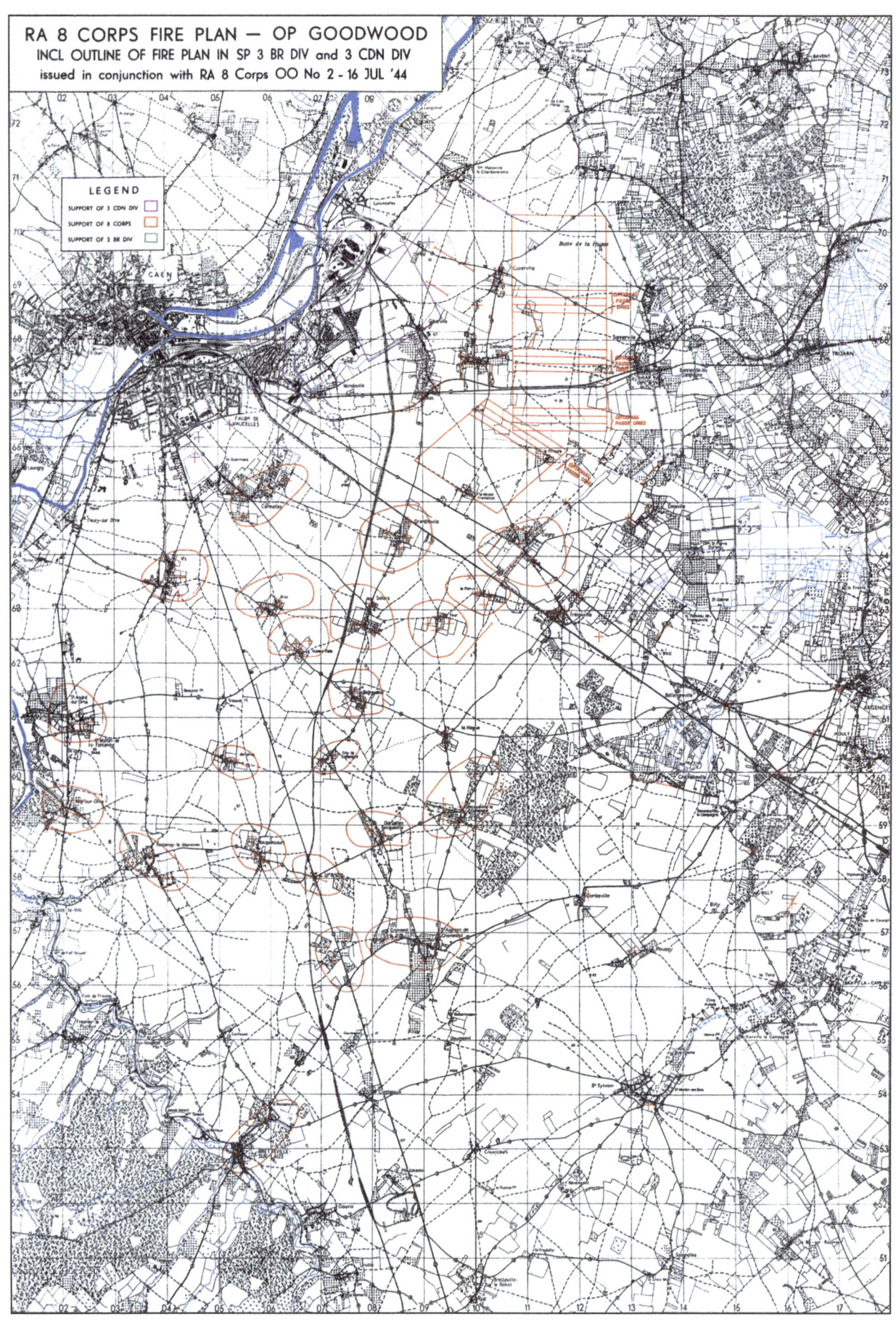

RA 8 CORPS FIRE PLAN — OP GOODWOOD
INCL OUTLINE OF FIRE PLAN IN SP 3 BR DIV and 3 CDN DIV
issued in conjunction with RA 8 Corps OO No 2 - 16 JUL '44

LEGEND
SUPPORT OF 3 CDN DIV
SUPPORT OF 8 CORPS
SUPPORT OF 3 BR DIV

RA 8 CORPS FIRE PLAN
OP GOODWOOD
Spread 1

RA 8 CORPS FIRE PLAN
OP GOODWOOD
Spread 2

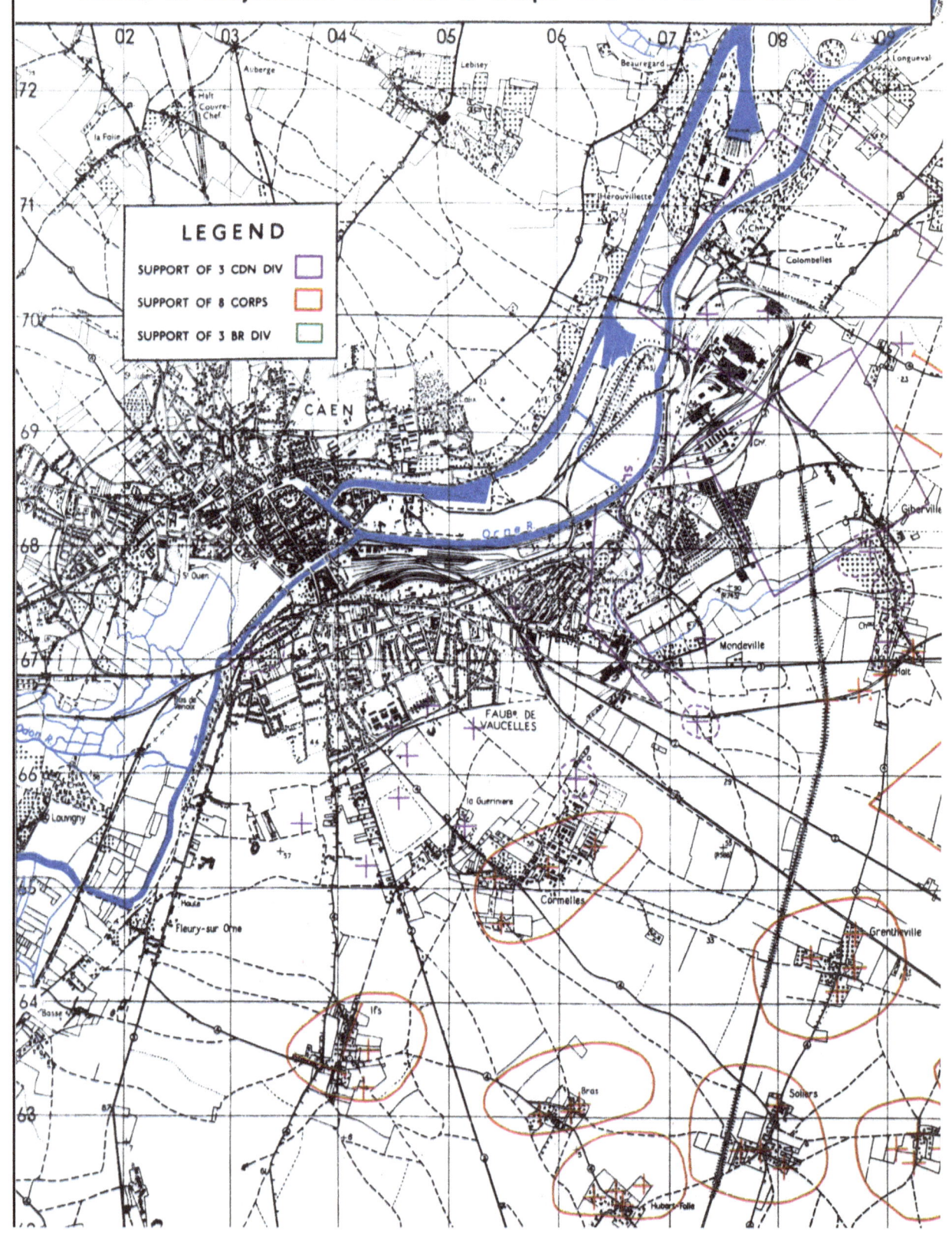

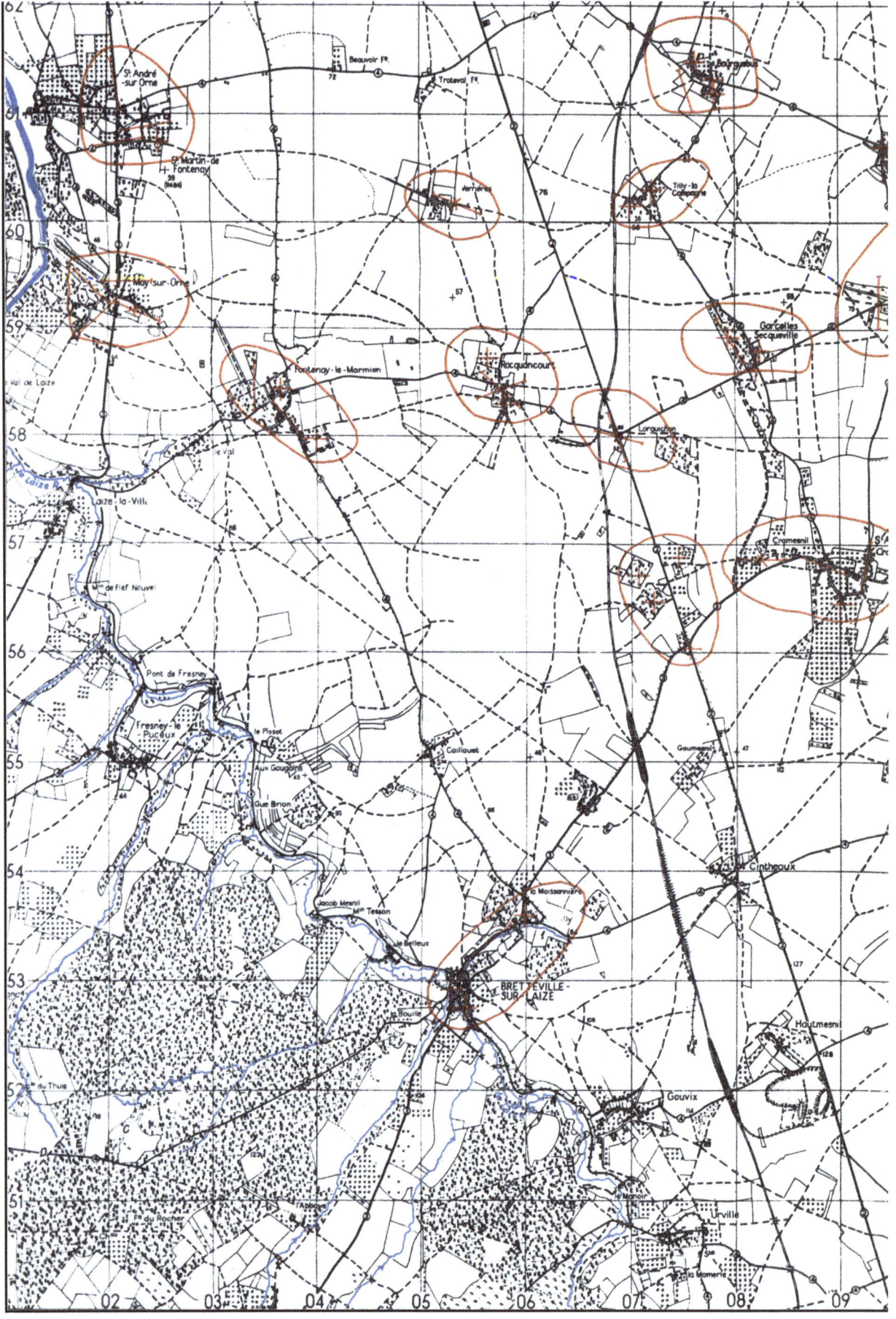

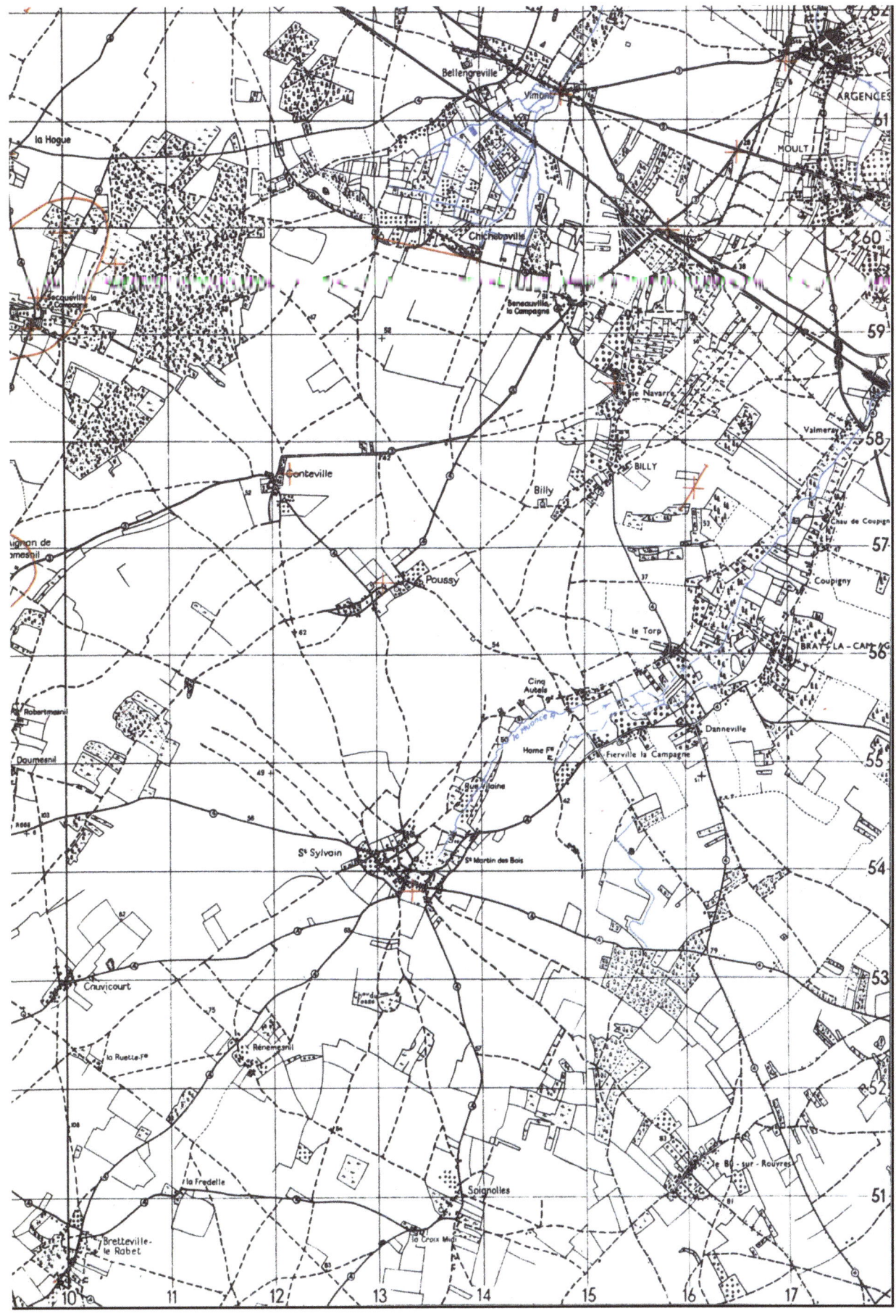

11 and Gds Armd Div were to have the same support from 8 AGRA as in the previous phase. Support for 3 Brit and 3 Cdn Divs was to be the same as in Phases III and IV.

Counter Battery Tasks

CCRA 1 Corps was charged with the co-ordination of all counter battery fire in support of Operation GOODWOOD.

For sub-division of counter battery tasks and resources, the area concerned was divided into two zones :—

RIGHT — 2 Cdn Corps Zone
LEFT — 1 Corps Zone

The boundary between the two zones was the railway CAEN–VIMONT. 12 Corps was to be asked to deal with hostile batteries between the Rivers ORNE and LAIZE and as far East as possible. The resources available were as follows :—

Phase	2 Cdn Corps Zone	1 Corps Zone
I and II	five field regiments	ten field regiments
	seven medium regiments	six medium regiments
	two heavy regiments	one heavy regiment
III	one medium regiment	one medium regiment
		one HAA regiment
IV and V	three medium regiments	four field regiments
	one heavy regiment	two medium regiments

In all phases, regiments engaged on counter battery tasks were controlled by 4 AGRA.

Anti-flak counter battery was to be fired in Phase I while the bombers were operating. The RAF reported later that this did not appear to reduce the flak very appreciably presumably because there were a number of hostile AA batteries unlocated.

The enemy gun areas as they were believed to be situated have been considered in Section III and are shown on Map No. 2. Those areas which were out of range of our guns were to be dealt with by fighter bombers of the RAF or by the Royal Navy.

Fighter Bombers

Fighter Bombers were to attack the hostile batteries North of TROARN and East of the River DIVES, and those South-East of TROARN in the area of JAUVILLE.

Attacks were timed for H+10 and H+40, and could be repeated if called for over ASSU nets.

Aircraft were also available to lay smoke screens to blind enemy OPs and batteries on the high ground East of the River DIVES immediately South of CABOURG.

Royal Navy

Three ships were available :—

HMS ROBERTS	2×15″ guns	(Range 30,000 yards)
HMS MAURITIUS	12×6″ guns	(Range 24,000 yards)
HMS ENTERPRISE	7×6″ guns	(Range 19,000 yards)

HMS ROBERTS was limited to 100 rounds of ammunition.

The ships were to deal with the coastal guns in the FRANCEVILLE and CABOURG areas.

Gun Areas

Owing to the small size of the bridgehead East of the River ORNE, most of our guns had to be sited to the West. This meant that the distance over which they could support the advance before they had to move was limited.

The plan was for three medium regiments to move to the area of CAGNY as soon as possible and for certain other regiments to move Southwards on the West bank of the river as soon as FAUBOURG DE VAUCELLES had been cleared.

Registration

Registration was only to be allowed for regiments of 2 Cdn and 1 Corps already in position, and was to be kept to an absolute minimum.

Air OP

652 Air OP Sqn was to provide up to 50 sorties over the 1 Corps counter battery zone during Phases III and IV. One flight of this squadron was in support of 3 Br Div; each armoured division was supported by a flight of 659 Air OP Sqn and 8 AGRA by a flight of 658 Air OP Sqn.

Ammunition Allotment

The allotment of ammunition was :—

    Field   500 rounds per gun,
    Medium 300 rounds per gun,
    Heavy   150 rounds per gun.

SECTION VIII
AIR PLAN

GENERAL

Operation GOODWOOD was to be preceded by the largest air effort ever made in direct support of ground forces.

The plan to employ such a large air force was not, in the first place, generally approved. The RAF, who were not strongly in favour, pointed out that there was little previous experience to draw upon, and that on two previous occasions, at CASSINO and CAEN, results had been disappointing. The bombing had not eliminated enemy opposition, and our own troops had been hampered by bad cratering and rubble-blocked roads.

The Army maintained that in view of the considerable opposition likely to be met from enemy artillery both in front of and on the flanks of the advance, and the long distance which had to be covered quickly if a breakout was to be achieved, the operation could not take place at all unless maximum air support could be given.

It was finally settled that the Royal Air Force could and would provide the support asked for and the Air Officer Commanding 83 Group RAF returned personally to UK to arrange it.

It was laid down that if the air support was not available on the proposed D Day, the operation would be postponed. The most likely cause of this would be the weather, which was not as "settled" as could have been wished, and a definite forecast as to whether it would be favourable on the day could not be expected more than about eight hours before H Hour. The possibility of postponement gave rise to several serious problems, which are brought out elsewhere in the book.

REQUIREMENTS

1. Aircraft other than 83 Group RAF

As already mentioned, 8 Corps was compelled to advance down a narrow corridor, the sides of which were held by the enemy. If the leading armour was not to be held up almost as soon as it had started, the enemy positions in and along the sides of the corridor had to be neutralised. The positions included the following :—

East of the corridor	TOUFFREVILLE
	SANNERVILLE
	BANNEVILLE LA CAMPAGNE
	EMIEVILLE
West of the corridor	GIBERVILLE
	Factory area (target 'A' on map) and South-East suburbs of CAEN.

These places were to be destroyed and cratering was accepted.

Two enemy strongpoints in the corridor, CUVERVILLE and DEMOUVILLE, were to be neutralised, but here cratering was not acceptable. Other areas in the corridor (marked C, D, E and F on the map) were also to be neutralised.

The village of CAGNY was to be destroyed and cratering was accepted.

Enemy gun areas (I, P and Q on map) were to be neutralised.

In order to assist in laying on attacks on these targets, the GSO I (Int) at Second Army was sent to the UK with traces and photographs of enemy positions and defences. The RAF was also assured that there would be no troops within 2,000 yards of HE bomb targets, within 2,500 yards of areas for fragmentation bombing, or any troops not dug in within 3,000 yards of any target area. This necessitated a slight withdrawal from our FDLs, which, owing to the small area of the bridgehead East of the river, was awkward but had to be accepted.

These demands were made on 14 July and it was particularly asked that Second Army should receive the answer by 1700 hours 16 July.

MAP No. 7
THE AIR PLAN
LEGEND
TARGETS FOR HEAVY NIGHT BOMBERS H.E. BOMBS
TARGETS FOR MEDIUM BOMBERS
TARGETS FOR HEAVY DAY BOMBERS (FRAGMENTATION BOMBS)
TARGETS FOR 83 GROUP R.A.F.
LIMIT OF BRIDGEHEAD EAST OF R. ORNE
LINE OF FORWARD TROOPS DURING AIR BOMBARDMENT
OUISTREHAM
GABOURE
DIVES-SUR-MER
FRANCEVILLE-PLAGE
SALLENELLES
BEUVILLE
BENOUVILLE
BREVILLE
BRUCOURT
CANAL DE CAEN
RIVER ORNE
RANVILLE
HEROUVILLETTE
ESCOVILLE
BOIS DE
GOUSTRANVILLE
COLOMBELLES
BURES
TOUFFREVILLE
SANNERVILLE
TROARN
CAEN
MONDEVILLE
DEMOUVILLE
BANNEVILLE LA CAMPAGNE
EMIEVILLE
JAUVILLE
FAUBOURG DE VAUCELLES
LOUVIGNY
CORMELLES
LE MESNIL FREMENTEL
CAGNY
FLEURY SUR ORNE
GRENTHVILLE
EVRECY
IFS
BRAS
SOLIERS
FOUR
FRENOUVILLE
HUBERT-FOLIE
ST. ANDRE SUR ORNE
BOURGUEBUS
VIMONT
ARGENCES
OVERRIERES
LA HOGUE
CHICHEBOVILLE
SECQUEVILLE LA CAMPAGNE
MAY SUR ORNE
ROCQUANCOURT
GARCELLES SECQUEVILLE
R. ORNE
FONTENAY-LE-MARMION
CLINCHAMPS SUR ORNE
THURY-HARCOURT
FALAISE
R. MUANCE
SCALE 1:100,000
MILES
ST. SYLVAIN

MAP No. 7
THE AIR PLAN
Spread 1

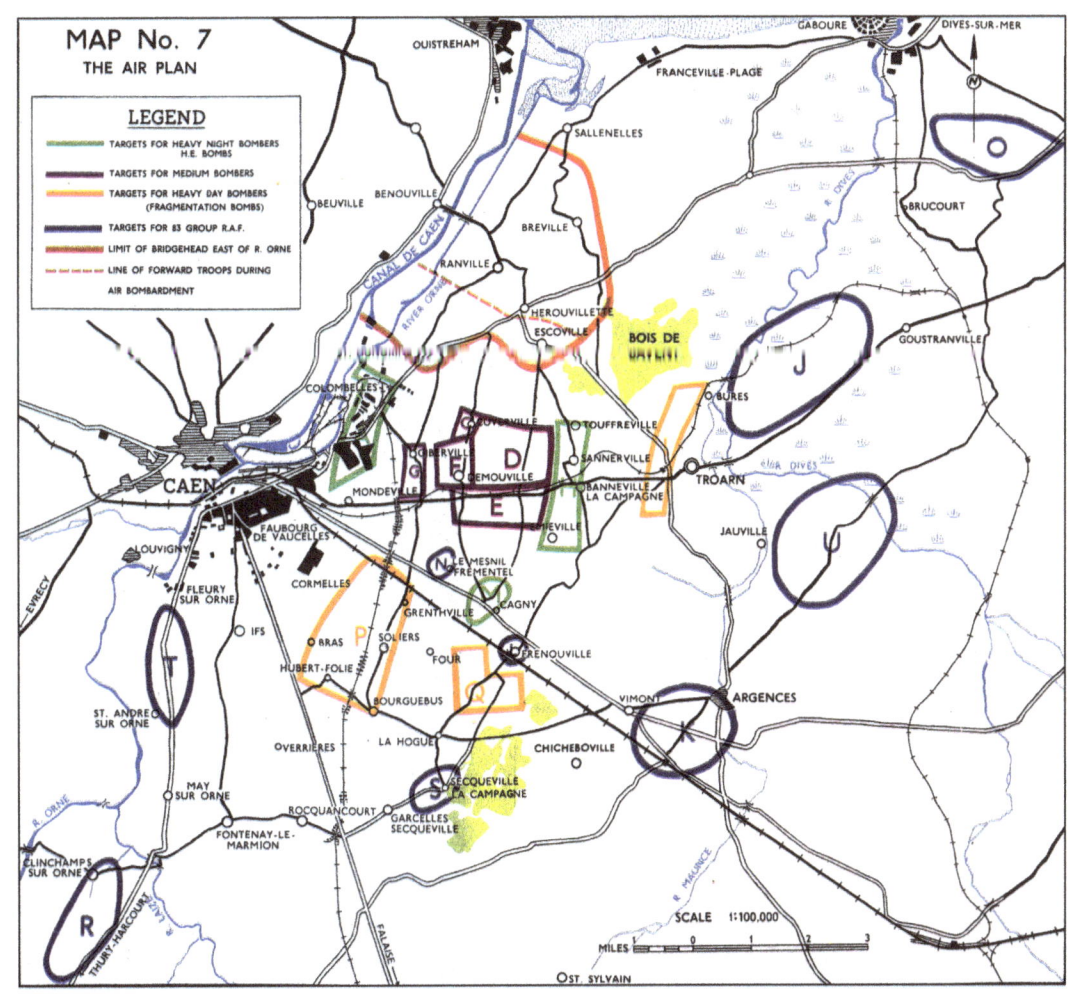

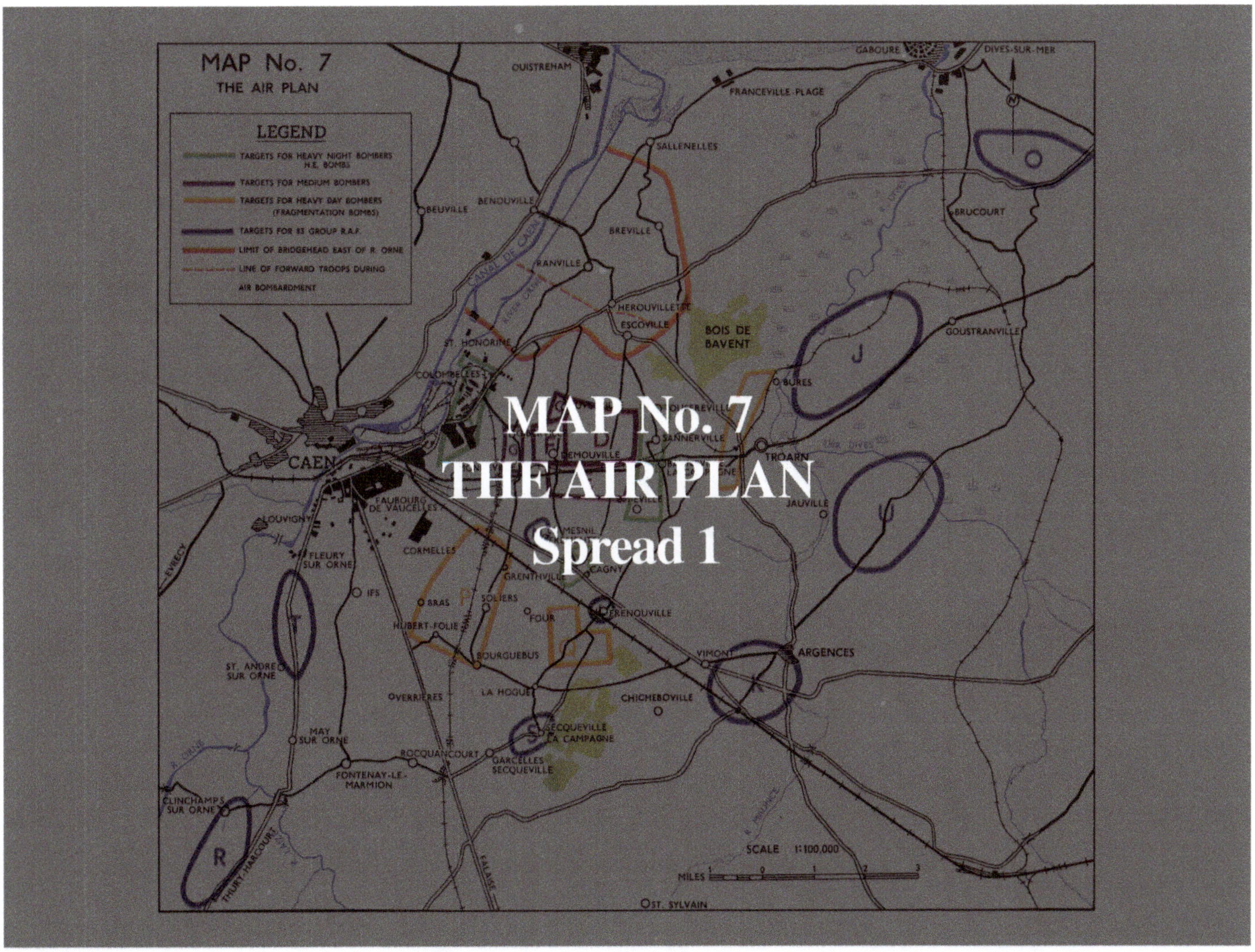

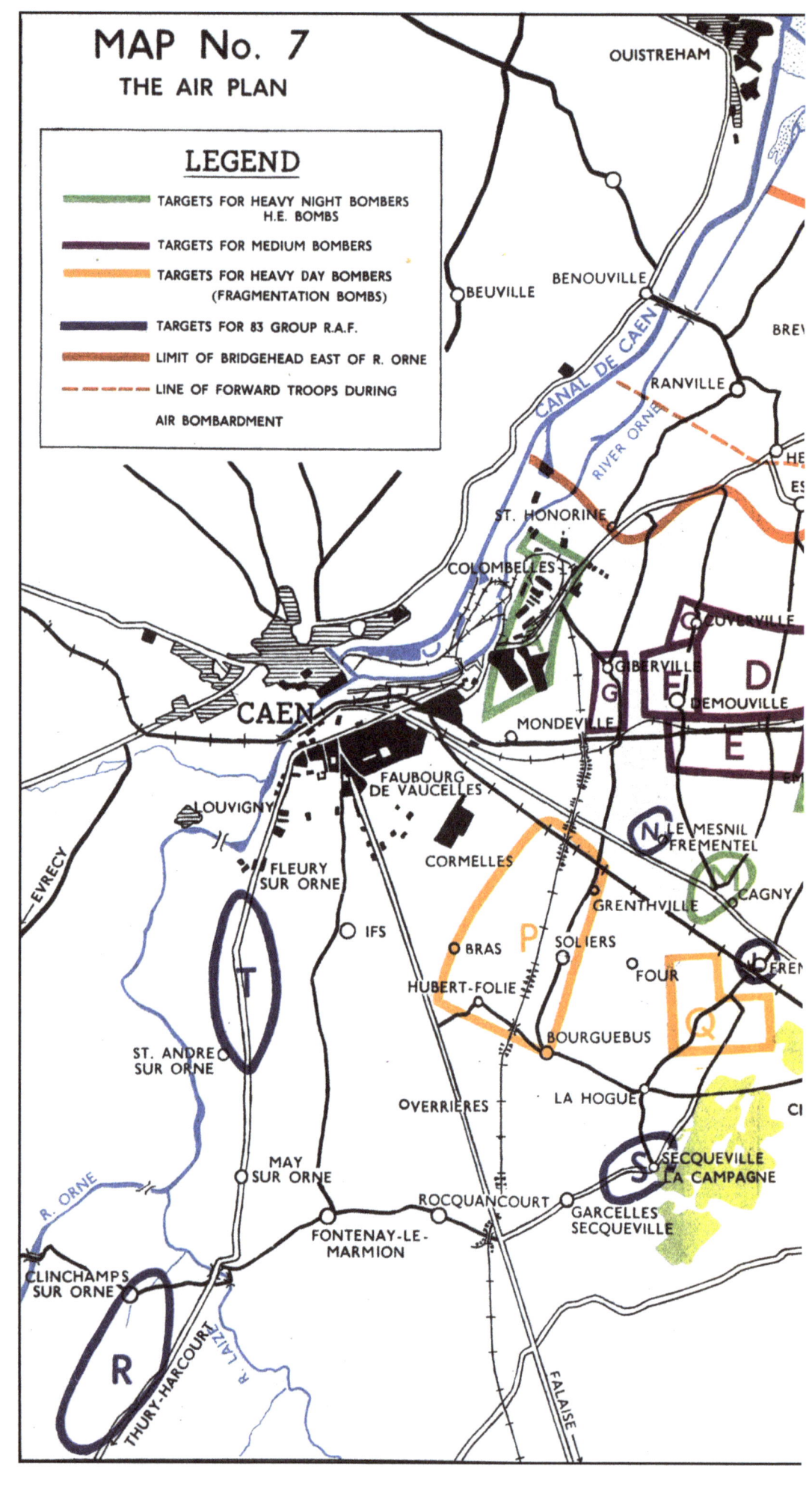

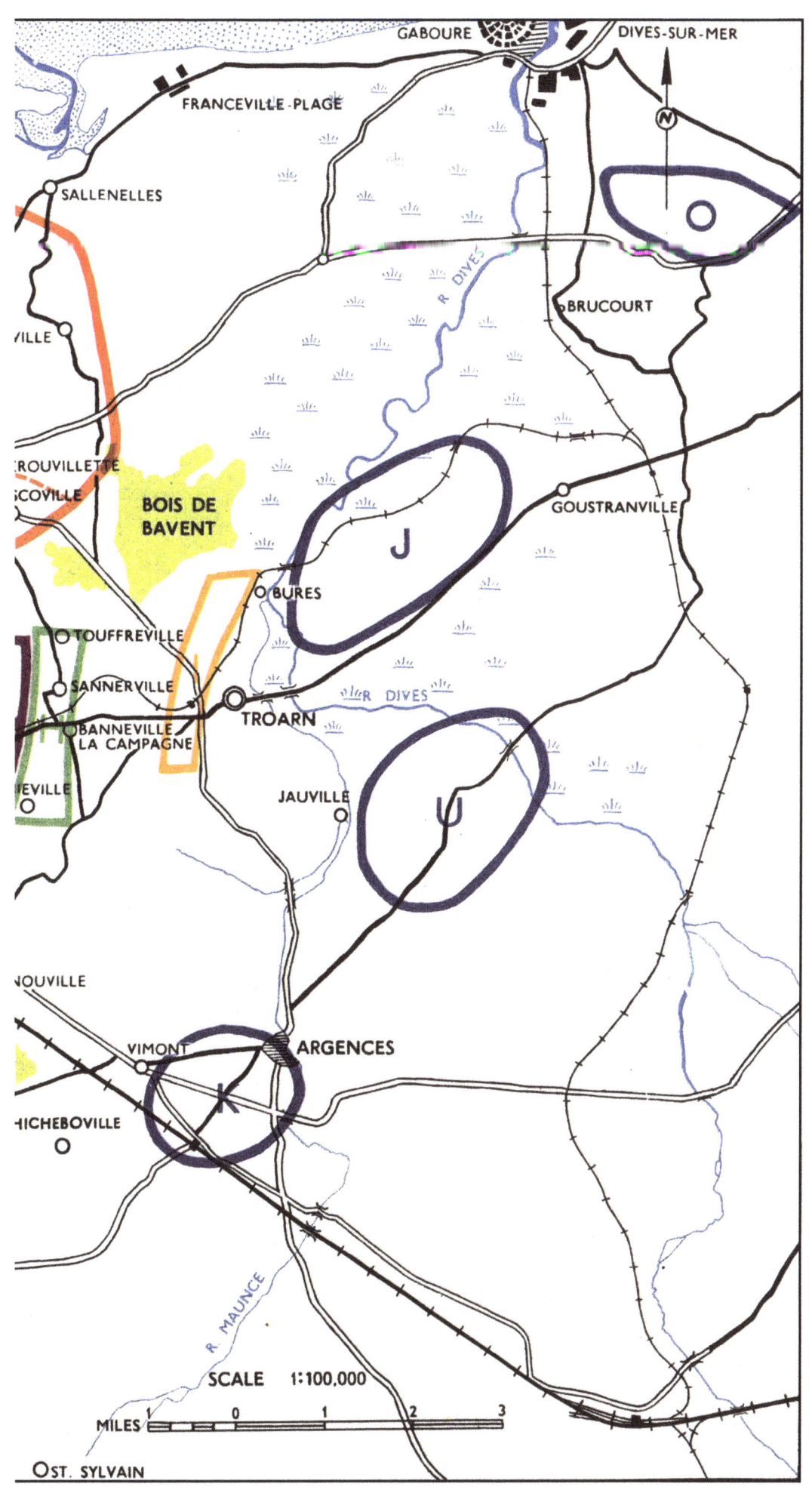

2. **Aircraft of 83 Group RAF**

83 Group, which was at that time controlling some squadrons of aircraft which had arrived as the leading elements of 84 Group, undertook to meet the other requirements. These included attacks on:—

(i) Enemy defended localities at LE MESNIL FREMENTEL, FRENOUVILLE, GRENTHE-VILLE and GARCELLES SECQUEVILLE.

(ii) Enemy gun areas, marked O, J and U on the map.

(iii) Enemy reserves areas—FLEURY SUR ORNE–ST ANDRE SUR ORNE; CLINCHAMPS SUR ORNE (between rivers ORNE and LAIZE) and VIMONT-ARGENCES.

Apart from pre-arranged targets, 83 Group was also asked to provide the normal impromptu direct air support.

Although the requirements have been split into those for aircraft provided by 83 Group and aircraft NOT provided by them, joint planning was done as normally at an Army/Tactical Group level, Tactical Group passing on requirements which they themselves did not meet.

THE PLAN

1. The target areas arranged for Medium, Heavy night bombers (Lancasters and Halifaxes) and Heavy day bombers (Flying Fortresses) are shown on the attached map. Other details were:—

Time of Attack	Number and type of Aircraft	Targets	Type of Bomb
0545–0630	1056 heavy night bombers (RAF Bomber Command)	A. H. M.	HE
0700–0745	482 medium bombers (IX USAAF)	C. D. E. F. G.*	Fragmentation
0830–0900	539 heavy day bombers (IX USAAF)	I. P. Q.	Fragmentation

* Target G (the village of GIBERVILLE) could not be bombed with HE.

2. **Aircraft of 83 Group RAF**

Aircraft of 83 Group were to attack the targets shown on the map while the other attacks were going in.

Other tasks of 83 Group included maximum interference with any enemy movement West from ARGENCES–VIMONT area and armed recce within an area of 25 miles of CAEN to interfere with movement into the battle area, with particular attention to area South of ST ANDRE SUR ORNE and the area between the rivers ORNE and LAIZE around CLINCHAMPS SUR ORNE.

It is of interest to record here that no enemy aircraft interfered with the air bombardment and losses amounted to 9 Heavy, 5 Medium and 11 Fighter Bombers, all caused by flak.

3. **Air Support Signals Unit (ASSU)**

The ASSU was deployed with tentacles, in certain cases, down to brigades. The exact layout is shown in the accompanying diagram.

The intention was to use a Visual Control Post (VCP), which was to move with HQ 29 Armd Bde. It was manned by a RAF Controller and an Air Liaison Officer (ALO), and its function was to guide airborne aircraft on to impromptu targets within visual range. In the event, the Controller was wounded in the early stages and as the ALO was new to the task, the Visual Control Post was not able to function as intended.

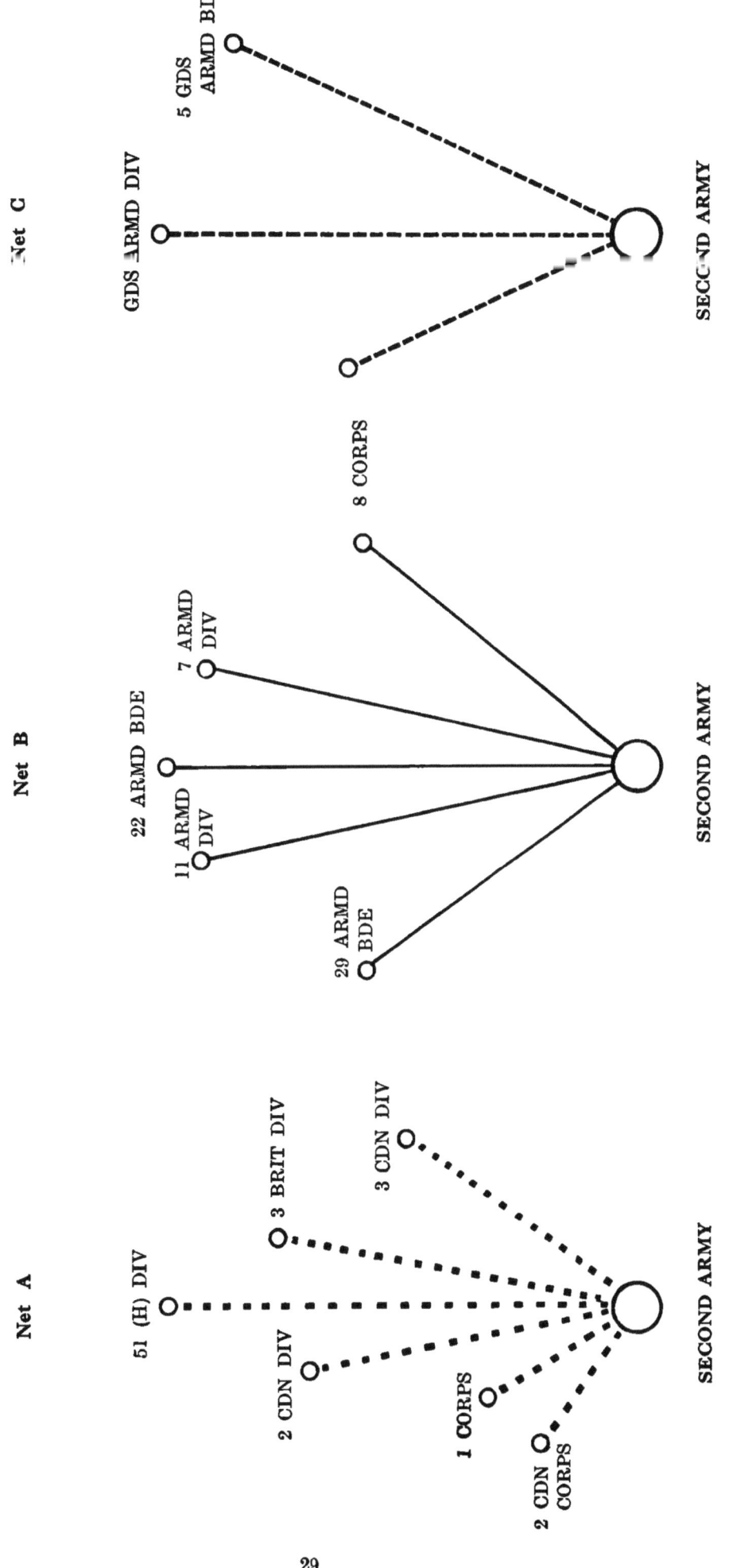

PART II

Account of the Battle

SECTION I

EVENTS PRIOR TO THE START OF OPERATION GOODWOOD

The events here described do not cover the planning of the operation, which has already been dealt with in Part I.

On 15 July (D—3), 7 Armd Div came under command of 8 Corps from 30 Corps, but remained in its present area North of TILLY SUR SEULLES.

During the day, 185 Inf Bde (3 Brit Div) were placed under command of 51 (H) Div and moved into the line on the ORNE bridgehead to relieve 153 Inf Bde which then concentrated West of the river.

During the night 16/17 July (D—2/D—1) the concentration before the operation commenced. As soon as it was dark, 9 Brit Inf Bde (3 Brit Div) moved across the ORNE, as planned, followed by Main HQ 11 Armd Div and the whole of 159 Inf Bde Group. The units of 29 Armd Bde moved up to their assembly areas West of the river, where they remained hidden throughout 17 July. 7 Armd Div also moved to the forward assembly area North of CULLY. Finally, 8 Brit Inf Bde (3 Brit Div) crossed the ORNE. All these moves were completed according to plan, and without incident, except for some shelling of the bridges.

During 17 July (D—1), emergency arrangements were made to contact 11 Armd Div, as the leading formation of the 8 Corps attack, in case the lines of communication across the river were broken, through HQ 1 Corps, which was West of the ORNE, by wireless to HQ 6 Airborne Div, where a LO from 11 Armd Div was located.

3 Brit Div also made arrangements to have a LO with 11 Armd Div during the early stages of the attack, transferring him to Gds Armd Div when that formation came into the battle.

The place, in which it had been decided to begin at H Hour the construction of the first of the two additional bridges South of LONDON Bridges (TAY), was in fact discovered to be on a route used by 9 Cdn Inf Bde, and the commencement of work could not therefore begin until H+3.

During the night 17/18 July (D—1/D), the concentration continued according to plan. 29 Armd Bde followed by 2nd Northamptonshire Yeomanry (2 N YEO) crossed the bridges, the move being slightly accelerated by enemy shelling. At about 0145 hours, information was received from HQ 8 Corps that Operation GOODWOOD would take place on 18 July, and H Hour was confirmed as 0745 hours.

During the night, Gds Armd Div moved forward and halted with the heads of the columns about 5,000 yards West of the bridges, ready to move on and start crossing the bridges at H Hour. Similarly, 7 Armd Div moved out of its assembly area, and also halted about 5,000 yards West of the ORNE. 8 Cdn Inf Bde crossed the river into its allotted area round LE BAS DE RANVILLE, while 9 Cdn Inf Bde concentrated on the West bank of the CANAL DE CAEN, in the orchards between BLAINVILLE and BENOUVILLE.

By 0515 hours 18 July, the additional gaps in the minefield, required for 29 Armd Bde and 159 Inf Bde to reach their Start Lines, were completed, and the stage was all set for Operation GOODWOOD.

SECTION II

OPERATIONS DURING THE MORNING OF 18 JULY

A. 8 CORPS

11 Armd Div

The morning of 18 July dawned bright and clear, a good augury for the air support programme and for the battle itself.

Punctually at 0545 hours, heavy bombers of RAF Bomber Command appeared and for 45 minutes bombs were dropped by a force of 1056 Halifaxs and Lancasters on the woods and villages on the East of the line of advance, particularly TOUFFREVILLE, SANNERVILLE, BANNEVILLE LA CAMPAGNE, EMIEVILLE and CAGNY, and also on the factory areas of COLOMBELLES and MONDEVILLE, which were 2 Cdn Corps objectives.

At 0700 hours 482 medium bombers of IX USAAF started an attack using fragmentation bombs on the villages of CUVERVILLE and DEMOUVILLE, and on the area over which 29 Armd Bde was to advance, from approximately the line CUVERVILLE—TOUFFREVILLE to a line about 1,000 yards South of the road CAEN–TROARN. This attack lasted for 45 minutes.

During this air programme, 29 Armd Bde started to move out of the concentration area through the gaps in the minefields and formed up on the Start Line South-West of ESCOVILLE. The leading regiment was The 3rd Royal Tank Regiment (3 R Tks) with under command one motor company (G Company, 8th Battalion The Rifle Brigade (Prince Consort's Own)) (8 RB), one SP battery (H Battery, 13th (Honourable Artillery Company) Regiment Royal Horse Artillery (13 RHA)), one squadron Flails (22nd Dragoons (22DGNS)), and one troop Assault RE (from 26 Aslt Sqn).

The remainder of the brigade followed in the order :—

Tac HQ 29 Armd Bde,

2nd Fife and Forfar Yeomanry (2 FF YEO) with under command F Coy 8 RB and

I Bty 13 RHA,

23rd Hussars (23 H) with under command H Coy 8 RB and G Bty 13 RHA,

8 RB less three companies.

Owing to the narrow gap, barely 1,000 yards wide, between the enemy positions at DEMOUVILLE on the Right, and LIROSE, West of BANNEVILLE LA CAMPAGNE, on the Left, 29 Armd Bde was forced to advance one regiment up for the first 4,000 yards. Each regiment was organized into three waves :—

First Wave	Two leading squadrons.
Second Wave	Recce Troop, RHQ, Carrier platoon of motor company.
Third Wave	Reserve squadron, motor company, RHA battery.

At the same time, 159 Inf Bde moved out from its concentration area North of LE BAS DE RANVILLE. The leading unit, 3rd Battalion The Monmouthshire Regiment (3 MON), with A Sqn 2 N YEO in support, formed up on its Start Line just South of the minefield and West of STE HONORINE LA CHARDONERETTE. 1st Battalion The Herefordshire Regiment (1 HEREFORD) with C Sqn 2 N YEO in support formed up at the track junction 900 yards North of 3 MON. 4th Battalion The King's Shropshire Light Infantry (4 KSLI) formed up in the orchards on the South edge of LE BAS DE RANVILLE.

As soon as the medium bomber programme finished at 0745 hours, (H Hour), the artillery programme started. Eight field regiments fired a rolling barrage in front of 29 Armd Bde. Two field, six medium, and two heavy regiments fired a programme of concentrations on the flanks of the barrage, particularly on the villages of CUVERVILLE, DEMOUVILLE, and GIBERVILLE on the Right, and EMIEVILLE and CAGNY on the Left. The remainder of the villages on the flanks were included in the artillery programmes for 3 Cdn Div on the Right and 3 Brit Div on the Left. In addition, three heavy regiments carried out harassing fire on all the villages South of the railway CAEN–VIMONT from BRAS on the West to FRENOUVILLE on the East, and as far South as GARCELLES SEQUEVILLE and SEQUEVILLE LA CAMPAGNE.

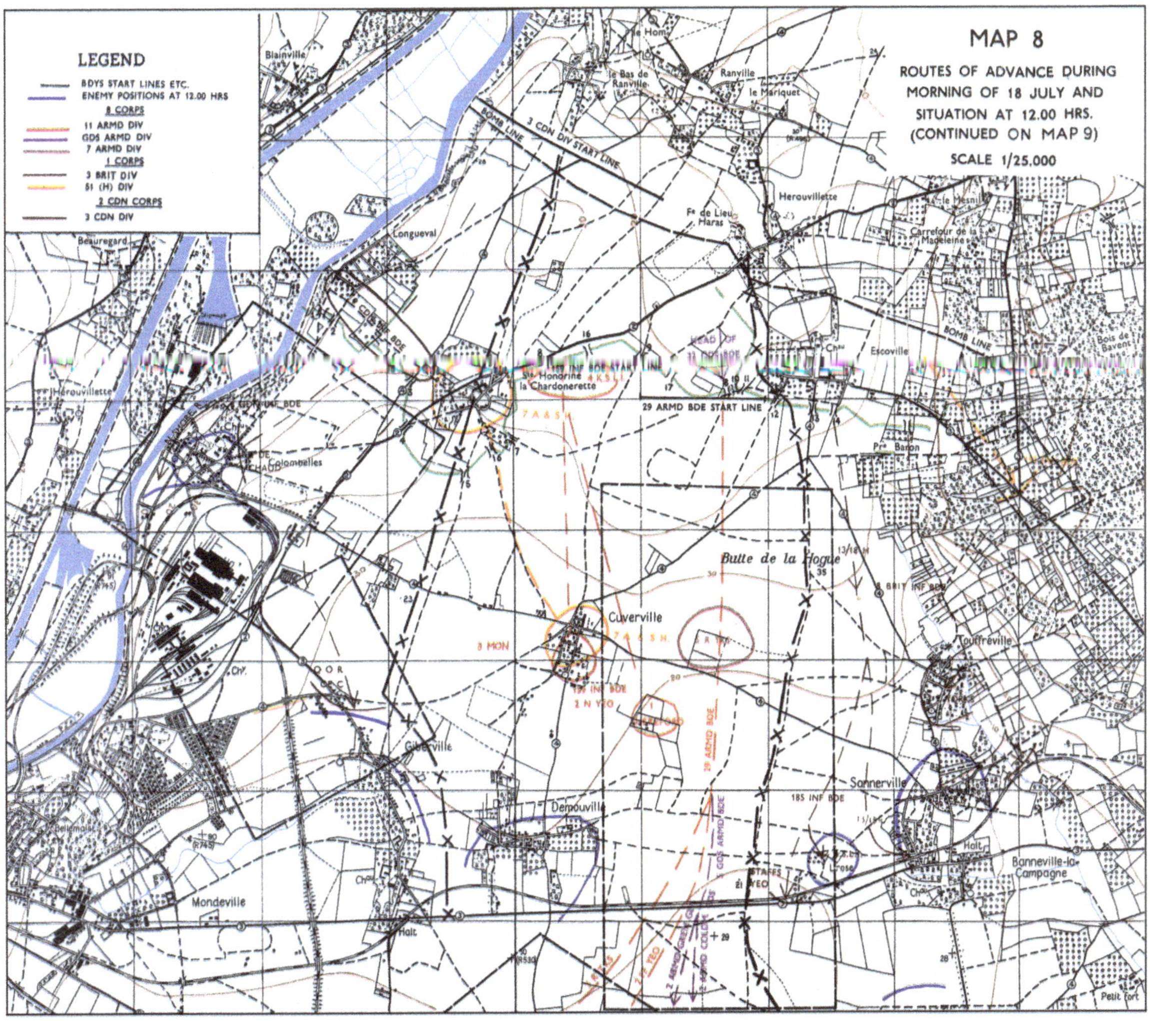
MAP 8
ROUTES OF ADVANCE DURING MORNING OF 18 JULY AND SITUATION AT 12.00 HRS.
(CONTINUED ON MAP 9)
SCALE 1/25,000
LEGEND
BDYS START LINES ETC.
ENEMY POSITIONS AT 12.00 HRS
8 CORPS
11 ARMD DIV
GDS ARMD DIV
7 ARMD DIV
1 CORPS
3 BRIT DIV
51 (H) DIV
2 CDN CORPS
3 CDN DIV
Ranville
Herouvillette
Longueval
Escoville
Cuverville
Butte de la Hogue
Touffreville
Giberville
Demouville
Sannerville
Mondeville
Banneville-la-Campagne
Colombelles
29 ARMD BDE START LINE
3 CDN DIV START LINE
BOMB LINE

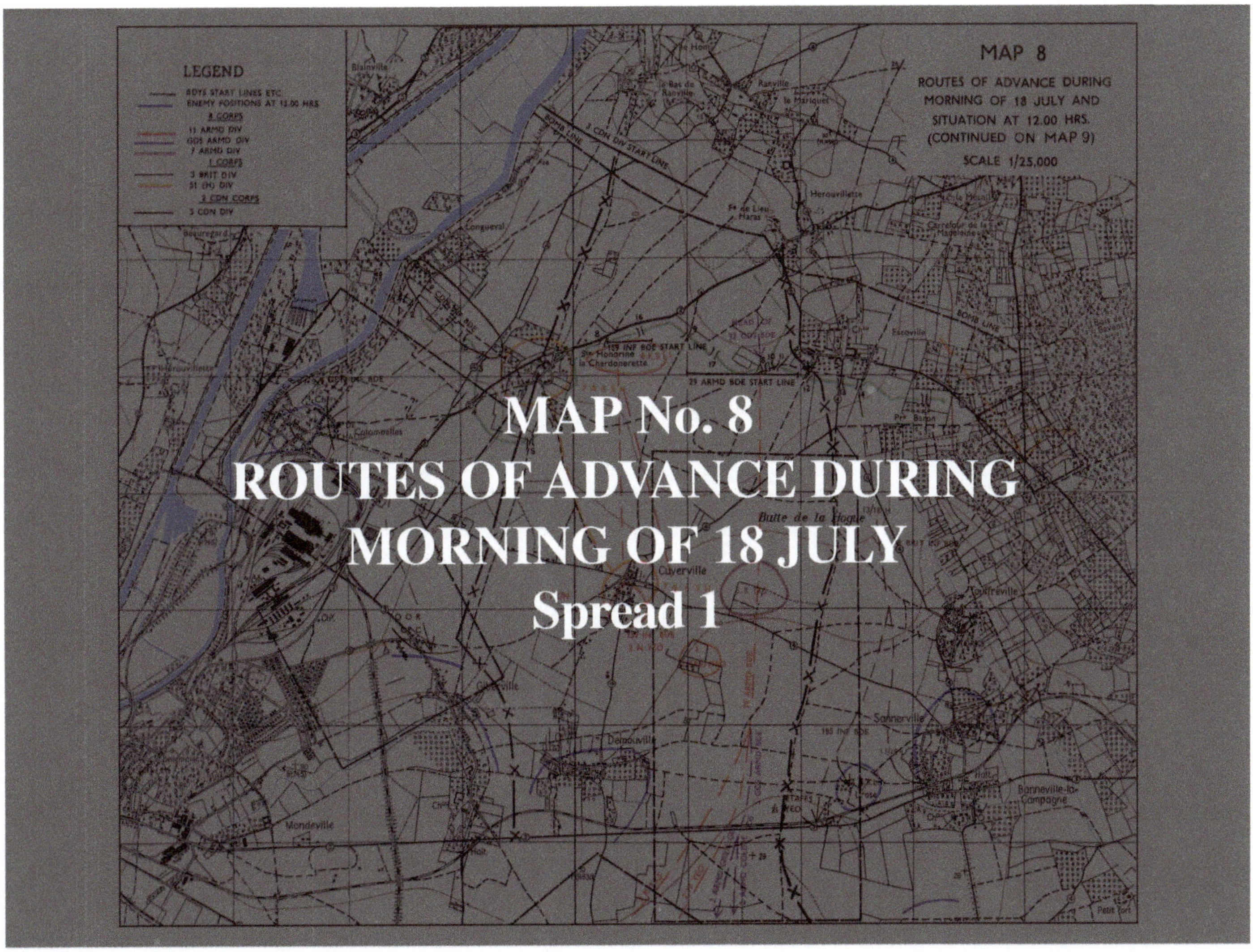
MAP No. 8
ROUTES OF ADVANCE DURING
MORNING OF 18 JULY
Spread 1

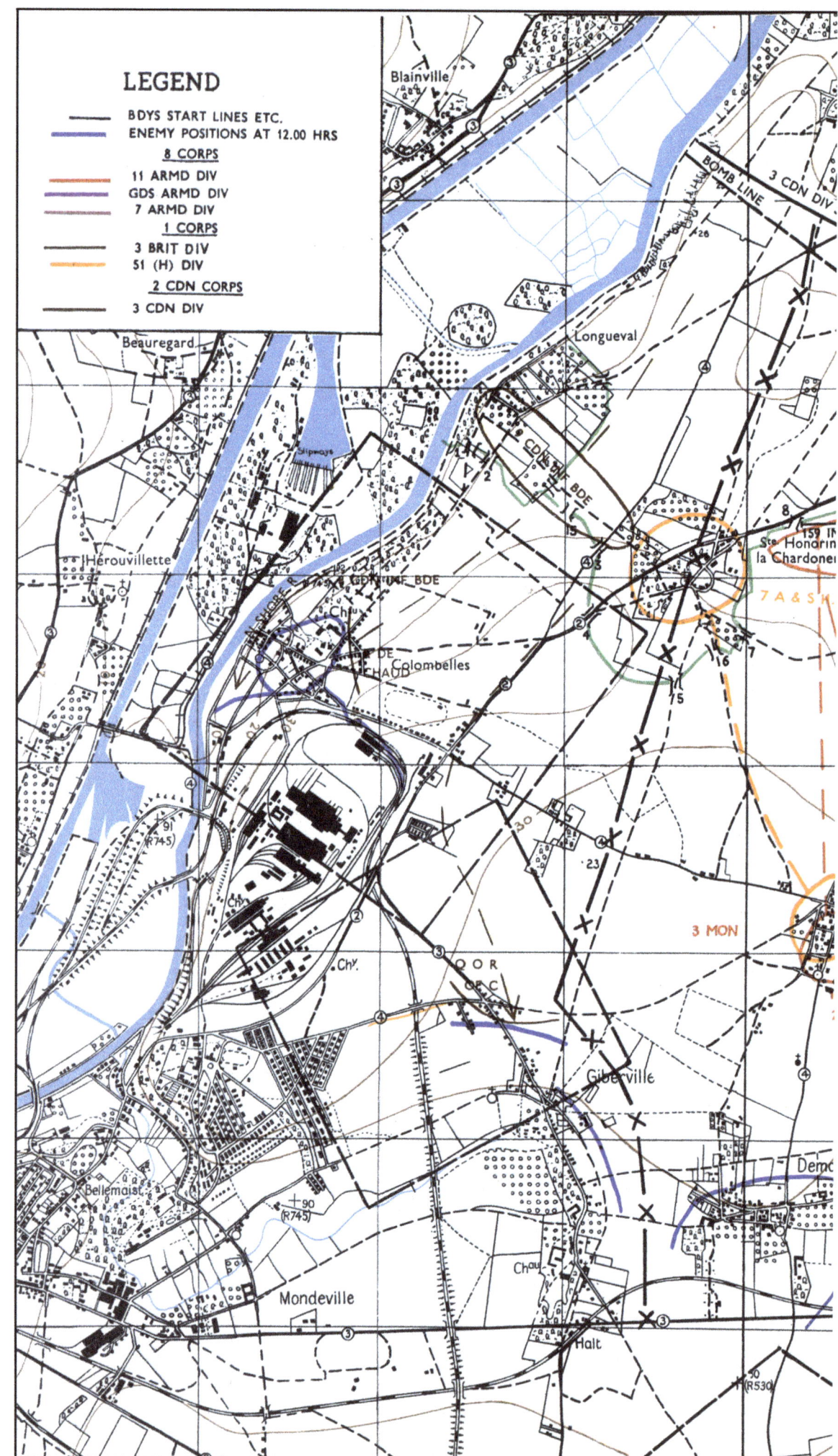

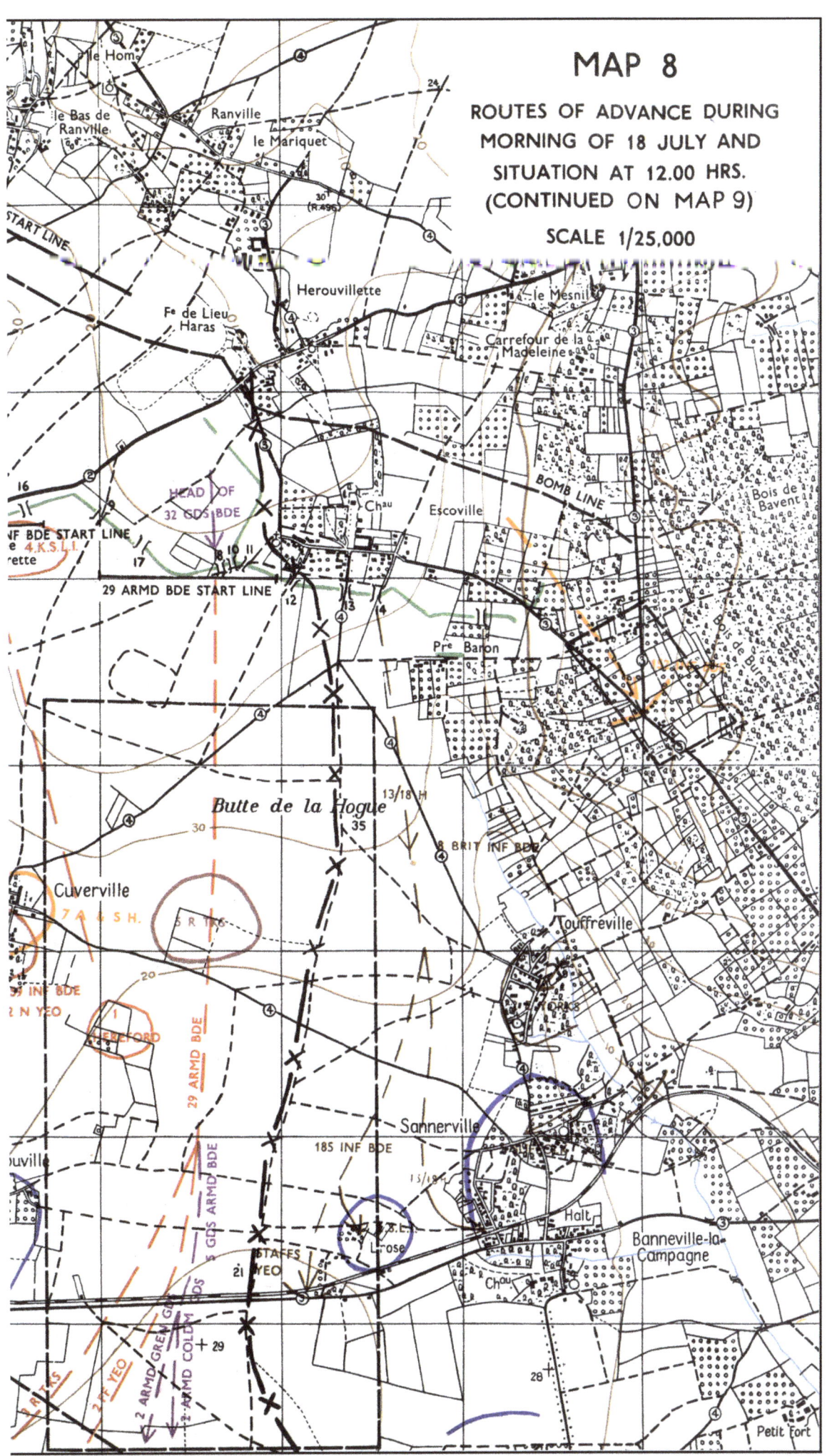

At H Hour, as soon as this artillery programme started, 29 Armd Bde and 159 Inf Bde moved forward from their Start Lines.

At 0800 hours, the third wave of the air support programme started. 539 heavy day bombers of VIII USAAF dropped fragmentation bombs on enemy guns in the areas of BOURGUEBUS and TROARN for 30 minutes.

The advance started well and at 0800 hours 3 R Tks were reported to be going well, closely followed by 2 FF YEO, and by H+35 the third regiment, 23 H, was passing through the minefield.

The first slight opposition was encountered by 3 R Tks from the orchards South-East of CUVERVILLE, where an enemy infantry platoon was soon dealt with, while two anti-tank guns in the same area were quickly knocked out. At 0830 hours the barrage had reached the end of the first phase, a line 300 yards South of the railway CAEN-TROARN. A pause of 15 minutes in the barrage had been arranged on this line to allow 2 FF YEO to come up on the Left of 3 R Tks, as from here onwards, it was possible for 29 Armd Bde to advance two up. During the first part of the advance, 3 R Tks had fallen slightly behind the barrage, and the pause was therefore increased by an extra five minutes to allow for this. The railway CAEN-VIMONT proved not to be a serious obstacle to tanks, but all the same it caused considerable delay, and at the end of the 20 minute pause, not all the tanks of 3 R Tks had crossed it. 2 FF YEO had not succeeded in getting up level, and the leading wave was still crossing the railway at the end of the pause.

At 0850 hours, the barrage moved forward South-West at the beginning of its second phase. During this phase each of the leading regiments found increasing difficulty in keeping up with the barrage, owing to the danger of the leading squadrons getting out of supporting distance of the reserve squadron, which was still trying to cross the railway.

Opposition was not very heavy: most of the enemy were completely dazed by the bombing attacks. A fair amount of abandoned enemy equipment was found, and many Germans surrendered, who were rounded up by the motor companies supporting the armoured regiments.

Meanwhile, 159 Inf Bde had also advanced without much opposition, although 2 N YEO lost four tanks while passing through our own minefield, and at 0835 hours, 3 MON was entering CUVERVILLE, which was completely cleared by 1020 hours. 1 HEREFORD also got on to its objective, the orchards South-East of CUVERVILLE, without any trouble, and was firmly established by 1015 hours, having taken about 50 prisoners.

A patrol of INNS OF COURT was then pushed out in the direction of DEMOUVILLE, and at 0930 hours reported that it had reached the North-West edge of the village, which was held by enemy infantry.

At about 1045 hours 8 Corps informed Div HQ that CUVERVILLE would be taken over as soon as possible by a battalion from 154 Inf Bde (51 (H) Div), and 3 MON was therefore ordered to be prepared to advance on DEMOUVILLE as soon as this had taken place. Meanwhile, 4 KSLI was held in reserve on the original Start Line East of STE HONORINE LA CHARDONERETTE.

At 0905 hours, the barrage finished on a line running North-West and South-East through LE MESNIL FREMENTEL. This was the end of the artillery programme as planned, and after this, support could be called for as required, although the field regiments were approaching their extreme range.

The two leading armoured regiments reached the railway CAEN-VIMONT at about 0920 hours, 3 R Tks having by-passed LE MESNIL FREMENTEL to the West, 2 FF YEO to the East. This railway proved to be a more formidable obstacle than the former, and crossings were not so easy to find. The banks were fairly steep, and in some places up to ten feet high, and an appreciable delay occurred while the leading squadrons negotiated this obstacle.

However, both leading regiments were reported to have their leading squadrons across the railway by 0935 hours. The third wave of 2 FF YEO suffered casualties from anti-tank guns in the CAGNY area, while crossing, but the two leading squadrons pushed on. At about the same time, 23 H were crossing the first railway CAEN-VIMONT, and while doing so were engaged by enemy tanks from EMIEVILLE.

As soon as they were across the railway, 3 R Tks on the Right encountered stiff opposition in GRENTHEVILLE, but by about 1010 hours the regiment had succeeded in working round to the West between the village and the railway running South to TILLY LA CAMPAGNE. This railway line runs on a high embankment and was a considerable obstacle to manoeuvre. 3 R Tks then pushed on towards SOLIERS, while G Coy 8 RB did some successful mopping up of enemy positions West of GRENTHEVILLE.

Meanwhile, 2 FF YEO also began to encounter opposition South of the railway, and reported enemy infantry and guns in SOLIERS and infantry and anti-tank guns in FOUR. F Coy 8 RB had been kept fully occupied mopping up enemy positions overrun by 2 FF YEO.

It appeared that, now the advance had gone beyond the area covered by the barrage, the opposition would be stiffer.

At 1020 hours, A Sqn 2 FF YEO on the Left sent two troops to cover FOUR from a position to the North-East, while B Sqn was trying to deal with SOLIERS. At the same time, SP guns and Panther tanks were seen in the area of BOURGUEBUS, and enemy guns were firing from FRENOUVILLE. Progress here was slow, but some tanks advanced down the middle, while SOLIERS and FOUR were kept occupied, and engaged the enemy tanks in the BOURGUEBUS area. Eventually by about 1115 hours, a troop succeeded in reaching the road BOURGUEBUS-LA HOGUE, about half-way between the two villages. F Coy 8 RB had been ordered to cross the railway and clear up the opposition in FOUR.

Meanwhile 23 H were crossing the railway CAEN-VIMONT and were trying to advance towards FOUR.

On the Right, 3 R Tks pushed steadily along the East side of the railway running South without having any serious trouble from SOLIERS. The leading squadron crossed under the railway 500 yards South-West of SOLIERS, and advanced up the hill towards HUBERT FOLIE. When about 400 yards North-East of the village the leading tanks were heavily engaged by enemy tanks from HUBERT FOLIE, and from the area of the road running South-East to BOURGUEBUS. Artillery concentrations were put down on HUBERT FOLIE, and the leading tanks of the regiment got across the road HUBERT FOLIE-BOURGUEBUS, and a few hundred yards South by 1115 hours, while a carrier section from G Coy 8 RB actually drove through the village.

As LE MESNIL FREMENTEL had been by-passed by the two leading armoured regiments, 8 RB Battalion HQ Group with about half E (Support) Coy was ordered to clear the village. One Sqn 22 DGNS and one troop 26 Aslt Sqn, were placed under command to support this operation, and at 1030 hours the clearance was commenced. The village had been held in some strength, but as a result of the air bombardment closely followed by the barrage, the enemy was too dazed to offer much resistance. By 1130 hours the village was well under control, although mopping up and routing out the enemy from slit trenches went on for some considerable time. The total yield was 134 prisoners. LE MESNIL FREMENTEL was then organized as a firm base against a possible armoured counter-attack.

At 1100 hours CUVERVILLE was mortared and shelled, and the move forward of the relieving battalion from 154 Inf Bde was therefore delayed, as Commander 159 Inf Bde considered that there was not sufficient room in the village for two battalions without incurring undue casualties. By midday, however, 7th Battalion The Argyll and Sutherland Highlanders (Princess Louise's) (7 A & S H) (154 Inf Bde) had completed taking over the village, and 3 MON was ready to resume the advance on DEMOUVILLE.

So far the advance had gone extremely well. Very few enemy tanks had been seen, and not much opposition had been encountered, and that which was met consisted, for the most part, of infantry with a few anti-tank guns, forming strong points in the various villages, which had been successfully by-passed by the armoured regiments, and left to be mopped up later. Unfortunately, 29 Armd Bde could not be closely followed up by 159 Inf Bde, for the latter had the rather lengthy task of clearing CUVERVILLE and DEMOUVILLE to complete, as there were no other infantry units which could be made available for this task. The motor companies under command of the armoured regiments were kept fully occupied mopping up the open ground over which the armour was advancing, and rounding up prisoners, and were numerically too weak to undertake at the same time the immediate clearance of the enemy in the villages LE MESNIL FREMENTEL, GRENTHEVILLE, SOLIERS, FOUR, HUBERT FOLIE and BOURGUEBUS. So these strong points perforce remained, and continued to inflict a few casualties on the armoured regiments by fire from anti-tank guns.

From now on, however, the situation changed, and the resistance offered by the enemy increased sharply. Reports were made by 29 Armd Bde of heavy enemy fire, and German tanks started to appear. At about 1130 hours 3 R Tks on the Right was engaged by heavy fire from enemy tanks and guns in both BRAS and BOURGUEBUS, and was not able to make any further headway.

2 FF YEO reported a Panther on the Left flank beyond FOUR, and heavy fire from enemy tanks and guns in FRENOUVILLE, which had pinned down its Left squadron. 2 FF YEO was ordered to try and disengage from FRENOUVILLE, which would be dealt with by 5 Gds Armd Bde, and to push on past BOURGUEBUS towards TILLY LA CAMPAGNE. This, however, was not possible and 2 FF YEO continued to report determined opposition by enemy tanks, four of which were moving South-

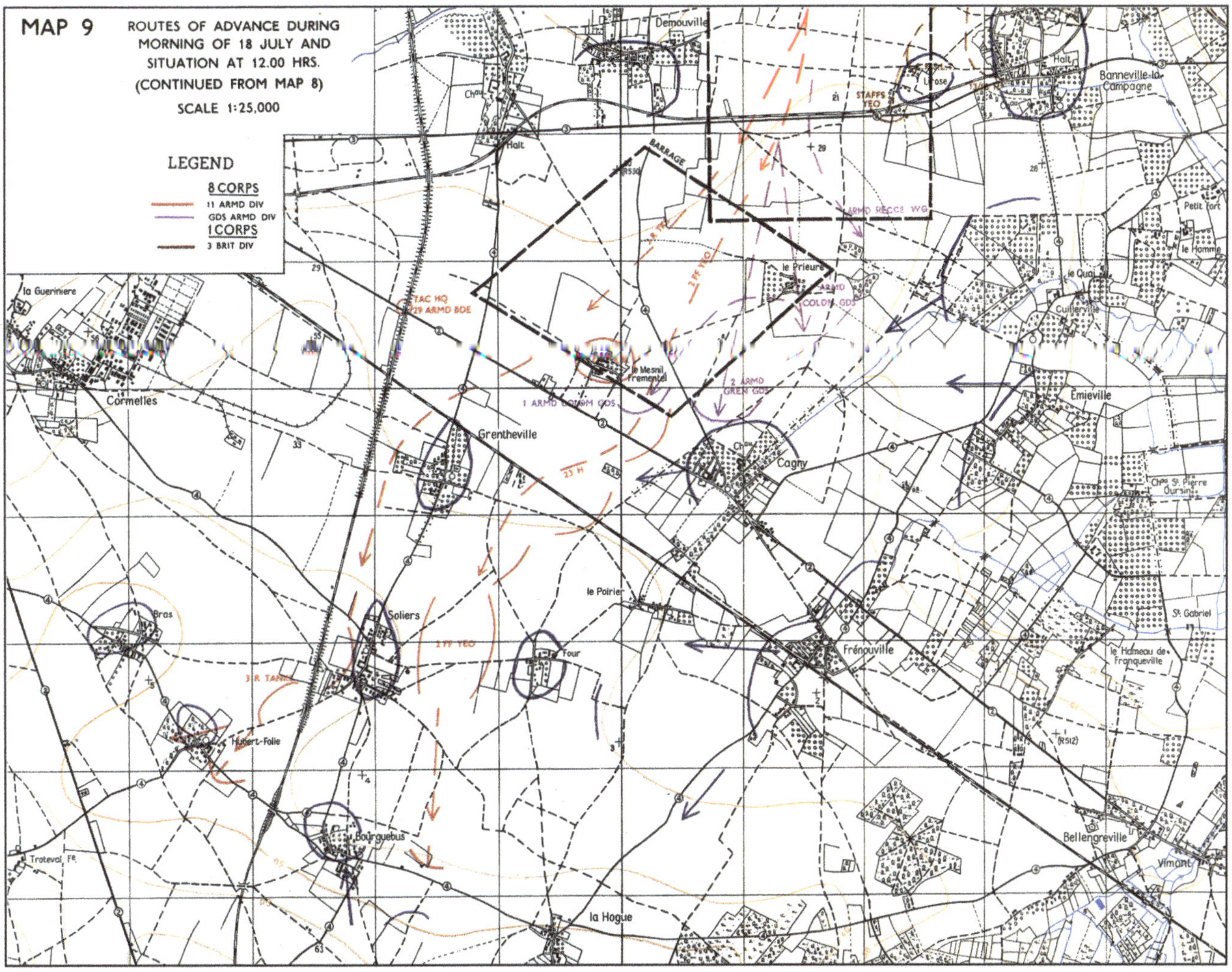
MAP 9
ROUTES OF ADVANCE DURING MORNING OF 18 JULY AND SITUATION AT 12.00 HRS.
(CONTINUED FROM MAP 8)
SCALE 1:25,000
LEGEND
8 CORPS
11 ARMD DIV
GDS ARMD DIV
I CORPS
3 BRIT DIV
Demouville
Banneville-la-Campagne
Holt
BARRAGE
Petit Fort
le Homme
le Prieuré
le Quai
Cuillerville
la Guerinière
TAC HQ 29 ARMD BDE
le Mesnil Frementel
Cormelles
Grentheville
Cagny
Emiéville
le Poirier
Soliers
Bras
Four
Frénouville
St. Gabriel
le Hameau de Franqueville
Hubert-Folie
Bourguébus
Bellengreville
Vimont
Troteval Fe
la Hogue

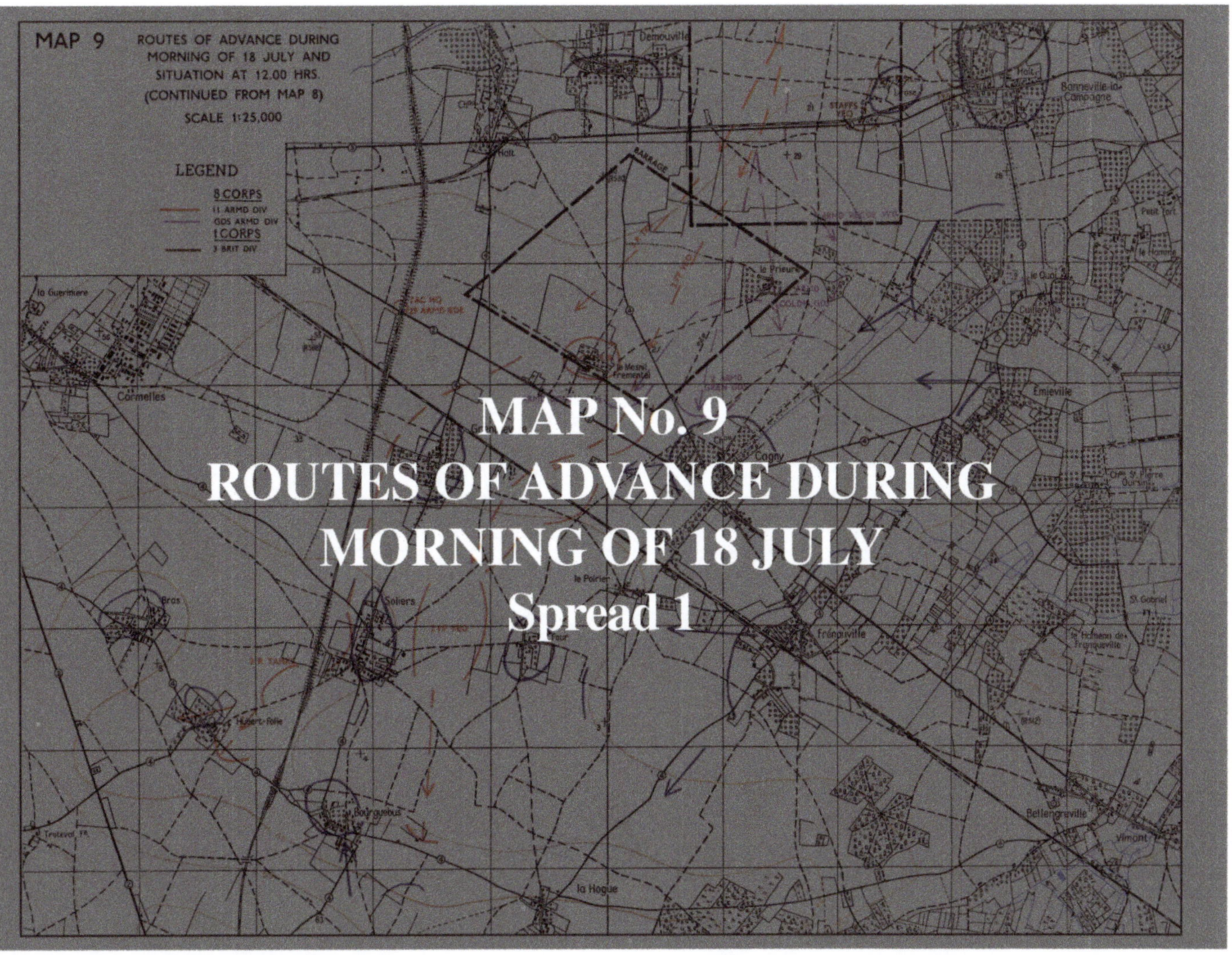
MAP No. 9
ROUTES OF ADVANCE DURING
MORNING OF 18 JULY
Spread 1

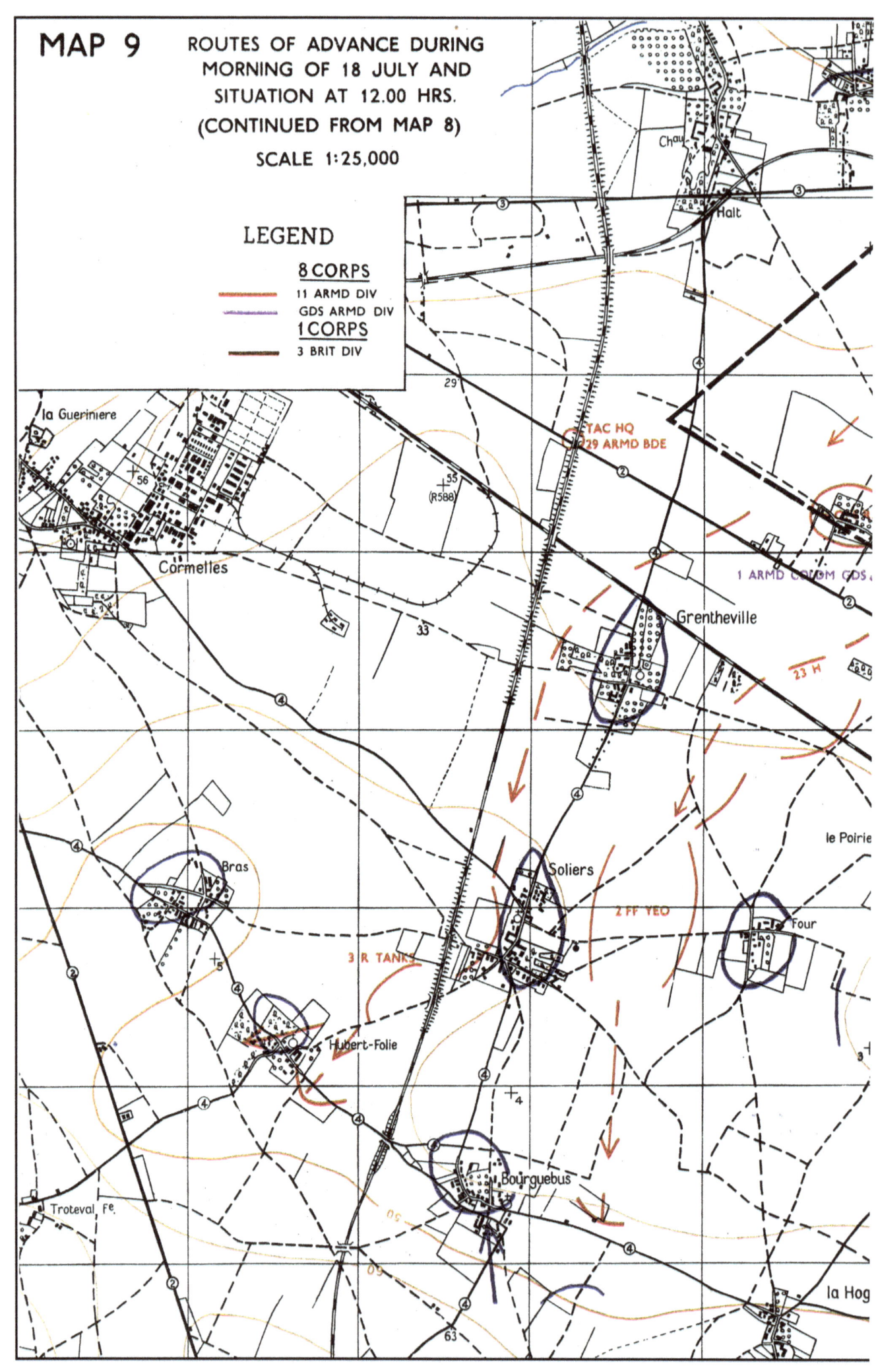

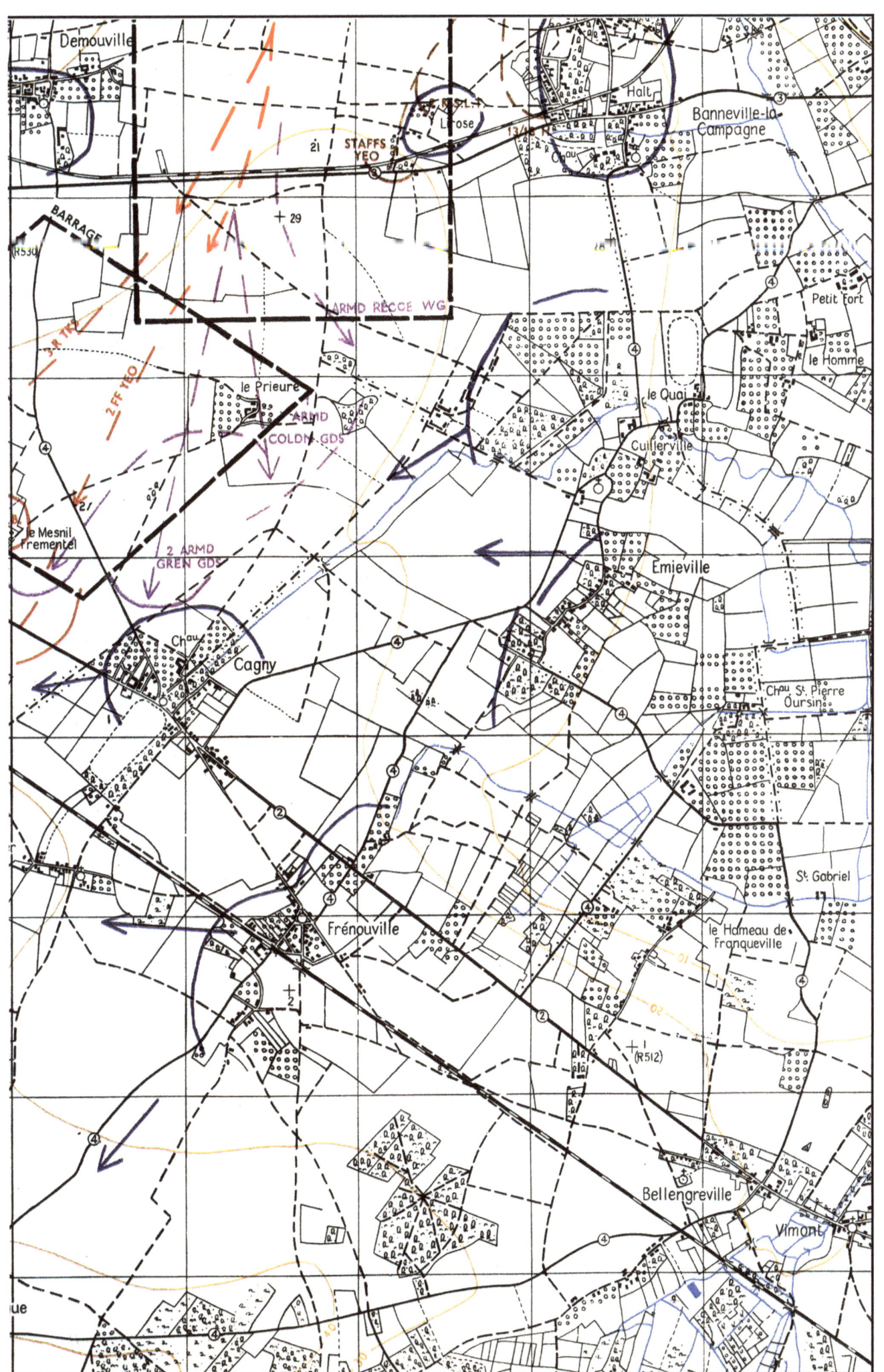

East from FRENOUVILLE, four were camouflaged in a position 1,000 yards South-East of BOURGUEBUS, while a little later four Panthers moved into BOURGUEBUS from the South-East, followed 15 minutes later by eight more tanks, thought to be Tigers. In the face of all this opposition, 2 FF YEO found it quite impossible to advance any further South from their present positions.

23 H, which had been ordered to screen CAGNY and FOUR from positions to the West astride the railway, also reported fire from two Panthers and some anti-tank guns, and was later engaged from North of CAGNY by two Tigers and anti-tank guns, but succeeded in knocking out one Tiger and one gun.

Thus, by midday, 29 Armd Bde, having advanced nearly 12,000 yards from the Start Line, was halted and firmly held by enemy tanks, sited on commanding ground and with good fields of fire, which had themselves escaped the effects of the preliminary air and artillery bombardments.

Gds Armd Div

There was some delay in moving forward from the assembly area 4,000 yards West of the ORNE, and the heads of the two columns instead of reaching the bridges (YORK and EUSTON) at H Hour as planned, did not arrive until H+45. However, the move was speeded up and by 0945 hours the head of 5 Gds Armd Bde was halted near DEMOUVILLE about 500 yards behind the tail of 29 Armd Bde (11 Armd Div), although a large part of the brigade was not yet clear of the bridges. There had been no hitch in following 29 Armd Bde through the gaps in the minefield and down past CUVERVILLE.

From here, 5 Gds Armd Bde was to advance two up. Right, 2nd Armoured Battalion Grenadier Guards (2 Armd GREN GDS) was directed on CAGNY to relieve 23 H (29 Armd Bde). Left, 1st Armoured Battalion Coldstream Guards (1 Armd COLDM GDS) was ordered to pass North and East of CAGNY and advance on VIMONT.

2nd Armoured Reconnaissance Battalion Welsh Guards (2 Armd Recce WG) was moving behind the two leading battalions, and 2nd Armoured Battalion Irish Guards (2 Armd IG) was the reserve unit of the brigade. 1st Motor Battalion Grenadier Guards (1 Mot GREN GDS) had one motor company under command each armoured battalion.

At about 1000 hours, 5 Gds Armd Bde was ordered to press on as soon as it was possible to manoeuvre on the Left flank of 29 Armd Bde. By 1045 hours the leading elements of 1 Armd COLDM GDS was moving South about 1,000 yards West of EMIEVILLE, from which village the battalion was engaged by enemy anti-tank guns.

At about the same time, 2 Armd IG was reported to be moving well on RAT track, but still about 7,000 yards West of the bridges.

At about 1115 hours, the leading troops of 2 Armd GREN GDS approached the Northern outskirts of CAGNY, but they were held up by anti-tank guns and could not get into the village itself.

By 1200 hours, all attempts by 1 Armd COLDM GDS to advance South-East between CAGNY and EMIEVILLE had been halted; the battalion was therefore ordered to disengage and to move West and South of CAGNY, and try to advance to VIMONT that way. 2 Armd GREN GDS was, at this time, ordered not to attack CAGNY if the place was strongly held, but to attempt to by-pass it, and 2 Armd Recce WG was told to move to the Left flank to try and find a way through the anti-tank screen to the East. 2 Armd IG was still held up by a traffic block, and was not yet clear of YORK bridges.

Meanwhile, 32 Gds Bde was halted with the leading troops on the Right level with ESCOVILLE, whilst on the Left, it was held up behind 2 Armd IG.

7 Armd Div

Shortly after H Hour, the leading unit of 22 Armd Bde. The 5th Royal Tank Regiment (5 R Tks) moved off again along CALF route, and started crossing LONDON bridges at H+60 behind 9 Cdn Inf Bde according to schedule. 5 R Tks was followed by Tac HQ 22 Armd Bde, Tac HQ 7 Armd Div, the 1st Royal Tank Regiment (1 R Tks) and 1st County of London Yeomanry (Sharpshooters) (4 CLY). The motor companies of 1st Battalion The Rifle Brigade (Prince Consort's Own) (1 RB) were under command of the armoured regiments and moved with them.

The advance of 22 Armd Bde proceeded rather slowly owing to the traffic congestion, and 400 yards beyond the bridges on the East side of the river, 5 R Tks was compelled to halt, to wait until the Canadians, moving down to their Start Line, had got clear. At about 0920 hours, the forward move of 22 Armd Bde started again, and continued steadily although rather slowly, for the next hour. By 1045 hours, 5 R Tks had got to a position to the East of CUVERVILLE, and Tac HQ 22 Armd Bde and Tac HQ 7 Armd Div were both across the bridges. For the next 45 minutes, 5 R Tks tried to get forward, but reported that it was unable to make progress, as it was held up by 2 N YEO assisting 159 Inf Bde on the Right, and the tail of 5 Gds Armd Bde on the Left.

At 1130 hours, 22 Armd Bde reported that 23 H (29 Armd Bde) had said that it was impossible for 5 R Tks to get through yet as there was too much congestion. Meanwhile, 1 R Tks was finding crossing the bridges a slow and tedious business, it taking more than two hours for the regiment to get across.

B. 1 CORPS

3 Brit Div

By first light, with the exception of a few posts to stop enemy patrols entering our lines, the forward battalion of 185 Inf Bde had been withdrawn from ESCOVILLE back into HEROU-VILLETTE. One battalion of 152 Inf Bde (51 (H) Div) in position further East was also moved North several hundred yards, behind the safe line laid down for the air bombardment. 152 Inf Bde had passed under command of 3 Brit Div and 185 Inf Bde had reverted to command.

The attack started at 0745 hours, after the air bombardment by the medium bombers, at the same time as the 8 Corps attack.

At H Hour, 13th/18th Royal Hussars (Queen Mary's Own) (13/18 H) (27 Armd Bde), which was supporting 8 Brit Inf Bde, crossed the Start Line ahead of the infantry. They crossed the trench system to the West of Task I without much opposition, and an hour later were approaching Task II, the enemy positions West of TOUFFREVILLE. Meanwhile, 8 Brit Inf Bde advanced, supported by heavy artillery concentrations on enemy centres of resistance, and by 0900 hours it was clearing Task I, the woods to the South of PRE BARON, and was meeting only slight opposition.

Also at H Hour, 152 Inf Bde, under command 3 Brit Div, advanced behind a barrage to clear the road triangle 1,500 yards South-East of ESCOVILLE.

At about 0900 hours, 13/18 H reported that it was collecting a number of prisoners in the area of Task II. 8 Brit Inf Bde successfully cleared the woods, and Task IIA was commenced about 0945 hours, 2nd Battalion The East Yorkshire Regiment (The Duke of York's Own) (2 E YORKS) attacking TOUFFREVILLE from the East.

At about the same time 13/18 H pushed South towards Task III, SANNERVILLE and BANNEVILLE LA CAMPAGNE.

At 0945 hours, one squadron The Staffordshire Yeomanry (STAFFS YEO) (27 Armd Bde), under command of 8 Brit Inf Bde, which had passed through 13/18 H on Task II, had reached the road CAEN-TROARN just West of LIROSE. About 40 minutes later infantry of 8 Brit Inf Bde reached the railway CAEN-TROARN about 700 yards East of SANNERVILLE, while by 1100 hours 13/18 H was approaching BANNEVILLE LA CAMPAGNE from the West.

During the rest of the morning 8 Brit Inf Bde made steady progress round TOUFFREVILLE and SANNERVILLE, while 152 Inf Bde was engaged in clearing the road triangle.

51 (H) Div

Before the bombing attack started, all three battalions of 154 Inf Bde were withdrawn from the area round STE HONORINE LA CHARDONERETTE, which the brigade was holding as part of the FDLs, North to the area of LE BAS DE RANVILLE. After H Hour, 7 A & S H had concentrated forward in the STE HONORINE area by 0915 hours, and was held in readiness to move forward to take over CUVERVILLE from 159 Inf Bde (11 Armd Div).

The remaining two battalions were not able to move forward to the original area, until 8 and 9 Cdn Inf Bdes had completed crossing the Canadian Start Line.

RE

During the morning, CE 1 Corps raised the question of the exact boundary for engineer responsibility for tracks and routes, and it was agreed mutually between Corps that 1 Corps would be responsible for all tracks and routes from the bridges as far South as the road LONGUEVAL-STE HONORINE-ESCOVILLE. Forward of that road, each corps would be responsible for the tracks within the corps boundaries. CE 1 Corps delegated the task to CRE 51 (H) Div.

It was reported that minor bridges on the routes in BENOUVILLE and RANVILLE had been damaged by the tanks of 11 Armd Div moving up at night, but that alternative bridges had been constructed, and were in use. A new bridge had also been constructed over the small stream between the two main LONDON bridges.

At 1035 hours the North bridge over the River ORNE (YORK) was reported out of action owing to a failure of the equipment, but 25 minutes later it had been repaired and was again open to traffic.

C. 2 CDN CORPS

3 Cdn Div was due to cross its Start Line 45 minutes after the attack of 8 Corps began. 8 Cdn Inf Bde was to advance behind a barrage fired by four field regiments, moving with two battalions up, Right Le Regiment de la Chaudiere (R DE CHAUD) and Left The Queen's Own Rifles of Canada (QOR OF C). 8 Cdn Inf Bde was supported by the 6th Canadian Armoured Regiment (1st Hussars).

At 0830 hours the two leading battalions crossed the Start Line 600 yards South-East of LE BAS DE RANVILLE. Twenty minutes later the leading elements of 6 Cdn Armd Regt reached the road LONGUEVAL–STE HONORINE without any trouble. By 0940 hours QOR of C on the Left had reached the line of the road COLOMBELLES–CUVERVILLE without much opposition, and half an hour later was approaching the Northern outskirts of GIBERVILLE.

On the Right, however, things did not go so well and R DE CHAUD met strong opposition in the Chateau North of COLOMBELLES and in the village itself.

Meanwhile, 9 Cdn Inf Bde had started crossing LONDON bridge at H Hour and one and a half hours later had reached the line LONGUEVAL–STE HONORINE close behind 8 Cdn Inf Bde.

The Corps Commander then ordered 3 Cdn Div to send a patrol from the reserve brigade (7 Cdn Inf Bde) across the River ORNE from CAEN into FAUBOURG DE VAUCELLES, and if this patrol met no opposition, one battalion of the brigade was to cross the river as soon as artillery support could be spared from the operations of the other two brigades.

At about 1100 hours, the preparations for the bridges over the ORNE between CAEN and FAUBOURG DE VAUCELLES were held up by intense mortar fire. Meanwhile, R DE CHAUD was still held up in COLOMBELLES, and the reserve battalion of 8 Cdn Inf Bde (The North Shore (New Brunswick) Regiment) (N SHORE R) tried to make its way to the West of R DE CHAUD, and push on into the factory area.

At about 1130 hours, QOR OF C was still in the Northern outskirts of GIBERVILLE having been held up by heavy machine gun fire, and it took it over two hours to clear up this opposition.

D. SUMMARY OF OPERATIONS DURING THE MORNING OF 18 JULY

The following summary of the operations of all three corps during the first few hours of Operation GOODWOOD is given in the Second Army Sitrep for the period 0001 to 1200 hours 18 July.

"At dawn probably the heaviest and most concentrated air assault ever launched in support of a military operation took place. Over 1,500 heavy bombers and nearly 600 mediums blasted a gap 7,000 yards wide through which a powerful armoured and infantry attack was launched. At 0745 hours, 8 Corps, with one armoured division up, attacked Southwards with infantry of 2 Cdn and 1 Corps attacking on each flank. The armoured division moved very fast, and was followed rapidly by two more. By midday, strong armoured formations of 8 Corps had advanced nearly seven miles to the South and had broken through the main German defences. The infantry on either flank were engaged in mopping up the COLOMBELLES factory and the villages between CAEN and TROARN. 83 Group RAF, with the assistance of units of IX USAAF, gave magnificient support throughout the morning, attacking in particular, gun positions and movement in the battle area."

The advances made by all three corps and the situation at 1200 hours 18 July are shown on Maps 8 and 9.

SECTION III

OPERATIONS DURING THE AFTERNOON OF 18 JULY

A. 8 CORPS

11 Armd Div

At midday 18 July, the situation of 29 Armd Bde was as follows. On the Right, 3 R Tks was within 800 yards of both BRAS and HUBERT FOLIE. The tanks which had got across the road between HUBERT FOLIE and BOURGUEBUS had either been knocked out, or forced to withdraw by fire from enemy tanks.

On the Left, 2 FF YEO had succeeded in disengaging from FRENOUVILLE, and the leading squadron was in a position about 800 yards East of BOURGUEBUS. Again, the tanks which had succeeded in reaching the road BOURGUEBUS-LA HOGUE had been forced to withdraw or been destroyed by heavy fire from enemy tanks. F Coy 8 RB (under command 2 FF YEO), having crossed the railway North-East of LE POIRIER, was attempting to get into FOUR, but was held up by fire from four Panther tanks. 23 H was crossing the railway CAEN-VIMONT East of GRENTHEVILLE, having left one squadron to protect its flank from the enemy in CAGNY.

Both the leading armoured regiments were again ordered to push on, 3 R Tks to cut the road CAEN-FALAISE South-West of HUBERT FOLIE, and 2 FF YEO to TILLY-LA-CAMPAGNE.

Resistance to the advance continued to stiffen, particularly from enemy tanks. 2 FF YEO on the Left, found itself in a difficult position. The majority of the regiment was deployed in an area between the villages of SOLIERS, BOURGUEBUS and LA HOGUE, all of which were on higher ground and overlooked the position. The enemy in LE POIRIER, FOUR and FRENOUVILLE also had observation over the area. Shortly before 1300 hours, a strong counter attack by fire from enemy tanks, supported by some anti-tank guns, was developed against 2 FF YEO from all these places, and the regiment suffered many tank casualties. 23 H was ordered to move up to the assistance of 2 FF YEO and to clear up the BOURGUEBUS area.

On the Right, 3 R Tks was unable to make any further progress, and came under heavy fire from 5 Panthers between CORMELLES and BRAS, SP guns in BRAS, tanks and anti-tank guns in HUBERT FOLIE, BOURGUEBUS, and South of SOLIERS, while fire was also coming from the area of LA HOGUE. BRAS, HUBERT FOLIE, BOURGUEBUS and SOLIERS were also held by enemy infantry.

In view of the strong counter attack launched by enemy tanks against 29 Armd Bde at about 1300 hours, a report from CCRA 2 Cdn Corps is of interest.

> At 1250 hours, a wireless intercept from the enemy was picked up in which an order was issued that the German armour in the BOURGUEBUS area was to withdraw to an area South of SECQUEVILLE LA CAMPAGNE. The reply was given that the armour in this area was unable to do so, as it was too heavily engaged.

A request was made for RAF assistance against the enemy tanks. A RAF Visual Control Post was located at Tac HQ 29 Armd Bde, but unfortunately the RAF officer, who was the Controller, was wounded during the morning. The Army Air Liaison officer endeavoured to function as Controller, but was not able to brief the aircraft in the air, and so the Post had to be used as an ordinary tentacle. At about 1330 hours, however, a successful attack was launched by Typhoons carrying rocket projectiles on enemy tanks in the BOURGUEBUS area, and a further attack a little later halted 9 Panthers which were moving North to the road between BOURGUEBUS and LA HOGUE.

When 23 H was ordered to move up to assist 2 FF YEO, the motor company under command, H Coy 8 RB, was given orders to clear GRENTHEVILLE. A number of prisoners from 125 PGR (21 Pz Div) and 14 Werfer Regiment and about 10 Nebelwerfer were captured.

At 1210 hours, 3 MON (159 Inf Bde) supported by both A and C Sqns 2 N YEO left CUVERVILLE for the attack on DEMOUVILLE. The attack was successful and by 1300 hours the Western half of the village was reported in our hands. Mopping up went on steadily, and an hour later, the village was reported clear except for three small pockets, which were finally reduced by 1530 hours.

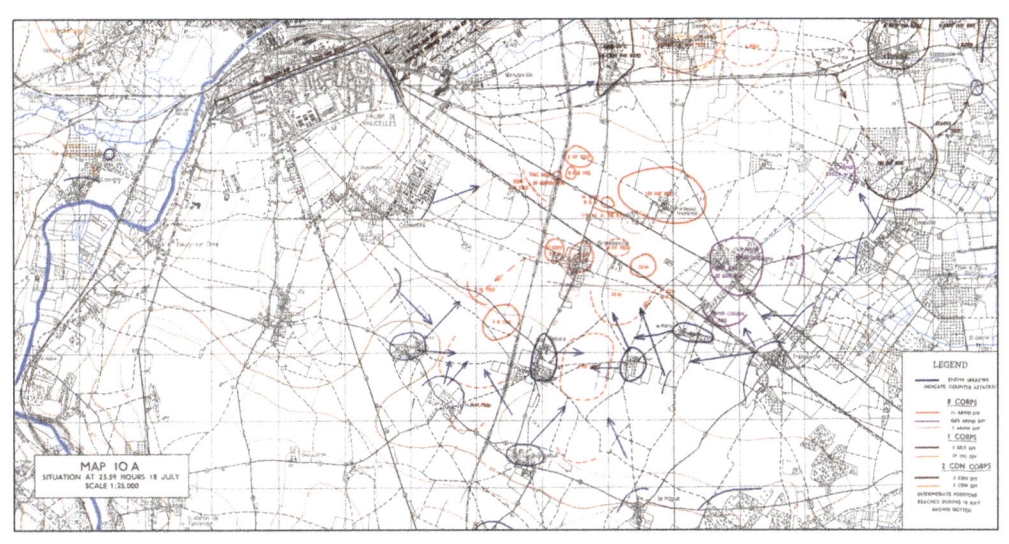

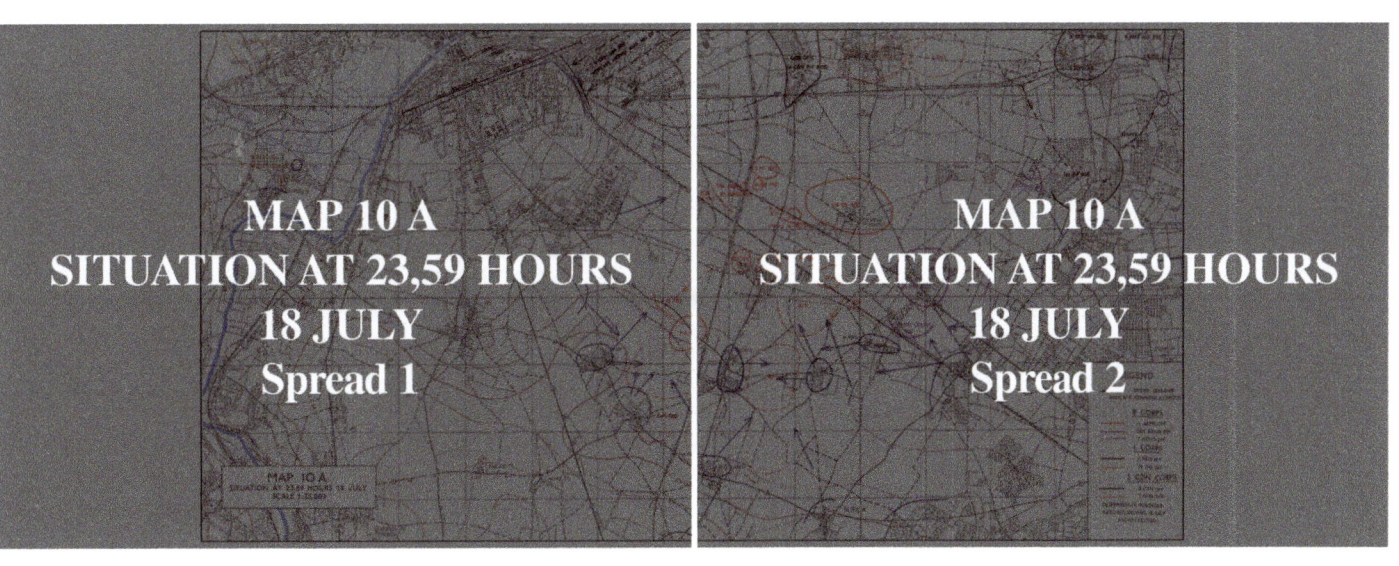

MAP 10 A
SITUATION AT 23,59 HOURS 18 JULY

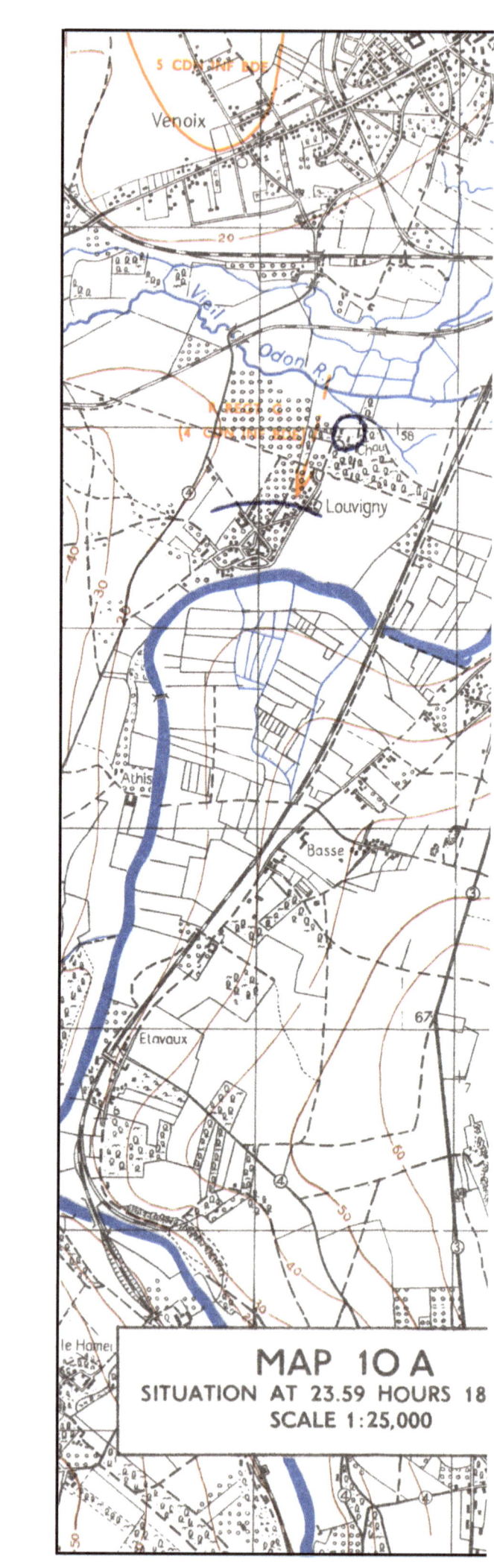

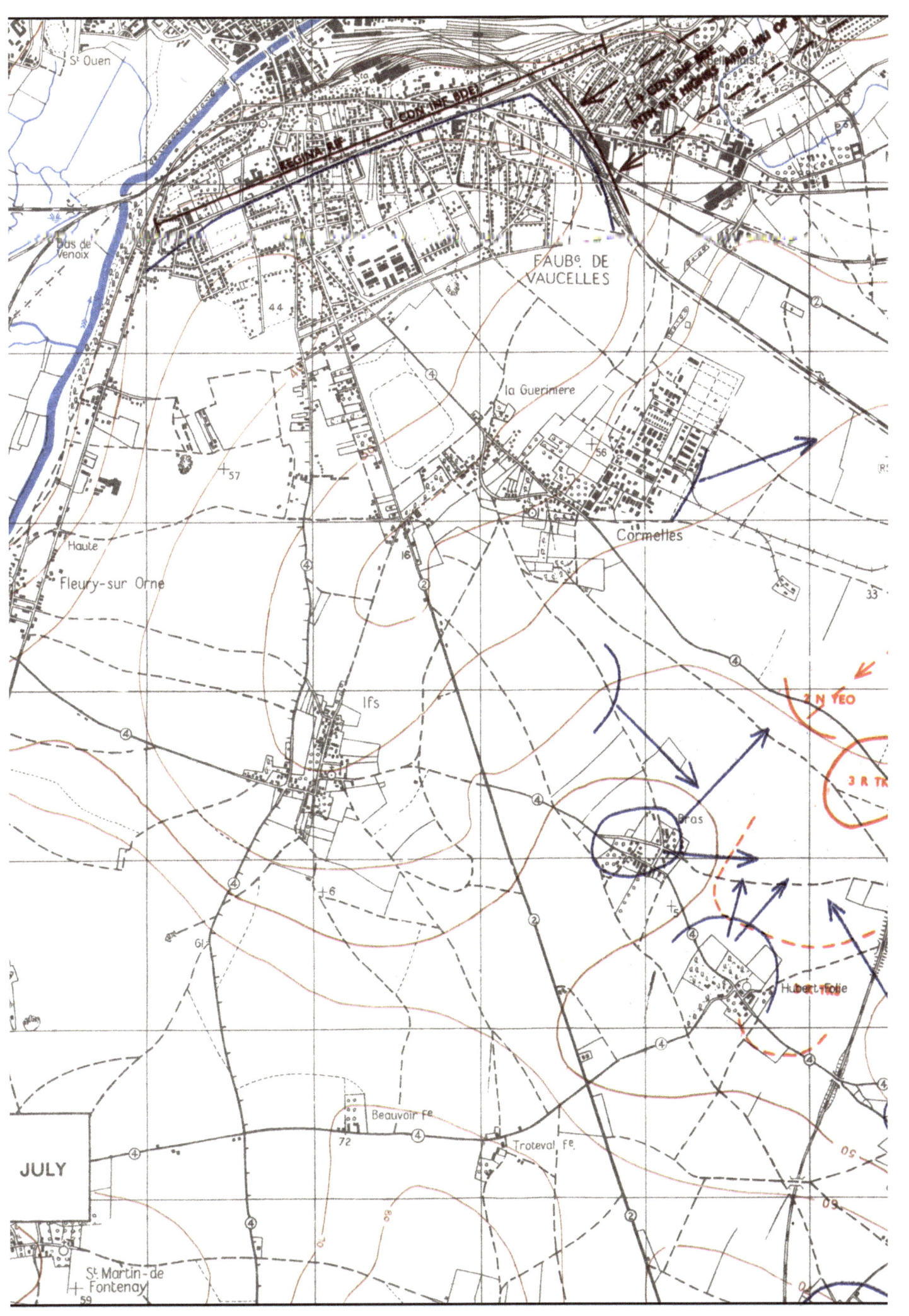

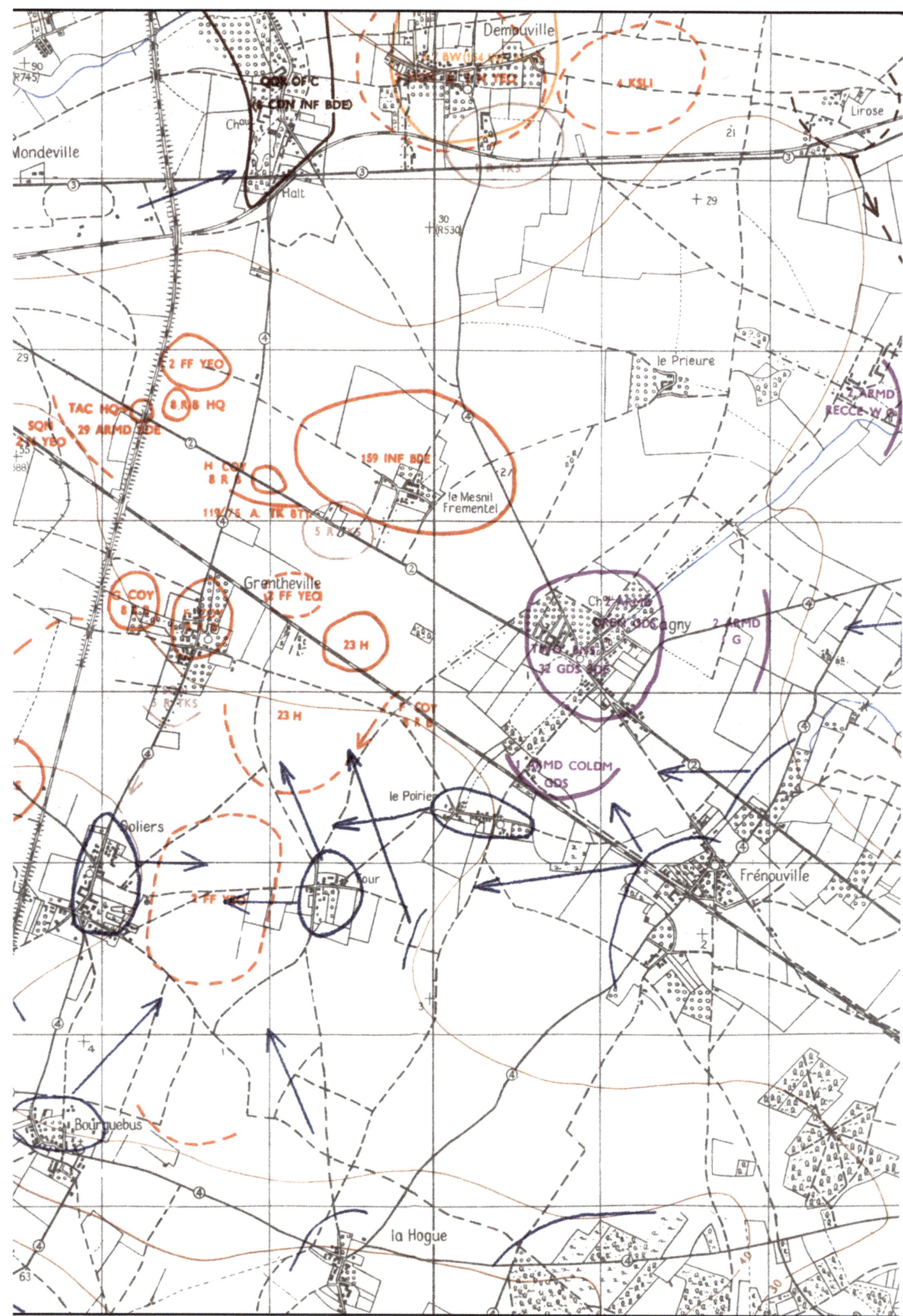

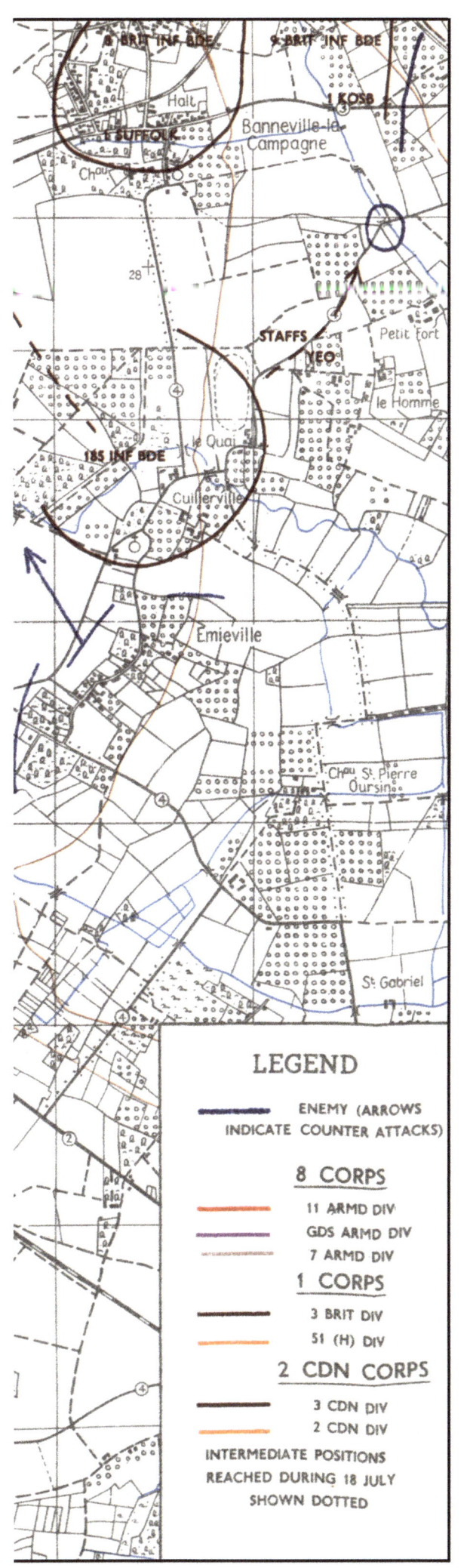

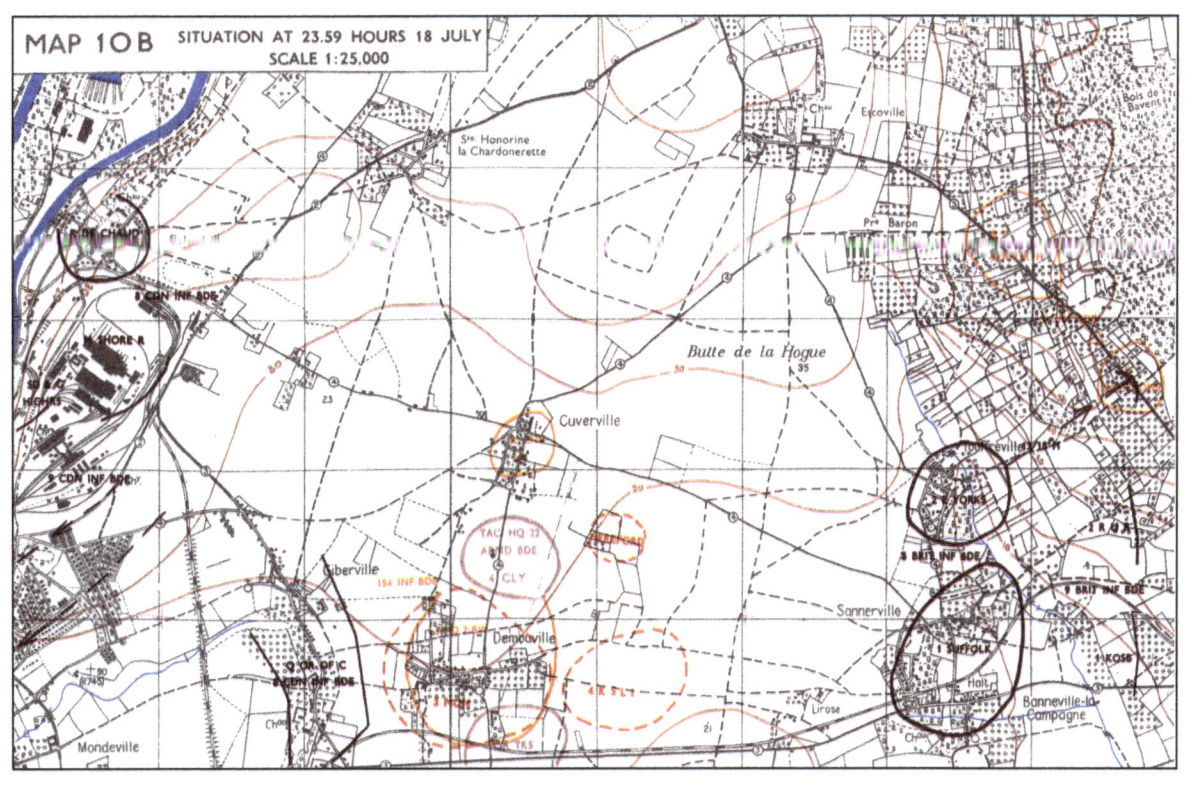

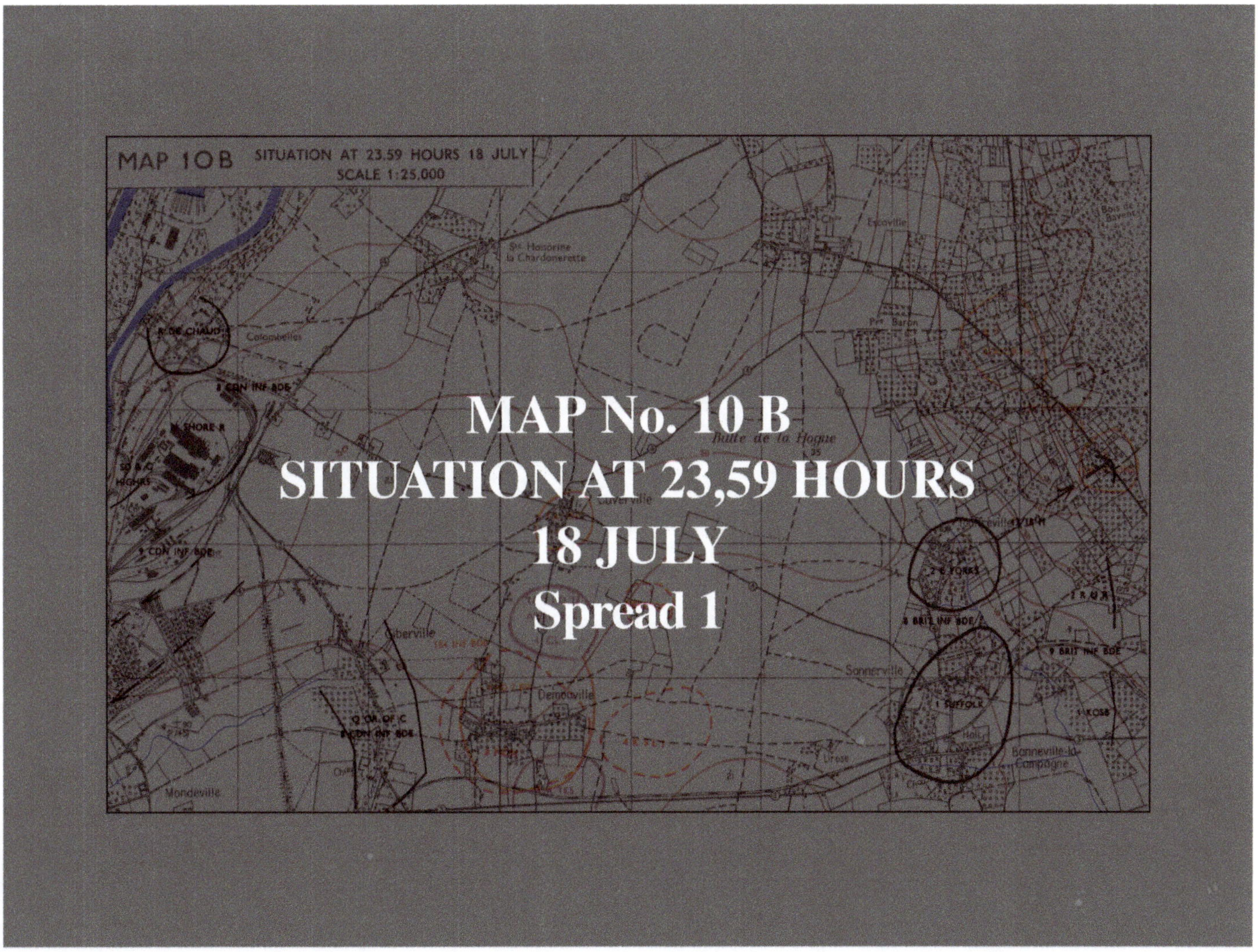

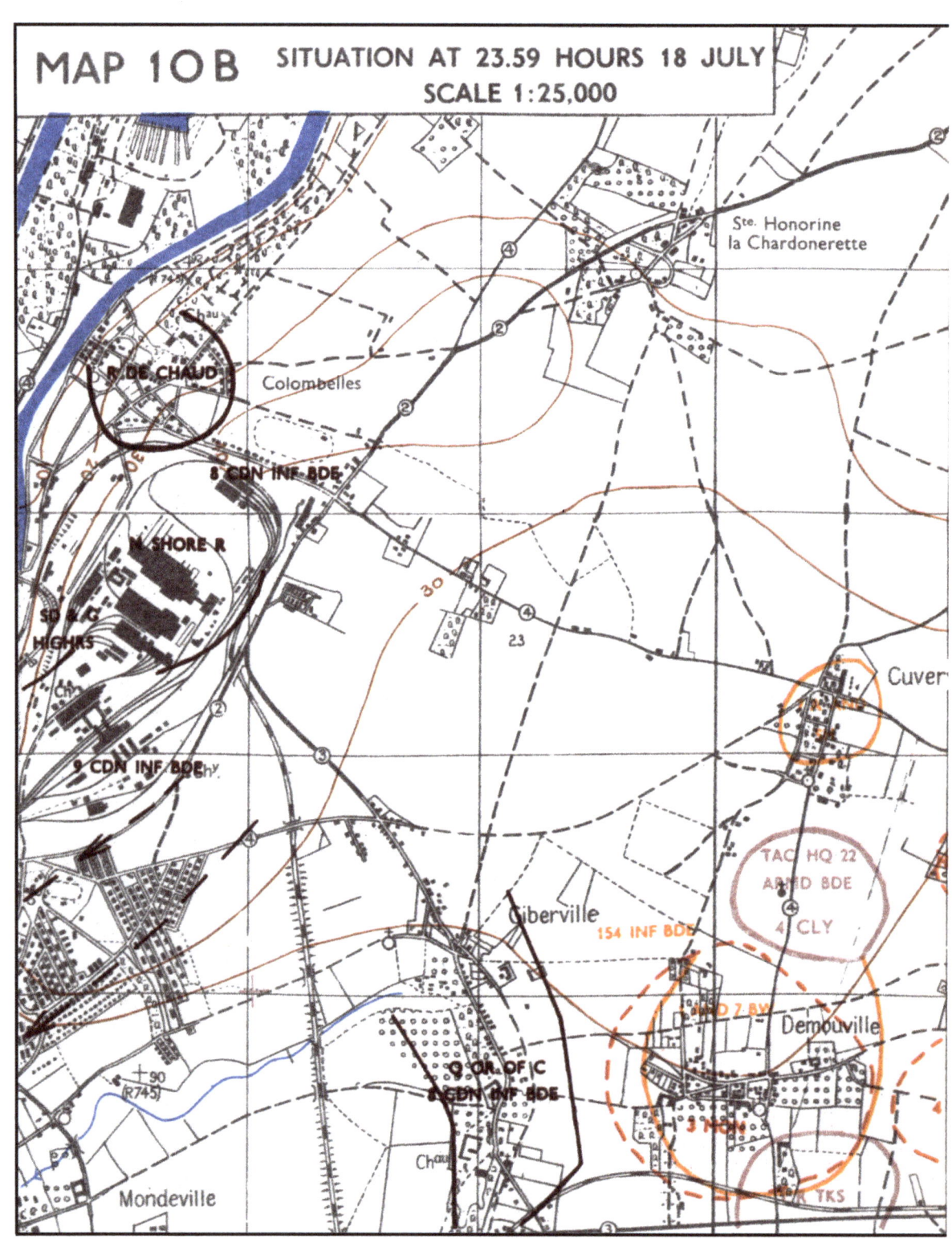

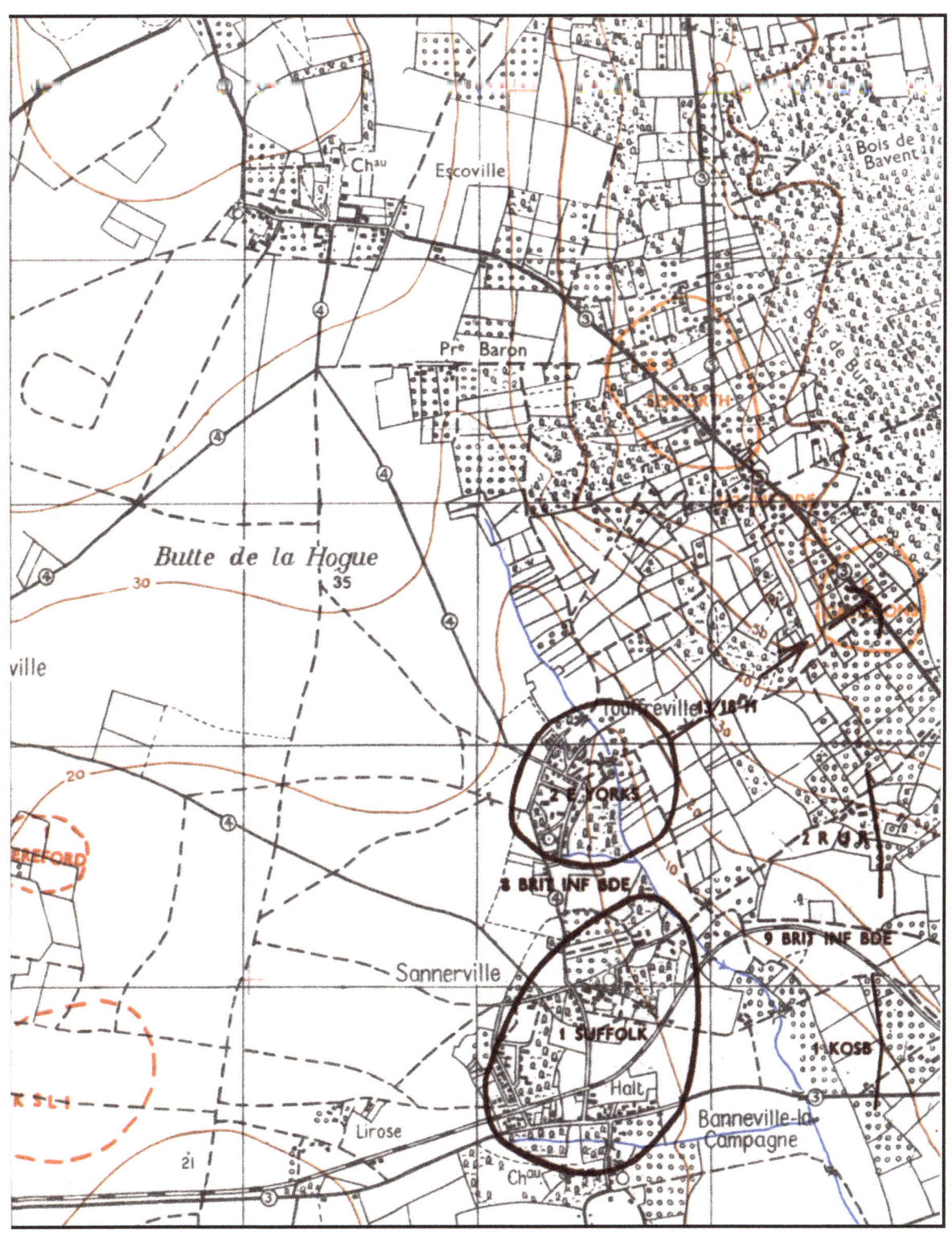

C Sqn 2 N YEO destroyed two enemy SP guns (105 mm) on the North-East edge of the village. B Sqn 2 N YEO was moved round to the orchards South-West of the village to cover the West flank. This squadron reported that part of GIBERVILLE had been cleared by the Canadians, but that there were still enemy in the Southern half of the village.

Some enemy anti-tank guns and infantry were later located in the orchards South of the village close to the railway, and these were eliminated by 2 N YEO with some help from 5 R Tks (7 Armd Div) from the East.

At 1400 hours, 4 KSLI was ordered to move up from STE HONORINE LA CHARDONERETTE and occupy a position 1,000 yards East of DEMOUVILLE. This move was completed an hour later.

Meanwhile, 1 HEREFORD remained in reserve in the orchards South-East of CUVERVILLE.

At about 1350 hours, as a result of a conference between the Corps Commander and Commanders 7 and 11 Armd Divs, a joint plan was made to continue the thrust towards HUBERT FOLIE, BOURGUEBUS and LA HOGUE with 29 Armd Bde on the Right and 22 Armd Bde on the Left.

23 H was then ordered to be prepared to move over to the Right flank on the Left of 3 R Tks and to attack SOLIERS and BOURGUEBUS along the East side of the railway, while 3 R Tks thrust on towards HUBERT FOLIE.

At 1425 hours, however, CO 23 H reported that he considered that it was now impossible to leave his present position, as 2 FF YEO was too thin on the ground in front, and to pull out would leave a hole. The situation of 2 FF YEO appeared to be that there were only about 20 tanks left, and nobody knew what had happened to the CO. A squadron leader of 2 FF YEO confirmed this a few minutes later by reporting that the regiment had again been heavily engaged at short range by a large number of Panthers making a counter attack from the direction of FRENOUVILLE, and also by other tanks from BOURGUEBUS and SOLIERS. About 6 Panthers had been destroyed, but many of our own tanks had been knocked out, including CO's and 2IC's, but the CO was alright. 23 H also reported the presence of Panthers in FOUR.

At about 1450 hours, 23 H reported a further counter attack by enemy tanks in some strength. One squadron facing BOURGUEBUS suffered heavy casualties, and another sqadron was in trouble from FOUR. CO 23 H was told that he was to hang on and try to hold the Left flank from his present position.

At the same time, 3 R Tks was in difficulties, its position East and North-East of HUBERT FOLIE being overlooked by enemy tanks and anti-tank guns. The regiment was also subjected to a sharp counter attack from enemy tanks from both HUBERT FOLIE and BOURGUEBUS, lost several tanks, and by 1530 hours, had been forced to withdraw about 500 yards to a position East of SOLIERS. Commander 11 Armd Div gave orders that it was to hang on as long as possible.

At 1500 hours, the remnants of 2 FF YEO were withdrawn through 23 H to a position North of railway CAEN-VIMONT and East of GRENTHEVILLE to reorganize.

As a result of these counter attacks from the South-East, and the threat of further danger from that direction, two troops 119/75 A Tk Bty were ordered, shortly after 1500 hours, to take up defensive positions North of GRENTHEVILLE to meet the threat: in addition, 2 N YEO was placed under command 29 Armd Bde and ordered to move up to the vicinity of Bde Tac HQ near the railway bridge North-West of GRENTHEVILLE.

More Typhoon RP attacks on enemy tanks in BOURGUEBUS and to the West were carried out, and some of the enemy tanks were thought to have been destroyed or forced to move, but owing to the dust it was not possible to get accurate reports. In spite of this, however 3 R Tks continued to be heavily engaged, both at 1545 hours and again at 1615 hours. The regiment managed to hold its ground in the position West of SOLIERS in spite of losses, and claimed to have knocked out at least two Panthers.

On the Left at about 1630 hours, there were again reports of some 20–30 enemy tanks moving North-East from SEQUEVILLE LA CAMPAGNE, while at the same time reports were received that tanks were withdrawing from SOLIERS to LA HOGUE and the woods to the East.

The attack by F Coy 8 RB on FOUR failed, and as 23 H was involved in a tank battle in the area between GRENTHEVILLE and FOUR, F Coy withdrew back to the railway and moved West along it towards GRENTHEVILLE. This village was being cleared by H Coy 8 RB. When F Coy appeared at about 1730 hours, the task was handed over to it, half the position having been mopped up, and H Coy withdrew to the North-East of the village. F Coy completed the clearance of the village, took a further considerable number of prisoners and captured another twelve Nebelwerfer.

G Coy, meanwhile, was waiting to the West of GRENTHEVILLE, having withdrawn from the area in which 3 R Tks was fighting its tank battle.

At about 1640 hours 2 N YEO started to arrive in the area just North of GRENTHEVILLE, and was ordered to move South along the railway COLOMBELLES–TILLY-LA-CAMPAGNE, and to link up with 3 R Tks.

One squadron went along the main CAEN road and under the railway to the West side, but then found that progress to the South was completely held up by the railway CAEN-VIMONT, which ran along an embankment about 15 feet high. This move was also harassed by fire from an anti-tank gun in the factory area of CORMELLES to the West.

Another squadron proceeded South on the East side of the railway, crossed under it due West of GRENTHEVILLE and then started to move towards BRAS. This squadron was eventually halted about 1,000 yards North-East of BRAS by enemy tanks and anti-tank guns from the BRAS–BOURGUEBUS ridge.

At about this time, INNS OF COURT patrols reported that LA HOGUE was lightly held, apparently by infantry only, while BOURGUEBUS appeared clear of the enemy, having been badly damaged by the Typhoon RP attacks.

At 1720 hours the situation of 29 Armd Bde was as follows. On the Right, 3 R Tks had elements within a few hundred yards of HUBERT FOLIE, but the remainder of the regiment was further back between BRAS and SOLIERS. On the Left, 23 H was in an area between GRENTHEVILLE, LE POIRIER and FOUR, a few hundred yards South of the VIMONT railway. The enemy still held the BRAS–HUBERT FOLIE–BOURGUEBUS ridge firmly, and some enemy tanks had infiltrated back into SOLIERS.

8 RB RHQ Group was then ordered to move out of LE MESNIL FREMENTEL to the area of Tac Bde HQ, near the railway bridge. At 1810 hours, 159 Inf Bde was ordered to hand over DEMOUVILLE to 154 Inf Bde (51 (H) Div) and move forward and establish a firm position about 1,000 yards North of the line GRENTHEVILLE–CAGNY. 3 MON therefore handed the village over to 1st Battalion The Black Watch (Royal Highland Regiment) (1 BW), and 159 Inf Bde moved forward, and by 1945 hours had taken up positions on the West, East and North of LE MESNIL FREMENTEL.

At 1800 hours, 22 Armd Bde appeared with 5 R Tks leading, directed on LA HOGUE, via FOUR. Shortly after, 29 Armd Bde was ordered to get firm on the line BRAS–HUBERT FOLIE–BOURGUEBUS, to conform to 22 Armd Bde thrust.

By this time, however, 3 R Tks was running out of ammunition, and as no echelon vehicles could be brought up to the tanks, it was not possible for the regiment to push forward any further.

By 1900 hours, continued counter attacks by enemy tanks between FOUR and FRENOUVILLE had forced all except two troops 23 H to withdraw North of the railway CAEN–VIMONT. The regiment also reported more enemy tanks infiltrating into SOLIERS. At about this time, 2 FF YEO was told to concentrate in the area just East of Tac Bde HQ, with I Bty 13 RHA.

At 2020 hours, a very heavy concentration from all guns within range was put down on SOLIERS, as a result of the reports about enemy tanks infiltrating into the village. In spite of this, and within an hour, yet another counter attack was launched by six Tigers and five Panthers from the area of SOLIERS against 3 R Tks, which knocked out one Tiger and one Panther and halted the attack.

Half an hour later a force of six Tigers and six Panthers moved North-East from SOLIERS, led by a Sherman. 119/75 (SP) A Tk Bty, in the area North of GRENTHEVILLE, saw this advance, was not misled by the presence of the Sherman, and quickly knocked out the Sherman and two Panthers. The remainder of the enemy tanks withdrew South.

3 R Tks was counter attacked once again by Tigers at about 2240 hours, but the visibility was very poor, and the enemy withdrew.

11 Armd Div remained firm for the night in the following positions :—

Tac HQ 29 Armd Bde, 8 RB RHQ	North-West of GRENTHEVILLE.
3 R Tks	1,200 yards South-West of GRENTHEVILLE.
23 H	1,200 yards East of GRENTHEVILLE.
2 FF YEO	1,500 yards North of GRENTHEVILLE.
159 Inf Bde	Area LE MESNIL FREMENTEL.

During the day, the A Echelons of 29 Armd Bde had crossed the ORNE and harboured in the area South-West of AMFREVILLE, where the tanks had concentrated the night before, and quite close to Main HQ 11 Armd Div, which had remained in the same position all day. During the day, many of the tank crews, who had had their tanks destroyed in the fighting, made their way back on foot to this echelon area to be reorganized as replacement crews.

At about 2330 hours, the enemy put in a sharp bombing attack in the area of the bridges. Main HQ 11 Armd Div suffered several casualties in this raid, and the ACV Rear Link to 8 Corps received a direct hit and was burnt out. The echelons of 29 Armd Bde also suffered a large number of casualties, particularly among the tank crews, who had escaped once during the day when their tanks had been knocked out, only to get hit in the evening air attack. There was, however, no damage done to any of the ORNE bridges.

The losses in tanks, damaged or destroyed, during the day's fighting were as follows :—

	SHERMAN 75 mm	SHERMAN 17 pr	CROMWELL 75 mm	95 mm	TOTAL
23 H	21	5	—	—	26
3 R Tks	33	8	—	—	41
2 FF YEO	35	8	—	—	43
2 N YEO	—	—	15	1	16
	89	21	15	1	126

Gds Armd Div

At 1230 hours, 2 Armd GREN GDS was still held up by the enemy on the outskirts of CAGNY, though a few tanks had worked round the North side of the village and penetrated about 1,000 yards to the South-East. 1 Armd COLDM GDS was still working its way down towards the West side of the village.

An hour later, 32 Gds Bde was ordered to proceed to an area South of DEMOUVILLE and to be ready to mount an attack on CAGNY.

2 Armd Recce WG was getting into position for its attempted penetration through the anti-tank screen to the East.

Fighting went on all the afternoon, and by 1445 hours, 1 Armd COLDM GDS had skirted the South-West edge of CAGNY and was pushing on towards FRENOUVILLE. 2 Armd IG, which had succeeded in getting South from the bridges, was trying to work its way past the North of CAGNY. 2 Armd Recce WG was engaging enemy anti-tank guns in the woods to the West of EMIEVILLE and CUILLERVILLE, and at 1600 hours, 2 KSLI (185 Inf Bde, 3 Brit Div) was also fighting in these woods, having entered from the North.

By 1800 hours, 2 Armd GREN GDS succeeded in getting into CAGNY, closely followed by two battalions of 32 Gds Bde, which completed clearing the village by 1930 hours, taking a number of prisoners from 21 Pz Div and 16 GAF Div and a few from 2 Pz Div.

2 Armd Recce WG had occupied a wood 1,000 yards West of CUILLERVILLE, but was unable to make any further progress to the East, and was trying to work its way South-East. 1 Armd COLDM GDS advanced between CAGNY and the railway, but met stiff opposition from both LE POIRIER and FRENOUVILLE. An attempt to capture the former village failed, and the battalion was eventually halted close to the railway and due South of CAGNY, by heavy anti-tank gun fire from FRENOUVILLE and the woods to the North-East.

2 Armd IG succeeded in getting round to the North of CAGNY to a position about 1,000 yards to the East and was also halted.

No further advance was made, and it was apparent, by 2200 hours, that Gds Armd Div was now facing a strong enemy position between FRENOUVILLE and EMIEVILLE, held by anti-tank guns supported by a few tanks, and with LE POIRIER as an additional strong point. The total losses for the day were 60 tanks.

7 Armd Div

The situation in front of 5 R Tks at midday seemed very obscure. There were reports of 29 Armd Bde being involved in a sharp battle, and of 5 Gds Armd Bde having trouble with enemy opposition in CAGNY. Meanwhile, 5 R Tks, in spite of continued exhortations from 8 Corps, was not able to get much further forward, and had its first incident when an enemy tank, about 800 yards East of DEMOUVILLE, knocked out a Sherman 17 pounder and a Honey. The enemy tank was soon eliminated and some further enemy resistance in the orchards South of DEMOUVILLE was dealt with by the combined efforts of 5 R Tks and 2 N YEO (11 Armd Div).

At about 1340 hours, Commander 8 Corps issued instructions for 22 Armd Bde to push 5 R Tks on towards LA HOGUE, leaving CAGNY on the Left, without waiting for the rest of the Brigade to concentrate. At this time, two squadrons of 4 CLY were still waiting to cross the bridges. 22 Armd

Bde, however, again reported congestion and being unable to move forward without becoming mixed up with 29 Armd Bde and 5 Gds Armd Bde. By 1500 hours, one squadron 5 R Tks had crossed the road CAEN-TROARN, and reached a position about 600 yards North-East of LE MESNIL FREMENTEL, and 45 minutes later the whole regiment was moving slowly forward to the GRENTHEVILLE area.

At 1615 hours, the remainder of 22 Armd Bde was ordered to move up from the position South of STE HONORINE, without interfering with Gds Armd Div. By 1700 hours, 1 R Tks had reached a position East of DEMOUVILLE, while 5 R Tks was reported to be in GRENTHEVILLE. 4 CLY was still held up by traffic back in the area of the bridges. Tac HQ 22 Armd Bde was at CUVERVILLE.

At 1745 hours, 5 R Tks was directed on LA HOGUE and 1 R Tks was ordered to be prepared to follow up. Twenty minutes later, it was reported that a squadron of 5 R Tks had reached SOLIERS, but this turned out not to be true, as in fact, it was not even in GRENTHEVILLE, but in a position to the East of the village. 22 Armd Bde then ordered the regiment to send one squadron towards FOUR where there were reports of 6 Panthers.

After a short engagement with some enemy infantry, A Sqn 5 R Tks succeeded in establishing itself in the Southern outskirts of GRENTHEVILLE, C Sqn took up a position from which it could watch and shoot into FOUR, while 'B' Sqn, which had so far been leading, came into reserve.

The enemy reacted strongly to this move, and at about 1900 hours, attacked from FOUR with two Panthers and two PzKw Mk IV, two of which were knocked out by C Sqn, while two of A Sqn tanks were destroyed. Artillery support was called for and the remaining two enemy tanks then withdrew into FOUR again. 5 R Tks was not able to use manoeuvre and ground to the best advantage in this engagement owing to tanks of 29 Armd Bde on both flanks.

At about 2000 hours, 131 Inf Bde was ordered to start crossing the ORNE bridges, and to concentrate in the area between LE BAS DE RANVILLE and STE HONORINE. This went on slowly all night as traffic congestion in the area of the bridges was still very acute.

Orders were again issued at about this time for 5 R Tks to try to get on to SOLIERS, and by 2200 hours, A Sqn was reported to be some distance South of GRENTHEVILLE, but had encountered approximately twelve tanks in the SOLIERS area, some of which were thought to be SP guns. Meanwhile, the remainder of 22 Armd Bde moved to night leaguer areas with both Tac Div and Bde HQ and 4 CLY North, and 1 R Tks South of DEMOUVILLE, and the remainder of 5 R Tks just South-West of LE MESNIL FREMENTEL. Eventually, A Sqn 5 R Tks leaguered for the night in the area South of GRENTHEVILLE.

At 2330 hours, the area of the bridges over the ORNE was subjected to a sharp enemy bombing raid, but units of 7 Armd Div did not suffer, although the passage of 131 Inf Bde across the river was delayed.

B. 1 CORPS

3 Brit Div

The situation on 3 Brit Div front at about 1230 hours was as follows :—

8 Brit Inf Bde :	2 E YORKS was in TOUFFREVILLE. 1st Battalion The Suffolk Regiment (1 SUFFOLK) started attacking SANNERVILLE at 1140 hours, and was still fighting in the village and hoped to clear it soon.
185 Inf Bde :	2 KSLI was mopping up LIROSE with one squadron STAFFS YEO, with the intention of moving on towards LE QUAI as soon as the village was clear.
9 Brit Inf Bde :	Had started to move forward and elements of 1st East Riding Yeomany (E RIDING YEO) in support had reached TOUFFREVILLE.
152 Inf Bde :	Was firmly established in the whole area of the road triangle.

1 SUFFOLK (8 Brit Inf Bde) continued successfully with the task of mopping up SANNERVILLE and the completion of the job was made quite clear at HQ 1 Corps shortly after 1300 hours by a wireless intercept, when an unknown speaker said rather tersely "Of course SANNERVILLE is clear. I wouldn't be here if it wasn't."

BANNEVILLE LA CAMPAGNE, however, was reported still held by the enemy, but at 1430 hours, 1 SUFFOLK was within 200 yards of the village. Meanwhile, 13/18 H had been clearing the woods to the North-East of TOUFFREVILLE, and at 1345 hours had reached a cross roads on the road ESCOVILLE-TROARN about 1,100 yards South-East of the road triangle.

At 1420 hours, 2 KSLI (185 Inf Bde) was still mopping up the last enemy resistance in the area of LIROSE, and was preparing to move forward to Task IV, LE QUAI and CUILLERVILLE. An hour later, it was reported by STAFFS YEO that the centre of the LE QUAI area was held by 4 Tigers, while at 1600 hours, 2 KSLI was fighting in the woods and orchards North-West of the village.

At 1630 hours, 1 SUFFOLK (8 Brit Inf Bde) was still mopping up in BANNEVILLE LA CAMPAGNE. 152 Inf Bde was exploiting Southwards from the triangle along the TROARN road, and the leading troops had joined up with 13/18 H. 9 Brit Inf Bde had started on their advance from SANNERVILLE towards TROARN 30 minutes previously. At about 1750 hours, 185 Inf Bde was reported to be on the edge of its objective in the orchards North-West of LE QUAI. Progress here was very slow, and a plan was made for an attack with support from STAFFS YEO and artillery to start at 2030 hours. While this attack was being prepared, STAFFS YEO tried to send a patrol from the LE QUAI area up the road running North-East to TROARN, but this patrol met slight enemy opposition about halfway in the area of the bridge over the COURS DE JANVILLE and was unable to make any further progress.

By 2000 hours, 152 Inf Bde had both 2nd and 5th Battalions The Seaforth Highlanders (Ross-shire Buffs, the Duke of Albany's) (2 and 5 SEAFORTH) in the area of the triangle, with 5th Battalion the Queen's Own Cameron Highlanders (5 CAMERONS) down as far as the cross roads 1,100 yards South-East, and had had a carrier patrol down to within 2 miles of TROARN.

8 Brit Inf Bde reported the whole area South-West of the positions held by 152 Inf Bde as far as TOUFFREVILLE completely clear of the enemy.

9 Brit Inf Bde was progressing slowly through the thick country East of TOUFFREVILLE and SANNERVILLE with 1st. Battalion The King's Own Scottish Borderers (1 KOSB) on the Right and 2nd Battalion The Royal Ulster Rifles (2 RUR) on the Left. There was a fair amount of cratering to overcome which made the progress of supporting weapons slow, and by 2130 hours, the forward troops had reached a line running North and South from the brickworks 1,400 yards East of TOUFFREVILLE, to the road CAEN-TROARN, where they were held up by enemy fire.

The attack by 185 Inf Bde was postponed for half an hour, but started at 2100 hours and the position was reported completely clear, and all opposition had ceased by midnight. 185 Inf Bde then consolidated the position and started patrolling North-East towards 9 Brit Inf Bde, which was pressing on steadily with its attack.

51 (H) Div

7 A & SH (154 Inf Bde) took over from 159 Inf Bde in CUVERVILLE by 1200 hours, and subsequently 1 BW took over DEMOUVILLE at 1930 hours, and was joined there by 7 BW before dark.

153 Inf Bde crossed the river and by midnight was concentrated in the area RANVILLE–HEROUVILLETTE.

RE

At 1225 hours, it was reported that TOWER bridge was 66% complete and the estimated time of completion was 2000 hours. TAY bridge was also going well. At 1415 hours, this estimated time of completion for TOWER bridge was altered to 1800 hours and that for TAY bridge given as 0200 hours 19 July. TOWER bridge was ultimately declared open to Class 40 traffic at 1745 hours.

The bridges were bombed at 2330 hours but no damage was done.

C. 2 CDN CORPS

At 1200 hours, R DE CHAUD (8 Cdn Inf Bde) was still held up in COLOMBELLES, and the Chateau just North of the village was resisting all attacks. N SHORE R was working its way past R DE CHAUD to the West, but in the factory area just South of COLOMBELLES, stiff opposition was also encountered.

By 1400 hours, QOR OF C, who had spent over two hours clearing opposition from the Northern outskirts of GIBERVILLE, was on the move again and had soon taken the Northern half of the village. Supported by B Sqn 6 Cdn Armd Regt, the whole village was steadily cleared, and by 1500 hours, the leading troops had reached the railway CAEN-TROARN on the Southern edge, and all opposition had been completely eliminated after a further forty minutes. The battalion was then ordered to occupy the village as a firm base.

At 1630 hours, R DE CHAUD had succeeded in capturing the Chateau, but was still mopping up in COLOMBELLES, while N SHORE R was still making very slow progress through the factory area.

The leading battalion of 9 Cdn Inf Bde (Stormont, Dundas and Glengarry Highlanders) (SD & G HIGHRS) had tried to assist R DE CHAUD in COLOMBELLES, and was involved in the fighting there during the next few hours. At about 1630 hours, the remainder of the brigade was ordered to by pass the factory area to the East and to push on and establish itself in the built up localities of MONDEVILLE and BELLEMAIS.

The patrol sent out by 7 Cdn Inf Bde crossed the river by the main bridge between CAEN and FAUBOURG DE VAUCELLES, and reported very little opposition, and early in the afternoon, the Regina Rifle Regiment (REGINA RIF) had got one company across, and the whole battalion was across by 1900 hours. The remainder of 7 Cdn Inf Bde was held back North of the river, and REGINA RIF was ordered to push South to the line of the main road through FAUBOURG DE VAUCELLES, in order to form a bridgehead, and drive back the enemy machine guns, which were holding up all work on the bridging sites. This task was commenced and some heavy fighting ensued in VAUCELLES, but by midnight, the battalion was firmly established on the line of LA RUE ROYALE from about 1,000 yards West of the road CAEN–FALAISE to about 400 yards East of the railway CAEN–VIMONT.

By 2359 hours, R DE CHAUD (8 Cdn Inf Bde) had finished mopping up COLOMBELLES, and was in reserve in the area of the Chateau : N SHORE R had cleared the enemy out of most of the factory area, in which there was a large fire burning, but was still trying to liquidate the remnants located in the railway cutting immediately East of the main factory area : QOR OF C was still firmly established in GIBERVILLE, having beaten off a heavy counter attack at 2100 hours, with the assistance of one squadron 6 Cdn Armd Regt, during which 500 prisoners were taken. It was reported that there was extensive mining and a large number of booby traps in the area.

By midnight, SD & G HIGHRS (9 Cdn Inf Bde), which had been working its way down the West bank of the ORNE, between the factory area and the river, was just South of the Southern railway bridge over the ORNE into the factory area. The other two battalions of 9 Cdn Inf Bde (The North Nova Scotia Highlanders (NORTH NS HIGHRS) and The Highland Light Infantry of Canada (HLI of C)) were completing the clearance of BELLEMAIS up as far as the railway CAEN–VIMONT.

4 Cdn Inf Bde (2 Cdn Inf Div) had been ordered to attack LOUVIGNY during the afternoon, and the attack was put in at 1900 hours by The Royal Regiment of Canada (R REGT C). The battalion had succeeded in getting into the orchards North of the village after about an hour, but resistance was stiff, and by 2359 hours there were three companies in the village, which was not yet clear, while some enemy in the Chateau North-East of the village were still holding out.

During the afternoon, 5 Cdn Inf Bde (2 Cdn Inf Div) moved to the area 2,500 yards West of CAEN, ready to carry out operations, and was subjected to heavy mortaring and shelling. It was ordered to try and cross the ORNE West of the town, and concentrate at the West end of FAUBOURG DE VAUCELLES, with the object of attacking the high ground South of FLEURY SUR ORNE.

From the RE point of view, the day was only partially successful. Recce parties for the bridges in CAEN were pinned to the ground by heavy machine gun fire from the South bank, and were not able to get information until late in the day. The Class 9 bridge and the DUKW crossing opposite HEROUVILLETTE were both given estimated times of completion as 0300 hours 19 July, but the bridges in CAEN were not likely to be ready until 0800 hours or 0900 hours on 19 July, which was later than had been hoped.

D. SUMMARY OF OPERATIONS DURING THE AFTERNOON OF 18 JULY

Second Army Sitrep for the period 1200 to 2359 hours 18 July have the following account :—

"During the afternoon, our rapid advance of the morning was slowed up by stiffening enemy opposition and the need for moving forward of infantry units to assist the armour. The air forces continued to give magnificent support for the remainder of the day, a record number of sorties being flown. Infantry had got a small bridgehead over the River ORNE in FAUBOURG DE VAUCELLES, were attacking LOUVIGNY, and were clearing the factory area. A heavy counter attack on GIBERVILLE was driven off, and approximately 500 prisoners captured. Enemy counter attacks with tanks developed against our own armour, which had been forced to take up positions in the area BRAS–BOURGUEBUS–GRENTHEVILLE. A strong anti-tank screen between FRENOUVILLE and EMIEVILLE halted the armoured thrust in the direction of VIMONT. The infantry on the Left were established as far South as CUILLERVILLE. The drive towards TROARN continues."

The situation at 2359 hours 18 July is shown on Map No. 10.

SECTION IV

OPERATIONS DURING 19 JULY

A. 8 CORPS

11 Armd Div

After the bombing, the rest of the night was fairly quiet, except for a little patrolling. 1 HEREFORD sent out a patrol due West from LE MESNIL FREMENTEL towards CORMELLES, but it met an enemy patrol, and could get no information. G Coy 8 RB, located West of GRENTHEVILLE, was ordered to send a patrol out to the road CAEN–FALAISE. This patrol managed to get as far as BRAS, but could not get further owing to a number of burning tanks, which lit up the route forward; it reported, however, that it did not think that the enemy were using that road.

At 0600 hours, 2 N YEO again attempted to reconnoitre South along the line of the railway, but came under fire and suffered casualties from enemy tanks and anti-tank guns on the BRAS–BOURGUEBUS ridge. At 0700 hours, a counter attack on 3 R Tks developed from BRAS and from North of HUBERT FOLIE. As a result of this attack, the regiment was withdrawn to a position between the railway and the road CAEN–VIMONT and West of the railway COLOMBELLES–TILLY-LA-CAMPAGNE. Later, reports were received of 400 enemy infantry in FOUR, and of enemy infantry digging in, and also tanks, in BRAS.

At 0845 hours, Main Div HQ moved away from the vulnerable area of the ORNE bridges to an area just South of the orchards, South-East of CUVERVILLE.

At about 0900 hours, 2 N YEO pushed a patrol out round the factory buildings halfway between CORMELLES and GRENTHEVILLE. Later on, C squadron followed this patrol, and by 1100 hours was established without any opposition in the orchards South of CORMELLES.

Meanwhile, A Sqn 2 N YEO had taken up a position of observation 600 yards South-West of GRENTHEVILLE. At about 1100 hours, enemy infantry were seen digging in on a line just North-East of BRAS and HUBERT FOLIE. These were effectively engaged by artillery fire.

During the morning, a considerable amount of fighting took place, but neither 3 R Tks nor 23 H was able to make any progress against the very strong screen of tanks and anti-tank guns in the villages of BRAS, HUBERT FOLIE, BOURGUEBUS and SOLIERS. All attempts to move South-West towards BRAS, and the high ground round VERRIERES, were stopped by fire from enemy tanks. 3 R Tks and 23 H therefore spent most of the morning in positions of observation South-West and South-East of GRENTHEVILLE. 2 FF YEO was in reserve North of this village, reorganizing.

During the morning, patrols of INNS OF COURT were very active, and produced various reports of enemy infantry and tanks in the villages on the BRAS–BOURGUEBUS ridge, and of some movement further South.

Early in the morning, Commander 11 Armd Div had informed 7 Armd Div that, owing to the large number of tanks lost during the previous day's fighting, and the consequent reorganization involved within the armoured regiments, 29 Armd Bde would not be undertaking much offensive action for the first few hours of daylight.

At about 1030 hours, Commander 11 Armd Div was informed that his first task for the day was to capture BRAS and to dominate the main road CAEN–FALAISE. Later in the morning, the Commanders Gds, 7 and 11 Armd Divs had a conference at Tac HQ 11 Armd Div to work out a combined plan. This plan was approved by the Commander 8 Corps when he visited this HQ at about midday. The plan in outline was as follows :—

> At 1600 hours, 11 Armd Div was to attack BRAS, and subsequently HUBERT FOLIE.
>
> At 1700 hours, 7 Armd Div was to attack BOURGUEBUS and FOUR.
>
> At 1700 hours, Gds Armd Div was to attack LE POIRIER and subsequently exploit to FRENOUVILLE.
>
> All these attacks were to have full artillery support.

Subsequently, Commander 11 Armd Div and Commander 29 Armd Bde discussed this plan at Tac HQ 29 Armd Bde, and the details of 29 Armd Bde tasks were agreed as follows :—

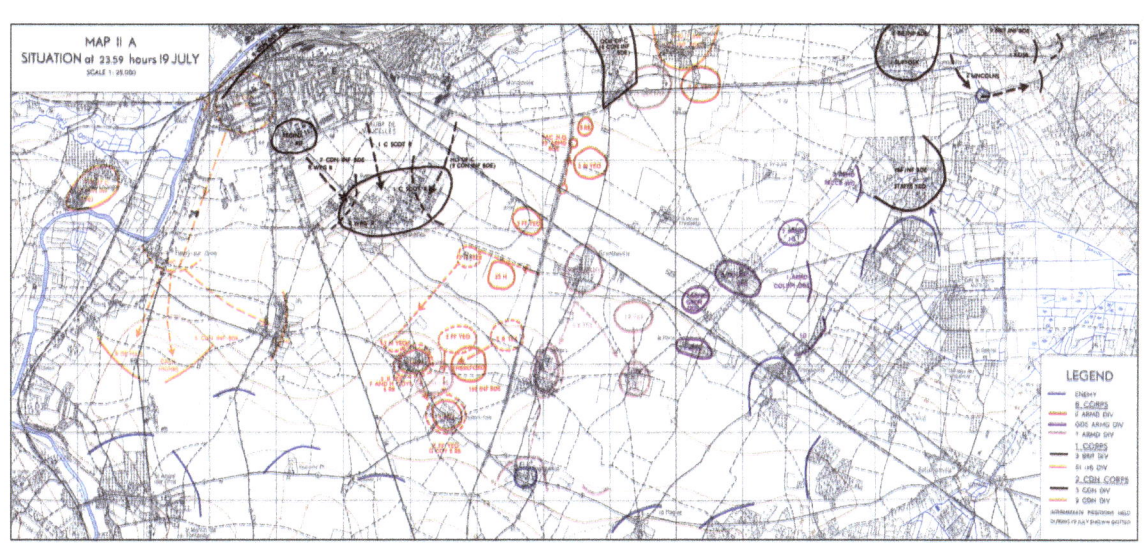

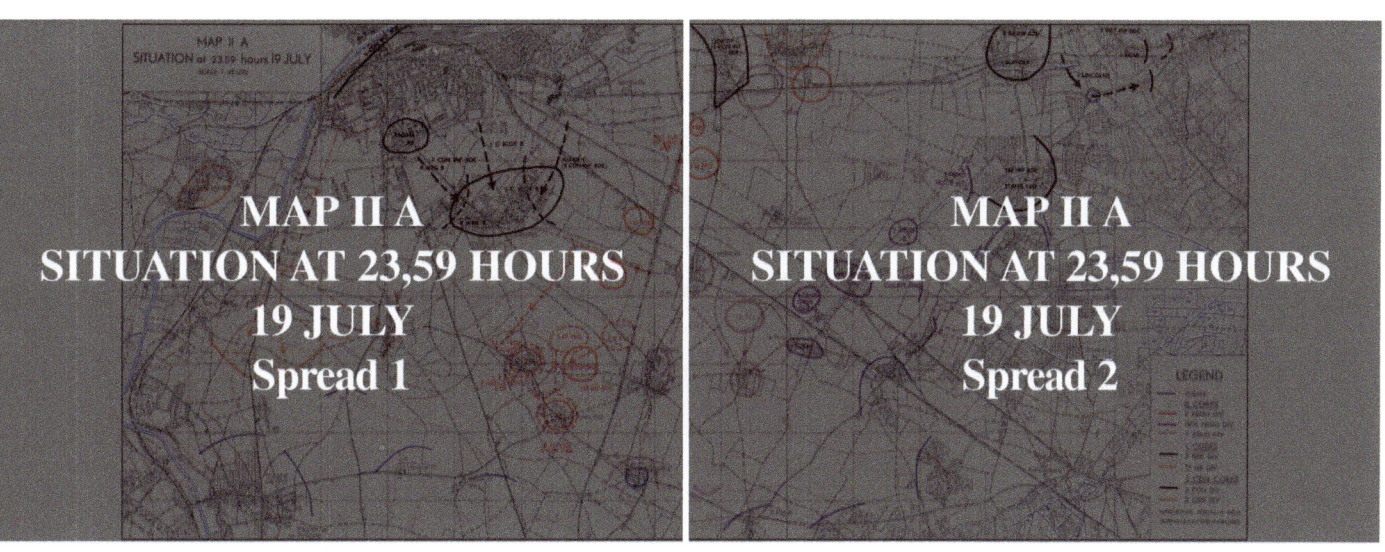

MAP II A SITUATION AT 23,59 HOURS 19 JULY Spread 1

MAP II A SITUATION AT 23,59 HOURS 19 JULY Spread 2

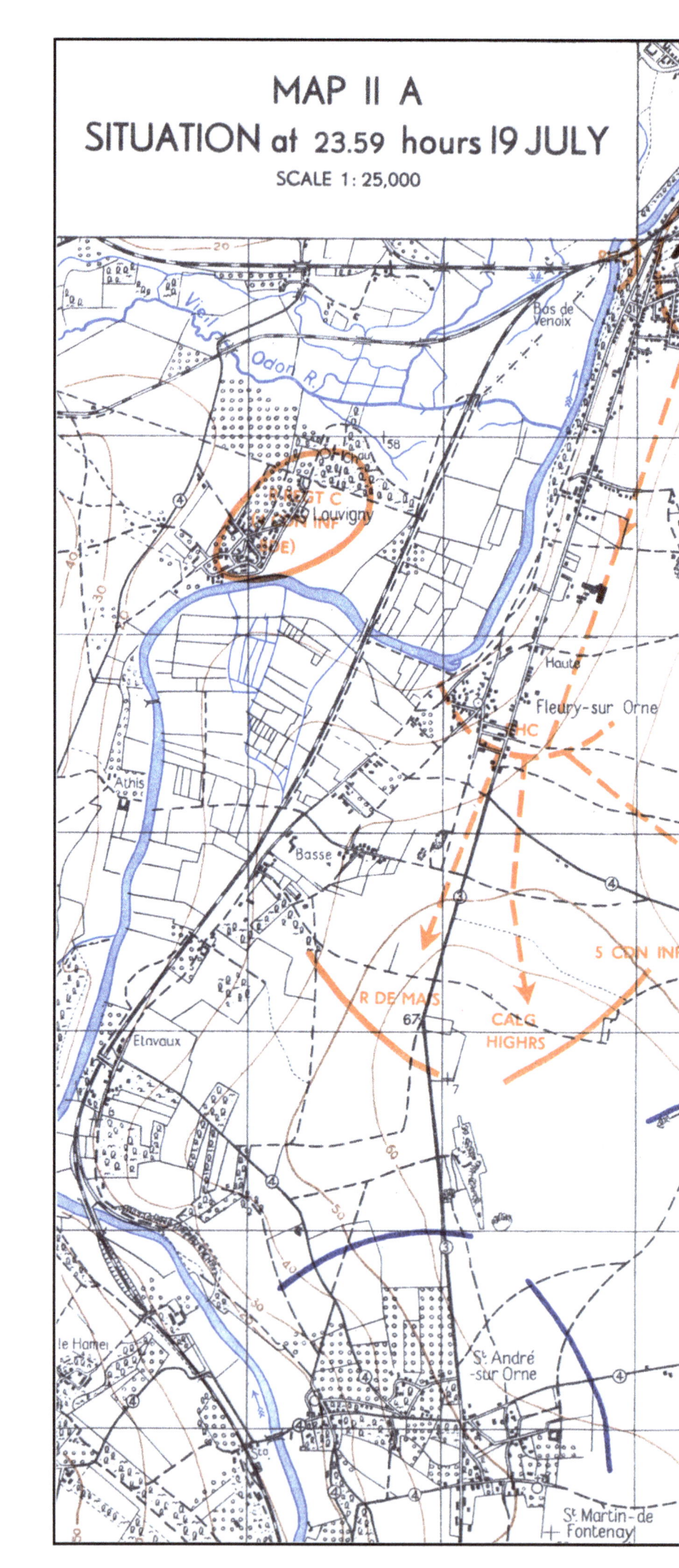

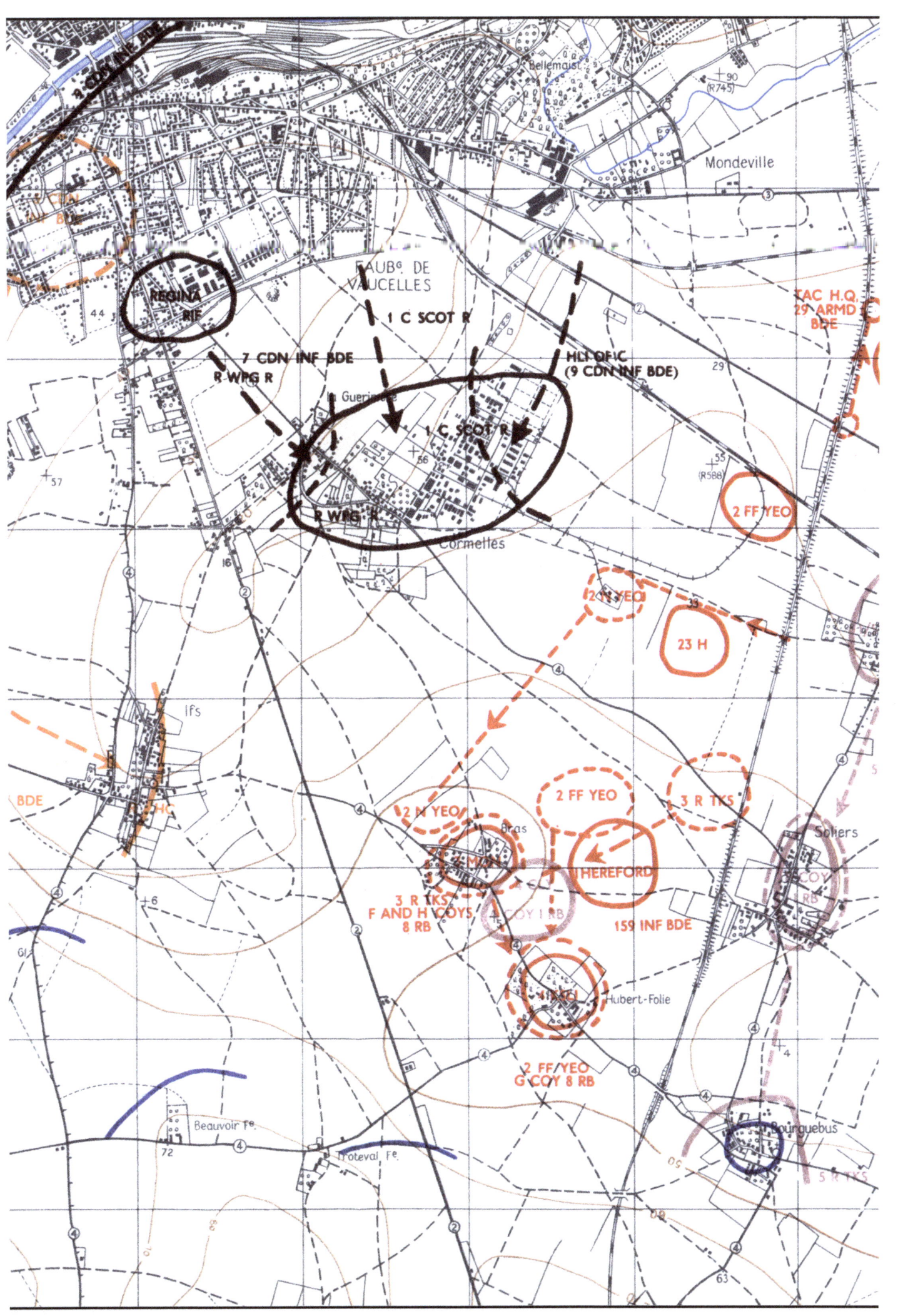

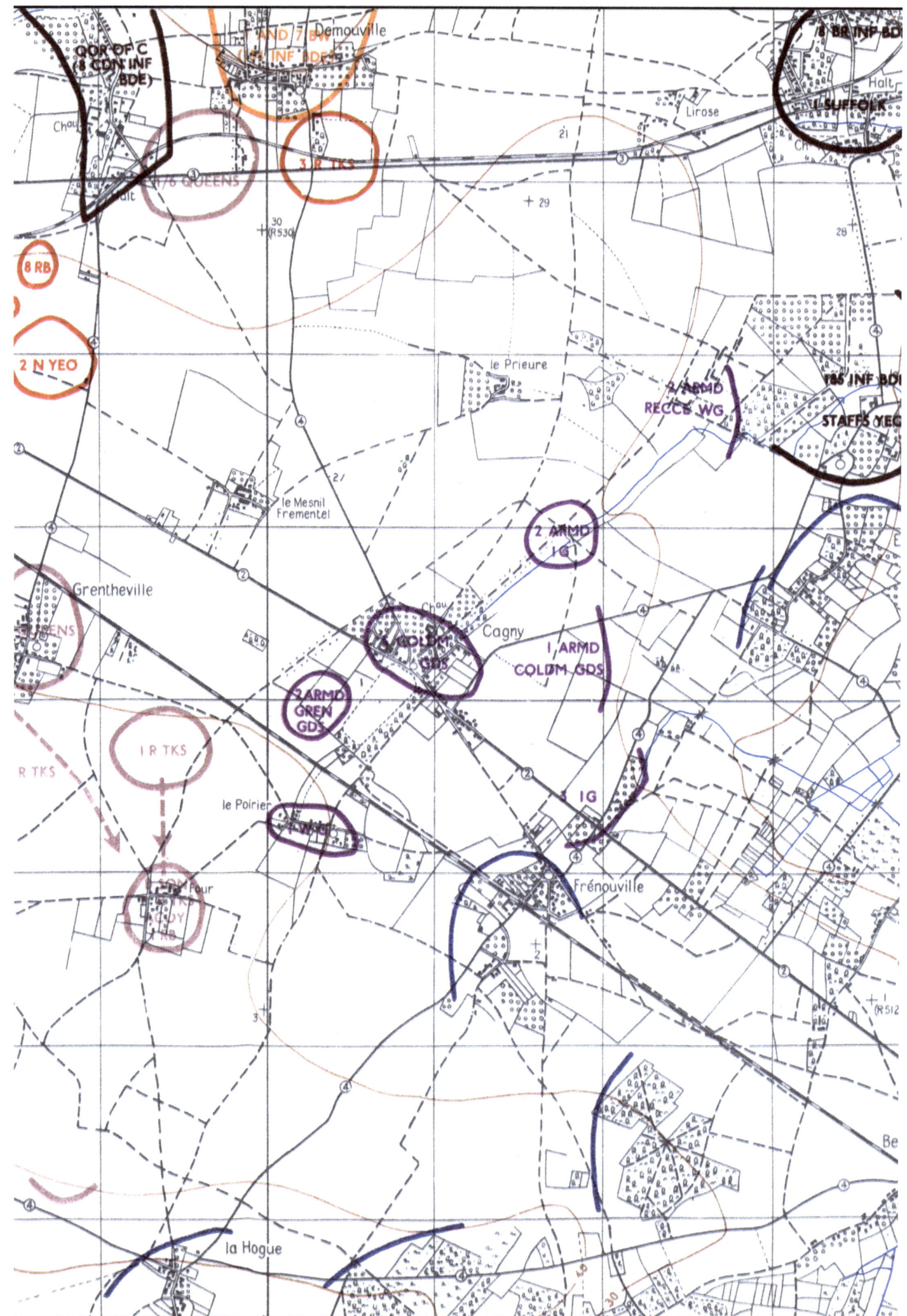

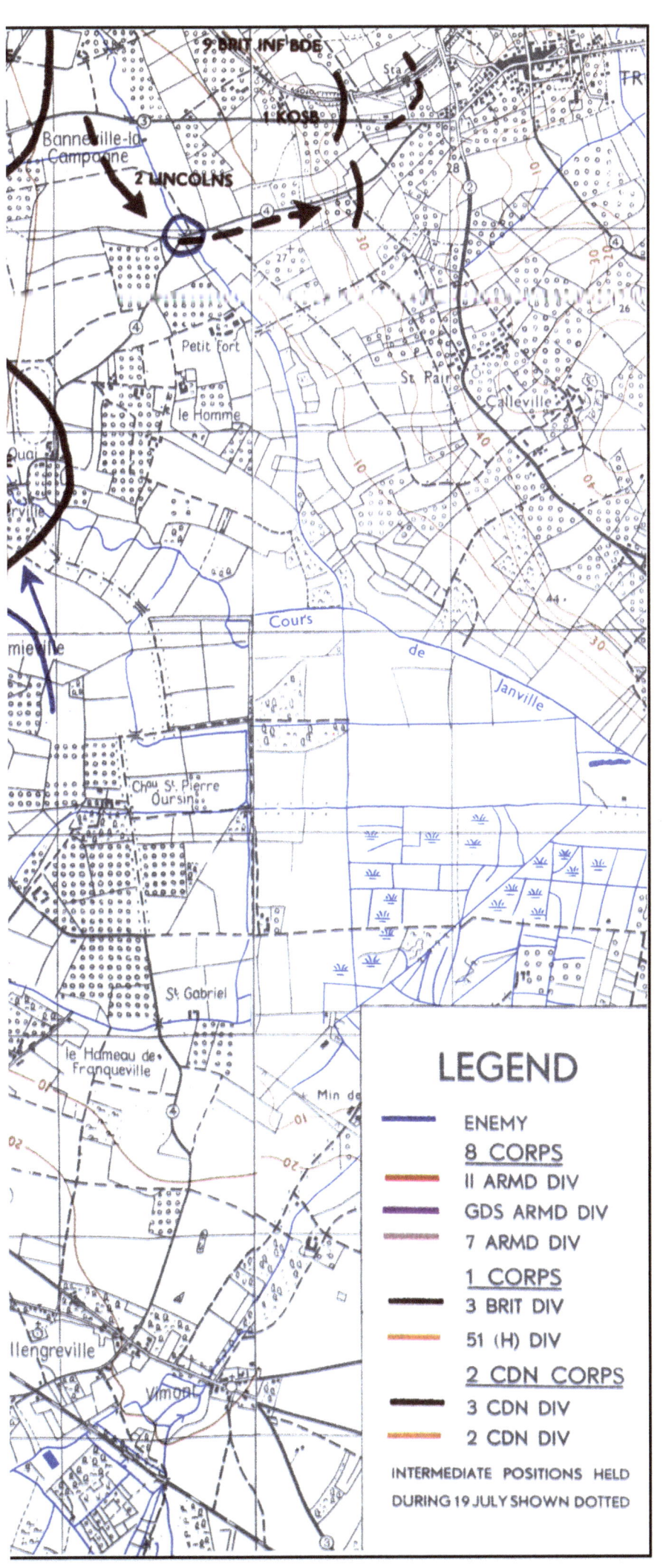

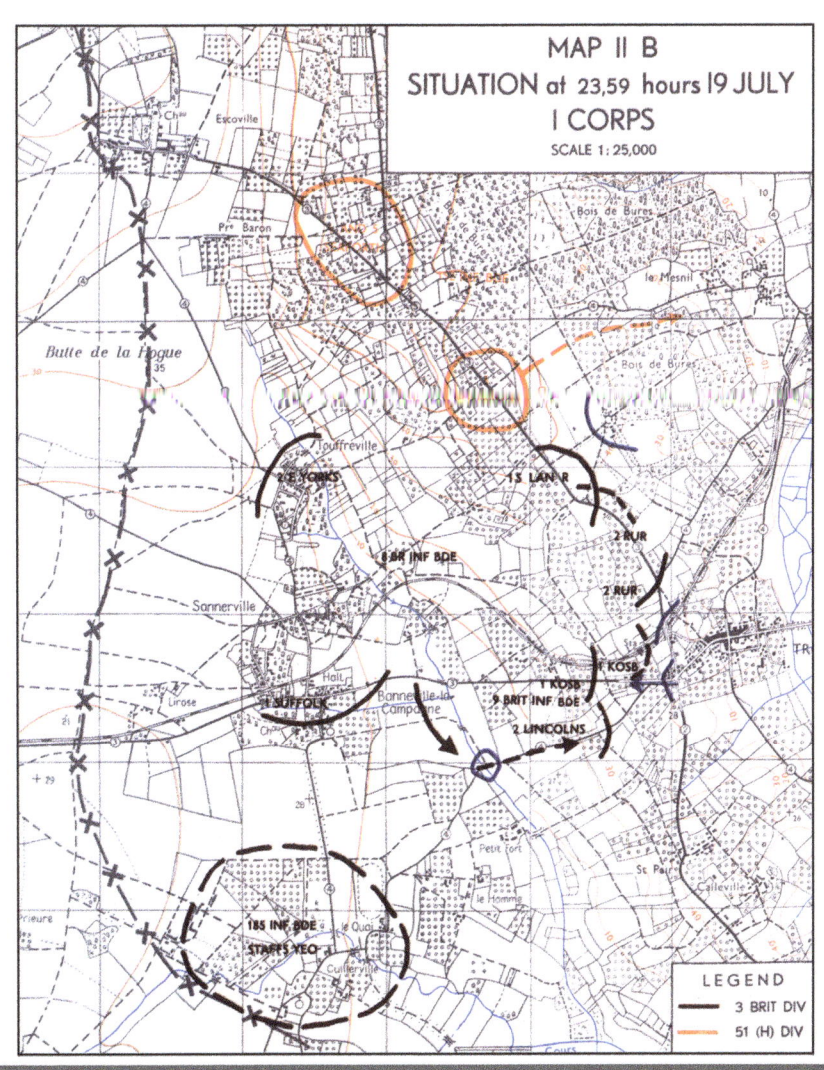

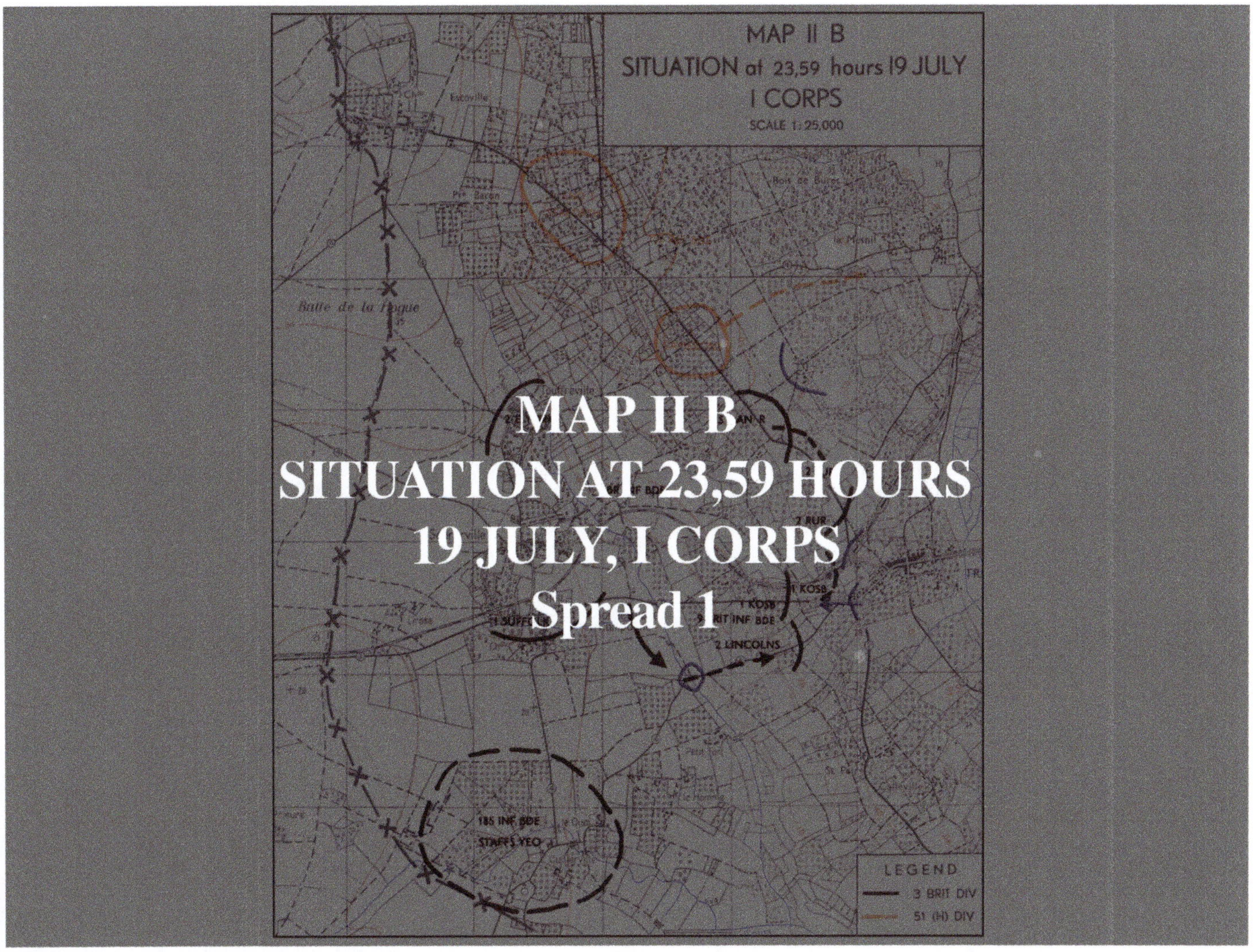

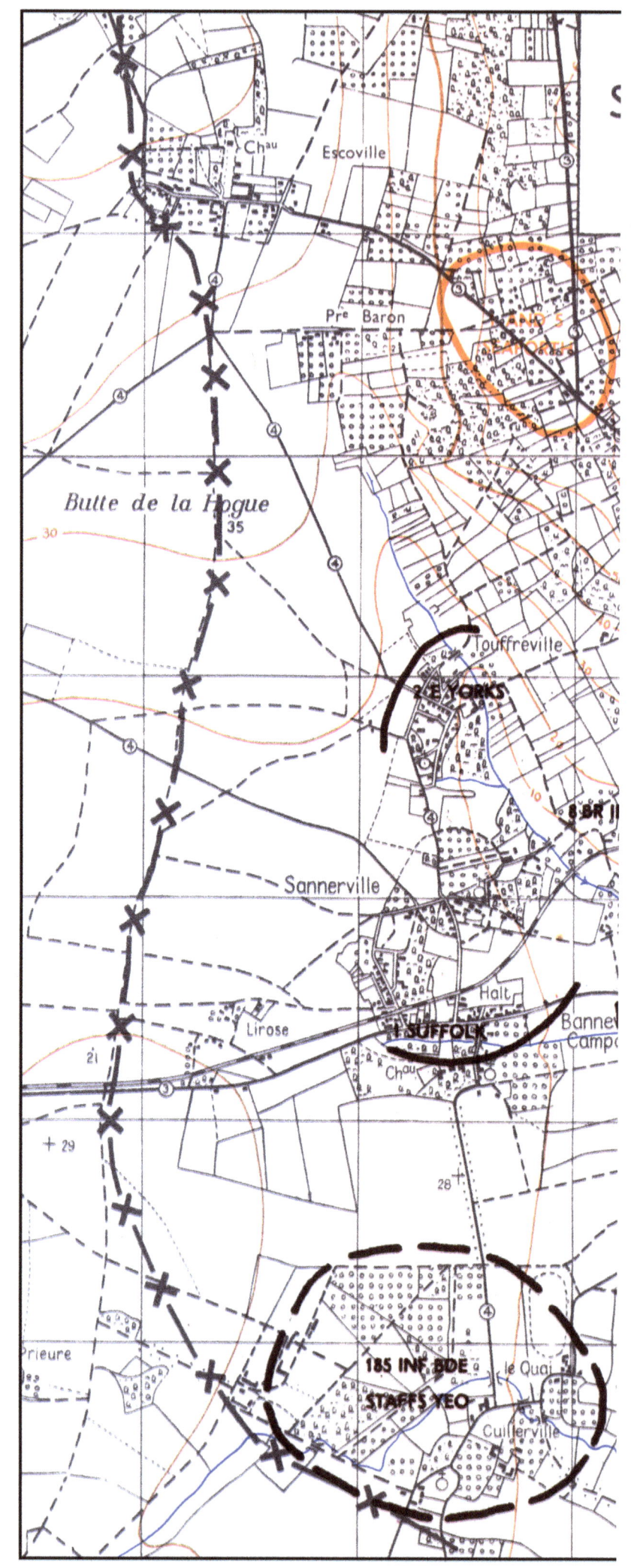

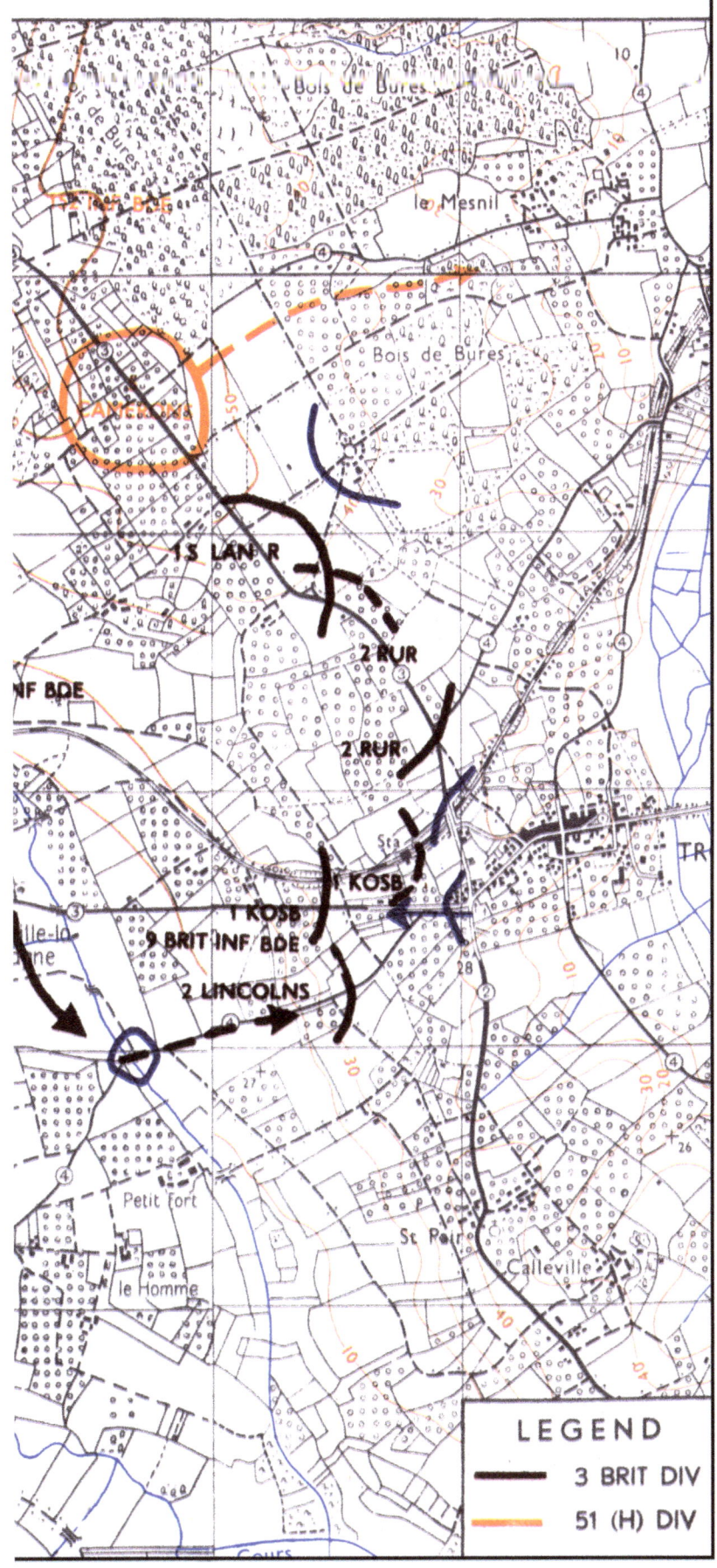

At 1600 hours, 2 N YEO was to advance and capture BRAS, followed by 8 RB, who would mop up the village. 2 N YEO was then to give fire support for the advance of 3 R Tks on HUBERT FOLIE, and 8 RB was again to follow up and clear the village.

At about 1400 hours, Tac HQ 29 Armd Bde, which was near the railway bridge North-West of GRENTHEVILLE, was heavily shelled, and subsequently moved back about 1,000 yards North along the railway.

The rest of 2 N YEO followed C Sqn, and by about 1400 hours the whole regiment was concentrated in the area of the factory buildings between CORMELLES and GRENTHEVILLE. By 1500 hours, the motor companies of 8 RB had been concentrated in the area West of the railway bridge. At 1600 hours, the attack on BRAS started, supported by artillery firing both HE and smoke, and twenty minutes later, the leading tanks of 2 N YEO reached the Western outskirts of BRAS, although it had been intended during planning that the regiment should attack the village from the East. It was then held up by heavy fire from the South-West.

Meanwhile, 3 R Tks was waiting just South-West of GRENTHEVILLE for the completion of the capture of BRAS, and its own subsequent advance on HUBERT FOLIE. When CO 3 R Tks saw that 2 N YEO was held up short of BRAS, he appreciated that he could make no progress with his attack until the village was captured. He therefore proposed that he should help 2 N YEO by attacking BRAS from the East. This proposal was approved, and at 1625 hours, 3 R Tks started to move forward. 15 minutes later, the leading tanks had started to enter the village.

The village was strongly held by about one battalion of enemy infantry well dug-in, and there was also a certain amount of opposition from anti-tank and Panzerfaust weapons. Progress through the village was slow because of the rubble, and some walls had to be demolished by the tanks firing 75 mm shells at them. By 1710 hours, however, the leading tanks had got right through the village to the South-West side.

F and H Coys, 8 RB, which were moving close behind 3 R Tks, debussed at the edge of the village and pressed on behind the tanks, H Coy on the Right and F Coy on the Left. The enemy belonged to 1 SS Pz (ADOLF HITLER) Div, one of the crack divisions of the Wehrmacht, and they fought bravely as they were expected to. However, owing to the speed with which 8 RB got into the village, they had little time to collect themselves. Some came out of their slit trenches with grenades in their hands and were rapidly dealt with. Inside the village, there were still machine gun posts and snipers holding out, and they too, were speedily mopped up. F Coy pressed right through the village, and was in time to get a good shoot at about fifty Germans, who were escaping to the South-West, but it seems that very few of the rest got away. The village was reported clear by 1800 hours, only 45 minutes after 8 RB entered. The speed of the attack by 3 R Tks and subsequent mopping up by 8 RB was such, that almost the whole garrison was killed or taken prisoner, and 3 Bn, 1 SS PGR, was considered to be almost completely written off.

Owing to the commanding position of BRAS, on a spur overlooking the whole of the ground to the North-East, it was considered a prize of very great value. The Army Commander therefore directed that it was to be firmly held by 159 Inf Bde, and eventually arrangements would be made for the village to be taken over by 2 Cdn Corps. Therefore, a battalion of 159 Inf Bde was ordered to follow up, and take over BRAS, as soon as it was cleared. At about 1800 hours, 3 MON entered the village and took over from 8 RB.

At 1810 hours, 2 N YEO was ordered forward to attack HUBERT FOLIE, under supporting fire from field and medium artillery. Shortly after the attack had started, information was received that the village was held by a unit of 22 Armd Bde. The attack was therefore halted, while this report was verified, but it turned out to be untrue, and 2 N YEO was therefore ordered to continue the attack. At 1830 hours, however, it was reported that the regiment was suffering casualties from Tigers from the South and was reduced to one squadron, that it was also considerably disorganised by the changes in orders, and was therefore unable to get forward.

At 1840 hours, 2 FF YEO was ordered to make the attack on HUBERT FOLIE and the CO went forward to contact CO 3 R Tks. The attack was timed to start at 2000 hours, with a barrage lasting for ten minutes. 2 FF YEO then moved up to a position just North-East of BRAS, being heavily shelled and mortared on the way. 8 RB, was still waiting in BRAS to follow up the attack, and the battalion was intermittently shelled the whole time, and also spent a very unpleasant ten minutes, when the village was shelled by a concentration from four medium regiments, which was intended for HUBERT FOLIE.

At 2000 hours the attack started, and C Sqn 2 FF YEO following up close behind the barrage, was able to enter the village without suffering any casualties, and was closely followed by A Sqn. There was very little opposition and at 2035 hours, G Coy 8 RB started to enter the village. The company was held up for a while by what seemed to be machine gun fire from a Sherman tank, and a good many hard things were said about 2 FF YEO. It turned out to be a German, who had got into one of our own Shermans knocked out the day before, and, once discovered, he was soon dealt with. The clearing of the village took a short time, as it appeared to contain only a few stragglers from BRAS, and by 2115 hours, the battle was over.

4 KSLI arrived to take over the village, which was completed by 2145 hours, while 1 HEREFORD moved up into a reserve position behind both 3 MON and 4 KSLI. 23 H was moved up to a position about 1,200 yards West of GRENTHEVILLE, from which it could support 159 Inf Bde if necessary.

29 Armd Bde then withdrew units to the following locations :—

    3 R Tks to echelon area just South of DEMOUVILLE.

    2 FF YEO just West of railway bridge North-West of GRENTHEVILLE.

    8 RB area of Tac HQ 29 Armd Bde, 2,000 yards North of GRENTHEVILLE.

At about 2250 hours, HUBERT FOLIE was subjected to a sharp attack of shelling and machine gun fire from the direction of SOLIERS. Otherwise the night passed quietly.

At about 2200 hours, orders were received that the area held by 11 Armd Div would be taken over on 20 July by 3 Cdn Div, including the villages of BRAS and HUBERT FOLIE.

The losses in tanks for 19 July were as follows :—

	SHERMAN		*CROMWELL*		*TOTAL*
	75 mm	17 pr	75 mm	95 mm	
23 H	4	—	—	—	4
3 R Tks	15	1	—	—	16
2 FF YEO	8	—	—	—	8
2 N YEO	—	—	35	2	37
TOTALS	27	1	35	2	65

Gds Armd Div

During the morning, reconnaissance confirmed the strength of the enemy position, which was still firmly held by anti-tank guns supported by a few tanks. Early in the morning, 2 Armd IG moved slightly to the North, but was unable to advance. 1 Armd COLDM GDS was ordered to resume the advance on VIMONT. The battalion was able to make no headway along the railway towards FRENOUVILLE, so moved North-East up on to the main road CAGNY-VIMONT by about 1000 hours. The resistance in this area from both FRENOUVILLE and the orchards to the North-East was just as strong, so 1 Armd COLDM GDS moved further North-East up on the Right of 2 Armd IG. Both battalions were firmly held in this area and could make no further progress.

An attack was made by 3 IG (32 Gds Bde) from CAGNY, supported by 2 Armd GREN GDS, on to the orchards North-East of FRENOUVILLE, which were successfully cleared. Meanwhile, 2 Armd Recce WG was still in a position to the West of EMIEVILLE and CUILLERVILLE, and about midday reported 5 Tiger tanks in the EMIEVILLE area.

At about 1700 hours, 1 WG (32 Gds Bde) attacked LE POIRIER and captured it. During the evening, two Panthers were destroyed, one South-East of LE POIRIER and one between that village and FOUR.

By last light, 32 Gds Bde held firm positions with 5 COLDM GDS in CAGNY, 1 WG in LE POIRIER, and 3 IG in the orchards North-East of FRENOUVILLE. 5 Gds Armd Bde was disposed with 1 Armd COLDM GDS 1,000 yards due East of CAGNY, 2 Armd IG having drawn back to a position 500 yards North-East of CAGNY, and 2 Armd GREN GDS withdrawn just West of the woods halfway between LE POIRIER and CAGNY.

During the evening, an attack on FRENOUVILLE with air support was planned for first light on 20 July.

7 Armd Div

During the night, units of 131 Inf Bde continued to cross the ORNE bridges and it was not until 0430 hours 19 July that all the infantry battalions and the remainder of the 65 A Tk Regt were reported clear.

At first light, 1 RB reported that FOUR was still occupied by tanks and infantry, but there were no signs of any digging. Commander 22 Armd Bde visited 5 R Tks at about 0600 hours in order to get the regiment moving again on SOLIERS. About 45 minutes later, the Commander 11 Armd Div informed Tac HQ 7 Armd Div that, owing to a loss of more than 100 tanks during the battle on 18 July, 11 Armd Div would be re-organizing, and would not be in a position to do any attacking for an hour or so.

At about the same time, 131 Inf Bde was ordered to move forward to the area of DEMOUVILLE, and at 0700 hours, Commander 7 Armd Div met Commanders 22 Armd Bde and 131 Inf Bde at Tac HQ 22 Armd Bde. It was then decided to hold GRENTHEVILLE as a firm base for further exploitation South, and that 1/5 QUEENS would be placed under command 22 Armd Bde for this purpose. Just after 0700 hours, a sharp counter attack was launched on 5 R Tks by enemy tanks from FOUR, but this was beaten off.

Shortly before 0800 hours, Tac HQ 22 Armd Bde and 4 CLY moved up close behind the area occupied by 1 R Tks just South of DEMOUVILLE. An hour later, 5 R Tks was reported to be a short distance South of GRENTHEVILLE, and on a line about 800 yards to the East, and at about 1000 hours was approaching FOUR.

Meanwhile, Commanders Gds, 7 and 11 Armd Divs met at Tac HQ 11 Armd Div, just North of LE MESNIL FREMENTEL, to work out a combined plan for the day.

By about 1100 hours, 1/5 QUEENS (131 Inf Bde) was located immediately North of CUVERVILLE. The rest of 131 Inf Bde was only able to make slow progress South from the bridges owing to traffic congestion.

At 1120 hours, 5 R Tks reported that one squadron was in SOLIERS with two platoons B Coy 1 RB, which were completing mopping up. It had not yet got into FOUR, which was offering strong resistance. Shortly afterwards, the area occupied by 1 R Tks and the remainder of 22 Armd Bde South of DEMOUVILLE was very heavily shelled and medium artillery was called on to reply. 5 R Tks reported that there were snipers in FOUR who were very hard to clear, and also Panthers to the East of the village, which were causing trouble.

5 R Tks did not manage to make any further progress against FOUR, and another battalion of 131 Inf Bde was ordered to move up from the concentration area so that it could assist.

After the conference at midday between the Corps Commander and the Commanders of the three armoured divisions, Commander 7 Armd Div arrived at Tac HQ 22 Armd Bde, halfway between DEMOUVILLE and LE MESNIL FREMENTEL at about 1400 hours. The following plan was then agreed. 5 R Tks to be called off from FOUR, and, using SOLIERS as a base, to attack BOURGUEBUS. 1 R Tks to attack FOUR, while 1/5 QUEENS, which had arrived in the area, occupied GRENTHEVILLE. The two attacks were to start at 1700 hours. 4 CLY was to be prepared to exploit South-West towards VERRIERES, after 11 Armd Div had captured both BRAS and HUBERT FOLIE. 131 Inf Bde was to be prepared to take up a brigade position in the areas GRENTHEVILLE and SOLIERS, as ordered.

At 1545 hours, 5 R Tks was still in the area SOLIERS, and West and North-West of FOUR, while 1 R Tks was astride the road CAEN–VIMONT. 131 Inf Bde was in the area of DEMOUVILLE.

The attack by 11 Armd Div on BRAS started as arranged at 1600 hours, and at 1700 hours, the two attacks on BOURGUEBUS and FOUR were begun. B Sqn 1 R Tks started well and met moderate opposition, but, as it got close to the village, the enemy resistance increased.

BRAS was reported captured by 29 Armd Bde by 1715 hours, and LE POIRIER was reported cleared by Gds Armd Div 15 minutes later.

B Sqn 5 R Tks moved on towards BOURGUEBUS, and at about 1840 hours the squadron was held up on the outskirts by 3 Tigers and 2 Panthers which had entered the village just before, and also by fire coming from LA HOGUE and the woods to the South. During the ensuing fight, 5 R Tks knocked out two Tigers and one Panther. By 2040 hours, the regiment had worked its way up to the North, East and West sides of BOURGUEBUS, but was still unable to capture the village. By about the same time, 1 R Tks had finally succeeded in completing the capture of FOUR assisted by C Coy 1 RB. Meanwhile, the attack by 11 Armd Div on HUBERT FOLIE had succeeded. As a result of the opposition against 5 R Tks from the direction of LA HOGUE, an air attack was requested and put in at 2155 hours. As a result of this attack, 5 R Tks succeeded in getting within 200 yards of the road BOURGUEBUS–LA HOGUE, about halfway between the two villages, but failed to capture BOURGUEBUS itself.

About 2200 hours, 11 Armd Div in HUBERT FOLIE complained that there was a good deal of fire coming in their direction from somewhere near SOLIERS. B Coy 1 RB was in SOLIERS, and the firing could not be traced.

It was possibly caused by one or two enemy tanks which had infiltrated at last light to a position North-East of BOURGUEBUS. 4 CLY supported by A Coy 1 RB had trouble trying to get forward between BRAS and HUBERT FOLIE from Tigers further South.

The position at last light 19 July was therefore as follows :— 5 R Tks on three sides of BOURGUEBUS, but the village still held by enemy tanks. B Coy 1 RB in SOLIERS. 4 CLY and A Coy 1 RB trying to patrol between BRAS and HUBERT FOLIE in the direction of VERRIERES. B Sqn 1 R Tks and C Coy 1 RB in FOUR with the remainder 1 R Tks concentrated North of the village. 1/5 QUEENS in GRENTHEVILLE. 1/6 QUEENS in the area GRENTHEVILLE–DEMOUVILLE and in touch with the Canadians on the Right. 1/7 QUEENS North of DEMOUVILLE.

D. 1 CORPS

3 Brit Div

By 0145 hours 19 July, the advance of 9 Brit Inf Bde had made good progress. On the Right, 1 KOSB was about 600 yards West of TROARN along the CAEN road. On the Left, 2 RUR was reported to be 500 yards North-West of TROARN. 2rd. Battalion The Lincolnshire Regiment (2 LINCOLNS) was in reserve behind 1 KOSB. Considerable delay had been caused by the cratering of roads which had occurred as a result of the bombing at the start of the operation. The Brigade was, however, held up on these positions and first light reports indicated no advance, 1 KOSB being held up by three machine guns sited on the South-West outskirts of TROARN, while 2 RUR was similarly halted by a machine gun on the Left flank North of the village.

The rest of 3 Brit Div front showed no change, 8 Brit Inf Bde being firmly established in the TOUFFREVILLE–SANNERVILLE–BANNEVILLE LA CAMPAGNE area, and 185 Inf Bde holding firm positions in the area MANNEVILLE–LE QUAI–CUILLERVILLE. EMIEVILLE, however, was still held by the enemy. STAFFS YEO was still with 185 Inf Bde while 13/18 H and E RIDING YEO were with 9 Inf Bde.

During the morning, the situation on 9 Inf Bde front became rather confused owing to the extremely close country, particularly on the Left, where 2 RUR got into further trouble from enemy opposition from some houses in the South-West edge of LE BOIS DE BURES, about 1,700 yards North of TROARN railway station. This opposition held up 2 RUR the whole morning, and eventually a battalion of 8 Brit Inf Bde took over this area, and released 2 RUR, which was then able to concentrate its efforts on the North-West outskirts of TROARN.

Meanwhile, at 1115 hours, 1 KOSB, which was still held up about 600 yards West of TROARN, put in an attack and succeeded in capturing the railway station, but it was subsequently held up at the cross roads about 300 yards further East by machine gun fire, and was unable to make any further progress.

During the morning, 152 Inf Bde sent patrols out towards BURES from the positions at the South-West corner of LE BOIS DE BAVENT, which found the bridges strongly held by the enemy. By 1430 hours, 2 RUR had been relieved and was continuing its advance towards the railway North of TROARN, while at the same time 2 LINCOLNS was trying to capture the bridge immediately South of TROARN by a Right flanking attack.

At about 1800 hours, 9 Inf Bde was still opposed by strong enemy positions :

(a) at the cross roads 300 yards South-East of the station,

(b) about the railway bridge 200 yards East of the station, and

(c) in the houses along the railway about 700 yards North of TROARN, including one 88 mm gun.

Opposition in this area had been so strong that 1 KOSB had been forced to withdraw about 500 yards West from the railway station, which had been captured during the morning. 2 RUR had not succeeded in getting any further towards TROARN than the road junction about 600 yards North of the railway station. At about the same time, C Sqn E RIDING YEO made contact with the rear company of 2 RUR, but was unable to give much support owing to the close nature of the country. 2 LINCOLNS was also held up by enemy at the bridge about 1,400 yards South-East of BANNEVILLE LA CAMPAGNE.

2 LINCOLNS put in another attack during the evening, and in spite of heavy machine gun fire succeeded in clearing the enemy from the bridge over the river, and advanced a further 500 yards up the road LE QUAI–TROARN, but was then halted at about 2015 hours by a strong enemy position in the orchards 500 yards South of the station. Neither 1 KOSB nor 2 RUR was able to advance any further, as the opposition was still very strong, and at about 2030 hours, 1 KOSB was subjected to very heavy shelling and mortaring.

At 2030 hours, therefore, 9 Inf Bde was ordered to cease attempts to attack TROARN and to adopt firm defensive positions in its present localities. 1 KOSB therefore took up a position covering the two roads to TROARN, 2 RUR in a position North-West of the village, while 2 LINCOLNS was withdrawn into reserve.

At about 1900 hours, STAFFS YEO and 2nd Battalion The Royal Warwickshire Regiment (2 WARWICK) (185 Inf Bde) reported a strong enemy counter attack developing from the South-East against their positions round CUILLERVILLE from about two companies of enemy infantry and six tanks. This attack was successfully beaten off with help from our own artillery.

51 (H) Div

At 2200 hours, 51 (H) Div was told, in answer to a query, that RE could commence clearing the minefields.

Orders were issued about 2300 hours that the co-ordination of the anti-tank defences between the locality held by 154 Inf Bde in the area DEMOUVILLE and that of 8 Brit Inf Bde at BANNEVILLE LA CAMPAGNE was to be done by 3 Brit Div.

RE

By 0230 hours, TAY bridges were open to Class 9 traffic, and by 0815 hours they were both pronounced fit for Class 40 traffic.

During 19 July, several attempts were made to shell TOWER Bridges. Although the shooting was accurate and shells fell all round, no damage was done to either bridge, and there were no casualties.

C. 2 CDN CORPS

At 0200 hours 19 July, the boundary between 2 Cdn Div and 3 Cdn Div for future operations was laid down as the road CAEN-FALAISE inclusive to 3 Cdn Div. Throughout the whole day, 8 Cdn Inf Bde remained in their present positions with QOR OF C in GIBERVILLE, N SHORE R in the factory area, and R DE CHAUD in COLOMBELLES and the Chateau.

Soon after first light, 9 Cdn Inf Bde continued to clear the remainder of FAUBOURG DE VAUCELLES, with HLI OF C and NORTH NS HIGHRS, and soon joined up with REGINA RIF (7 Cdn Inf Bde) who had crossed the ORNE the previous evening.

During the night 18/19 July, The Black Watch (Royal Highland Regiment) of Canada (RHC) (5 Cdn Inf Bde) had managed to capture intact the railway bridge across the River ORNE East of FAUBOURG DE VAUCELLES. RHC therefore crossed the river and by 0300 hours had linked up with the REGINA RIF (7 Cdn Inf Bde) in VAUCELLES. During the morning the remainder of the brigade crossed over this bridge and concentrated in the West end of VAUCELLES, prior to mounting an attack on FLEURY SUR ORNE and the high ground further South round Point 67.

Both 7 Cdn Inf Bde and 9 Cdn Inf Bde were ordered to send patrols South from VAUCELLES into CORMELLES to see if it was occupied by the enemy. 9 Cdn Inf Bde spent the whole morning clearing mines and booby traps in VAUCELLES, and at about 1130 hours received a warning order that if CORMELLES was clear of the enemy, it was to be occupied immediately. About half an hour later, the patrol from 9 Cdn Inf Bde reported that CORMELLES was clear. HLI OF C was therefore ordered to occupy it, and advanced South from BELLEMAIS, and by 1630 hours had one company established in the North-East part of the area, followed half an hour later by another company.

However, the battalion found CORMELLES rather a bigger task than had been expected, for it was not entirely clear of enemy as had been reported. 7 Cdn Inf Bde who by this time had a second battalion in VAUCELLES, was therefore ordered to complete the task. The Royal Winnipeg Rifles (R WPG R) therefore advanced up the road CAEN–FALAISE, until it got to the Western outskirts of CORMELLES, where at about 1500 hours, it was held up by heavy enemy fire. The third battalion of 7 Cdn Inf Bde, 1st Battalion The Canadian Scottish Regiment (Highlanders) (1 C SCOT R) was moved to a position just South of FAUBOURG DE VAUCELLES, and both battalions then made a joint attack on CORMELLES, R WPG R from the West and 1 C SCOT R from the North-West. By 1900 hours, CORMELLES was captured and HLI OF C was relieved. The town was occupied with R WPG R in the Western portion and 1 C SCOT R in the East.

Meanwhile, 9 Cdn Inf Bde relieved 7 Cdn Inf Bde of all commitments in VAUCELLES, and occupied a reserve position just South of the River ORNE from the West edge of VAUCELLES to the South of the factory area. REGINA RIF (7 Cdn Inf Bde) remained in a reserve position in the Southern part of VAUCELLES.

By 1100 hours, R REGT C (4 Cdn Inf Bde) had succeeded in clearing the village of LOUVIGNY but the Chateau to the North-East was still holding out, and it was not until two hours later that all resistance in that area had ceased. During the night 19/20 July, this area was taken over by 129 Inf Bde (43 Div, 12 Corps) and R REGT C joined the rest of the brigade in the area immediately West of CAEN.

During the night 18/19 July, The Royal Canadian Engineers (RCE) of both divisions and corps troops, had been working at high speed to construct crossings over the River ORNE, which were successfully completed, in spite of delays caused by enemy interference, as follows :

(a) Class 9 bridge into West end of FAUBOURG DE VAUCELLES by 0800 hours.

(b) Class 40 raft into West end of FAUBOURG DE VAUCELLES, 150 yards North-East of Class 9 bridge by 0915 hours.

(c) Class 40 bridge just South-West of the main road bridge between CAEN and VAUCELLES by 1100 hours.

(d) Class 9 bridge between CAEN and VAUCELLES near the railway station by 0900 hours.

(e) A DUKW crossing and a Class 9 bridge between HEROUVILLETTE and the Island West of the factory area were also completed during the morning.

Owing to the damage to the railway bridge in FAUBOURG DE VAUCELLES, over the main road running South from the Class 40 bridge, the Class 40 route from this bridge to the main road CAEN–FALAISE involved a detour of some four miles in all. The route ran along the South bank of the ORNE as far as the railway bridge over the river in BELLEMAIS, then back along the main lateral road running South-West through VAUCELLES.

H Hour for the attack of 5 Cdn Inf Bde (2 Cdn Div) was postponed one hour, and at 1300 hours the attack started. One hour and a half later the leading troops of RHC were entering FLEURY SUR ORNE. They encountered a lot of enemy resistance and heavy mortaring, but by 1600 hours the village was cleared.

Immediately, an attack was made on Point 67 and the high ground running East, about 1,500 yards South of FLEURY, by two more battalions from 5 Cdn Inf Bde. On the Right was Le Regiment de Maisonneuve (R DE MAIS), and on the Left The Calgary Highlanders (CALG HIGHRS). By 1830 hours, the high ground had been captured without any opposition and the position was firmly established. At 2300 hours the enemy put in an armoured counter attack on this high ground, and recaptured most of the ridge. CALG HIGHRS then put in a further very strong attack, and after some stiff fighting, completely recaptured the whole area. Half an hour later, RHC attacked IFS from the West. The leading troops entered the village at midnight, and by 0130 hours 20 July the mopping up was completed.

At 2200 hours, 3 Cdn Div was given orders to take over the area of 11 Armd Div, including the villages of BRAS and HUBERT FOLIE, which had just been captured. 9 Cdn Inf Bde in VAUCELLES was ordered to carry out this relief at 1000 hours 20 July.

D. SUMMARY OF OPERATIONS 19 JULY

From Second Army Sitreps :—

"Our position South of CAEN was greatly strengthened today by the capture of VAUCELLES from the East and North, and the establishment of a strong infantry bridgehead South of the town. Bridges were built in CAEN and routes through VAUCELLES were completed. The armour fought all the morning against strongly defended villages, where enemy tanks, anti-tank guns, and infantry resisted fiercely. Progress was slow. On the East, after fierce fighting all the morning, our troops were on the outskirts of TROARN, but not in the town."

"The bridgehead South of CAEN was extended and our position strengthened after heavy fighting during the afternoon. Infantry attacking along the East bank of the River ORNE captured the high ground overlooking ST ANDRE SUR ORNE. A line of village strong points had held up our armour all the morning, but during the afternoon, six of these were captured by armoured formations with infantry leading. Enemy anti-tank guns and tanks in carefully selected ground has resulted in slow progress by armoured formations, and forced their infantry into the lead."

The situation at 2359 hours 19 July is shown on Map No. 11.

SECTION V

OPERATIONS DURING 20 JULY

A. 8 CORPS

11 Armd Div

At about 0715 hours 20 July, the enemy put in a small counter-attack on HUBERT FOLIE, which was effectively repelled by 4 KSLI. The relief of 159 Inf Bde by 9 Cdn Inf Bde (3 Cdn Div) started at 1000 hours. Before the hand-over was completed, 3 MON in BRAS was counter-attacked by seven Tigers, but three of these were knocked out, and the rest withdrew. By midday, the relief by the Canadians was complete, and 159 Inf Bde then took up positions in reserve, with two battalions in the area of LE MESNIL FREMENTEL, and the third in GRENTHEVILLE. The brigade came under command 7 Armd Div at 1600 hours.

During the morning, 29 Armd Bde remained in reserve, reorganizing and carrying out maintenance in the area West of GRENTHEVILLE, where it had concentrated the previous evening. At about midday, the brigade was ordered to concentrate in the area North of GIBERVILLE and East of the factory area, and to observe wireless silence. 2 N YEO also concentrated in the same area, but reverted to command 11 Armd Div. During the afternoon Main HQ 11 Armd Div moved back to the area just South of STE HONORINE.

That night, orders were received that 11 Armd Div would concentrate West of R ORNE moving on 21 July. At about 1600 hours a very heavy thunderstorm started, and in a few hours all tracks except metalled roads were impassable.

Gds Armd Div

During the night 19/20 July, patrols showed the enemy still holding EMIEVILLE and the orchards immediately South. The flak batteries in the general area EMIEVILLE–ARGENCES–VIMONT–FRENOUVILLE were found to be unoccupied.

At 0545 hours, the RAF put in an air attack on FRENOUVILLE and supported by artillery 5 COLDM GDS and 1 WG attacked the village. It was found that the enemy had withdrawn during the night, and the village was occupied without opposition, and 5 COLDM GDS was established firmly on the line FRENOUVILLE cross-roads 700 yards North-East. 1 WG subsequently returned to its original position at LE POIRIER.

Then patrols from 2 HCR tried to get out to recce areas LE HAMEAU DE FRANQUEVILLE and ARGENCES, but were unable to get forward from the FDLs.

At about 1115 hours, some enemy were seen forming up in the woods 1,500 yards South-East of FRENOUVILLE and were most successfully engaged by the whole divisional artillery, while at about midday 2 Armd Recce WG, still carrying out their screening role, engaged six Panthers in the woods 600 yards South-West of EMIEVILLE and at least one was knocked out.

During the day, orders were received that 153 Inf Bde (51 (H) Div) would take over the area at present held by Gds Armd Div. In order to avoid unnecessary road movement, the infantry anti-tank guns of 32 Gds Bde were to be left in position and taken over by the battalions of 153 Inf Bde. The artillery of Gds Armd Div, including the RA anti-tank guns, was also remaining in its present positions to support 153 Inf Bde.

That night, 32 Gds Bde held firm positions at FRENOUVILLE, LE POIRIER and just East of CAGNY, and the armoured regiments were withdrawn into concentration areas between CAGNY and the orchards 1,500 yards North. 1 Armd Recce WG also concentrated in the same area, with one squadron in some orchards on the Southern outskirts of EMIEVILLE.

Late that night, orders were received from 8 Corps that Gds Armd Div was to be prepared to concentrate further North and East of the River ORNE on 21 July, in corps reserve, and would then come under command 2 Cdn Corps.

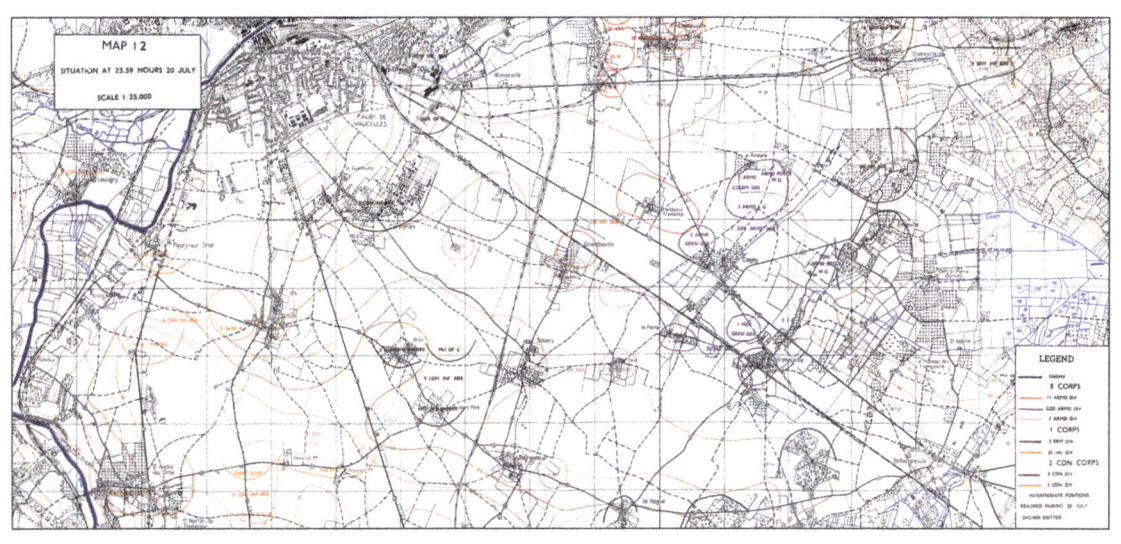

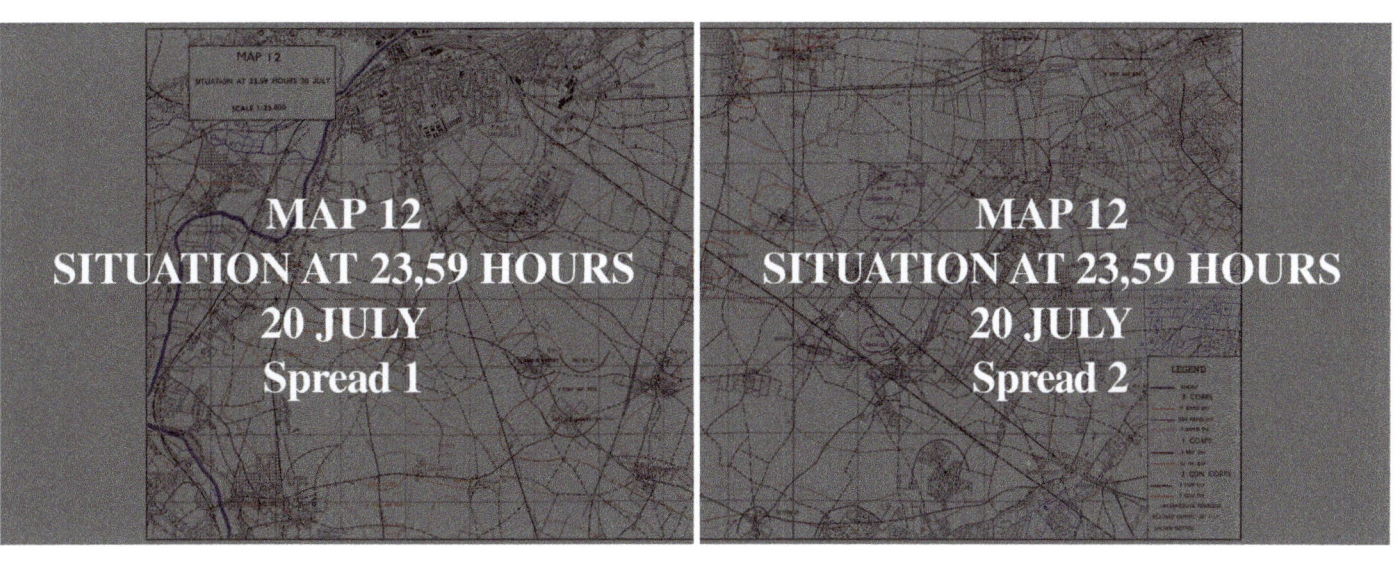

MAP 12
SITUATION AT 23,59 HOURS
20 JULY
Spread 1

MAP 12
SITUATION AT 23,59 HOURS
20 JULY
Spread 2

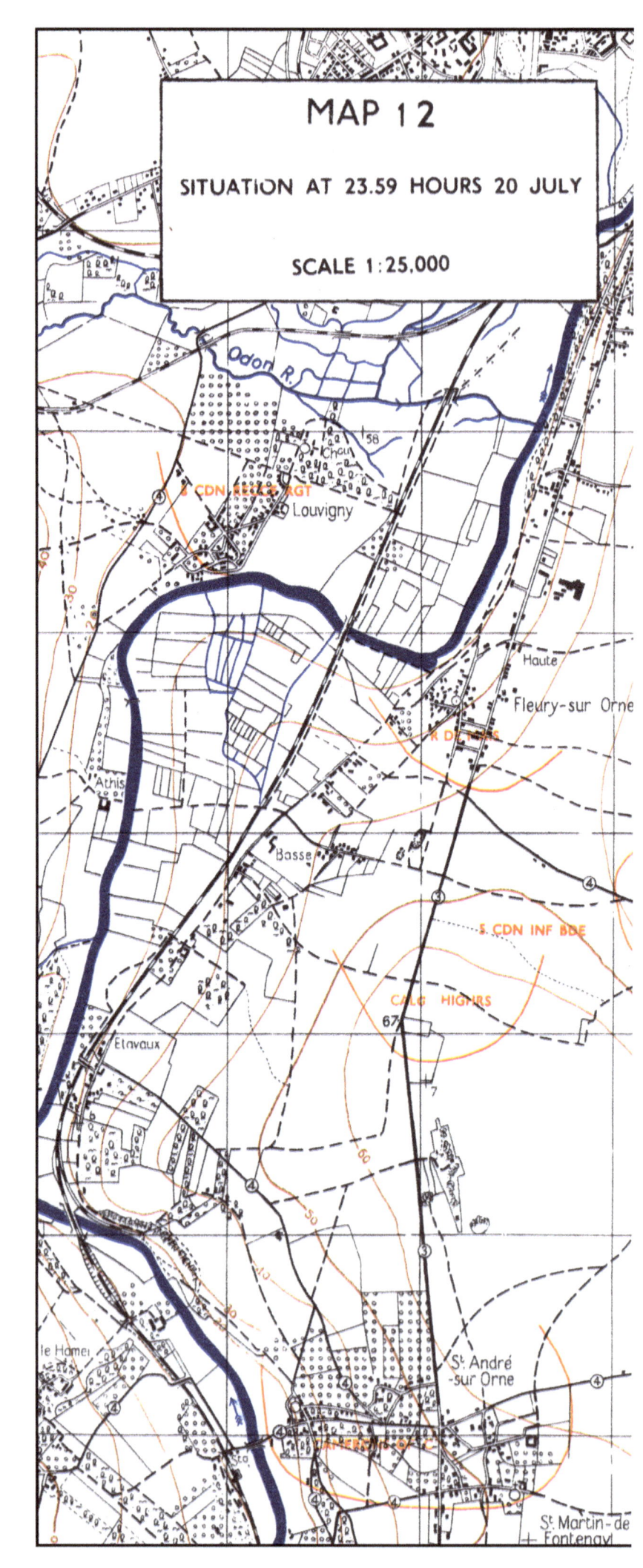

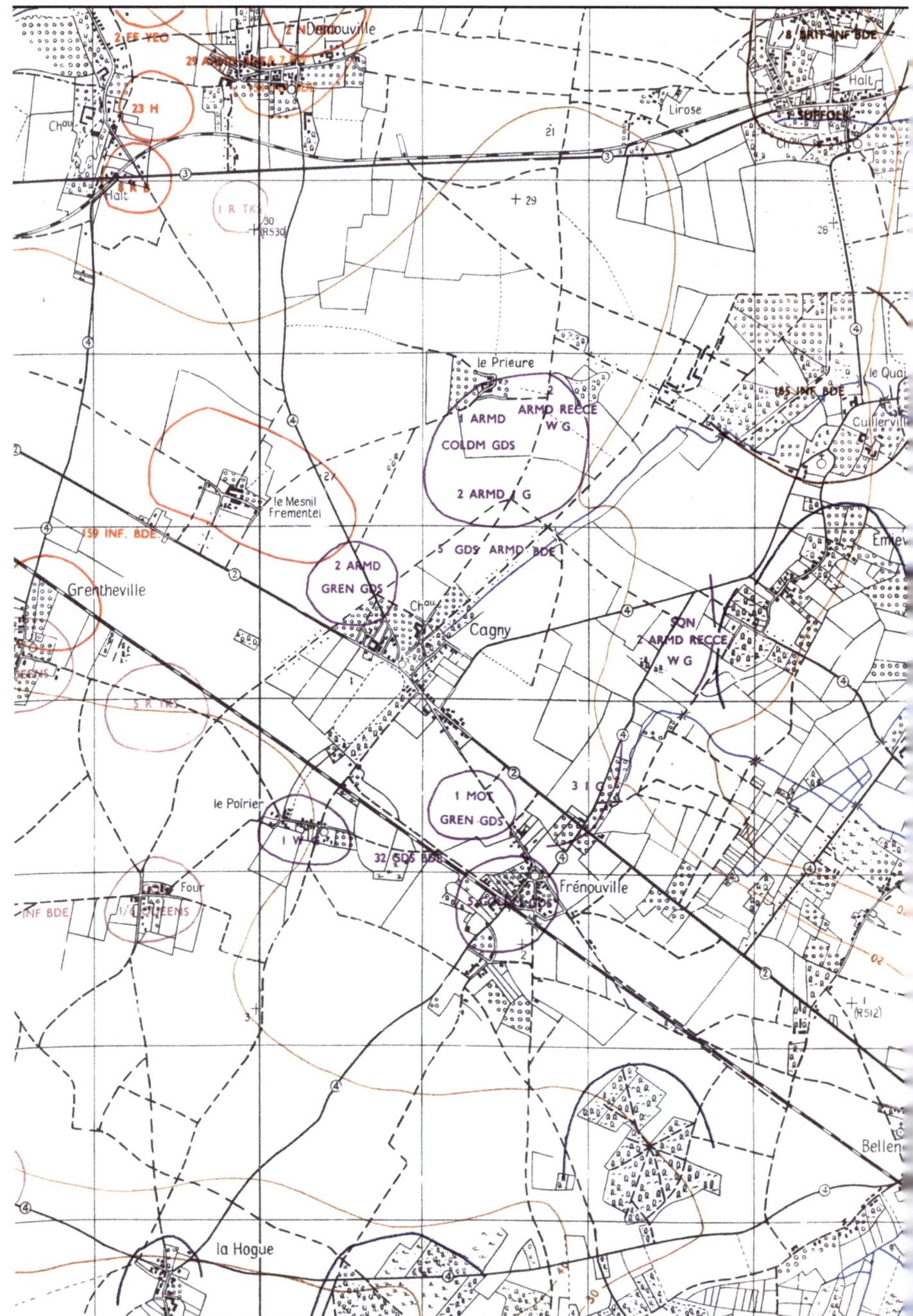

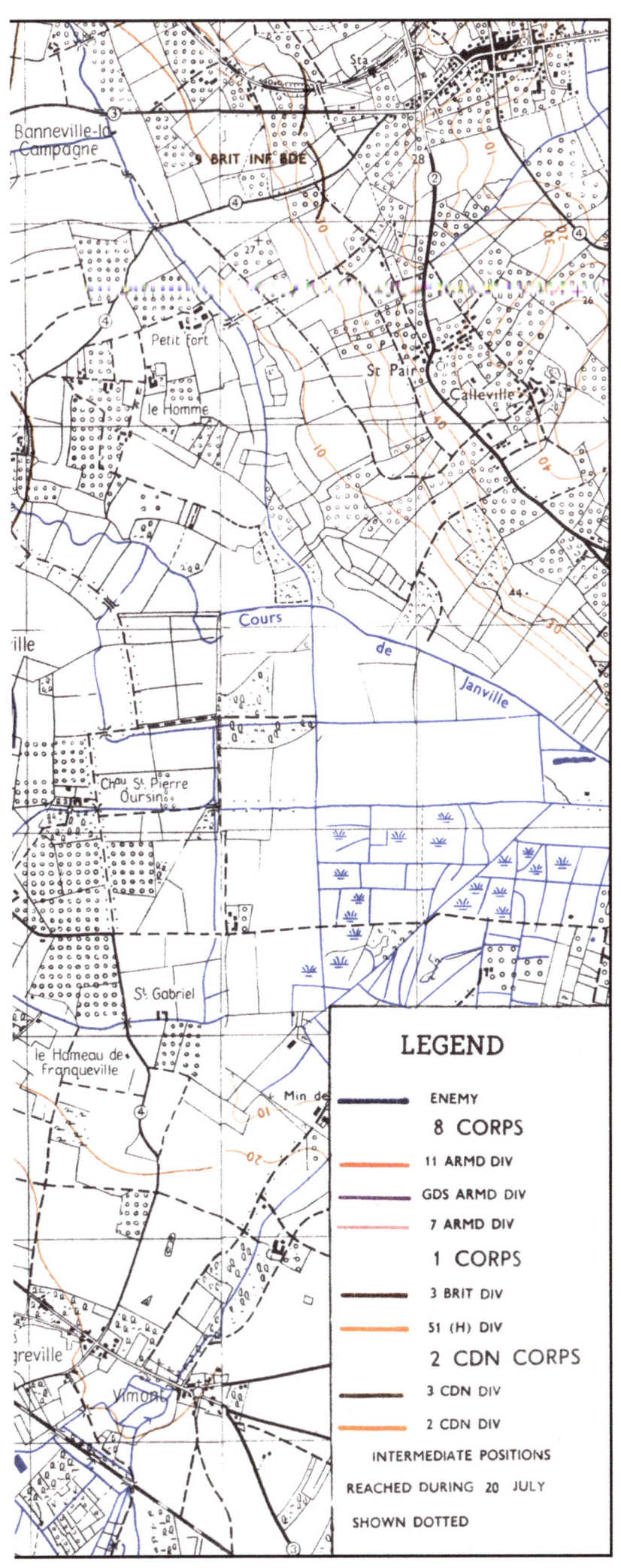

7 Armd Div

At first light 20 July, B Sqn 5 R TKS again attacked BOURGUEBUS, and after a short fight with a Tiger, which was destroyed, it entered the village without further opposition, to find no enemy except two abandoned Panthers. 1/5 QUEENS in GRENTHEVILLE was ordered to send one company to relieve B Coy 1 RB in SOLIERS.

At 0900 hours, 1/7 QUEENS came under command 22 Armd Bde and relieved the company 1/5 QUEENS in SOLIERS, and later sent two companies to BOURGUEBUS.

Soon after first light, 4 CLY succeeded in getting forward between BRAS and HUBERT FOLIE, and cutting the road CAEN–FALAISE. B Sqn occupied Point 72, 1,300 yard South-West of BRAS, and had mopped up the houses in the vicinity of BEAUVOIR FERME by 1000 hours, in spite of opposition from infantry anti-tank guns and one Mk IV tank.

An attempt was then made to attack in a South-Westerly direction on to VERRIERES. A heavy barrage was put on to the area around the farm buildings TROTEVAL FERME, 500 yards East of Point 72, and A Coy 1 RB advanced with the tanks of C Sqn 4 CLY in support. Opposition proved to be too strong, and the motor company was therefore successfully withdrawn. A and C Sqns 4 CLY then withdrew to a position East of the road CAEN–FALAISE and North-West of BRAS.

Soon after this, about eight enemy Mk IV tanks moved across the front of A and C Sqns to attack B Sqn on Point 72. These were effectively engaged and one immobilized. The remaining German tanks passed over the hill and out of sight, but they were most successfully engaged by medium artillery and all were knocked out.

At about 1340 hours, 4 CLY pulled back all troops to the East of the FALAISE road, so as to make way for the Canadians who were mounting an attack on VERRIERES from IFS. Eventually, support was given to the Canadian infantry by C Sqn 4 CLY, which helped to shoot them on to their objective, TROTEVAL FERME. Later, the whole regiment was withdrawn into reserve in the area of the factory buildings between COLOMBELLES and GRENTHEVILLE.

At 1400 hours, a conference was held and orders were given for holding the area gained during the day's fighting, as follows :—

131 INF BDE : (1/5 QUEENS and 1/7 QUEENS reverted to command at 2000 hours)
              1/5 QUEENS area GRENTHEVILLE
              1/6 QUEENS area SOLIERS and FOUR
              1/7 QUEENS BOURGUEBUS

22 ARMD BDE : 5 R Tks between DEMOUVILLE and LE MESNIL FREMENTEL
              8 H in support 131 Inf Bde in area BOURGUEBUS
              1 R Tks in support 32 Gds Bde on Left
              4 CLY factory buildings West of GRENTHEVILLE

159 INF BDE : under command at 1600 hours in reserve—
              two battalions area LE MESNIL FREMENTEL
              one battalion area GRENTHEVILLE

When 1 R Tks went to liaise with 32 Gds Bde, it was discovered that this brigade was being relieved by 51 (H) Div, and that armour support was being provided by 148 RAC. 1 R Tks therefore concentrated about 1,000 yards South of DEMOUVILLE.

There were several cases of tanks being badly bogged owing to the torrential rain, and being unable to withdraw with their regiments. The Divisional Commander ordered that such tanks were to be fought as pill-boxes.

At 2140 hours, 7 Armd Div was put under command of 2 Cdn Corps, and was ordered to be prepared to concentrate in the area West of GRENTHEVILLE during 21 July. 131 Inf Bde was to be relieved during the morning 21 July by 8 Cdn Inf Bde (3 Cdn Div).

The situation on the front of 8 Corps at 2359 hours on 20 July is shown on Map No. 12.

B. 1 CORPS

3 Brit Div

No offensive operations were carried out during the day. The gap between 2 RUR (9 Brit Inf Bde) North-West of TROARN, and 5 CAMERONS (152 Inf Bde) at the cross roads, 1,500 yards South-East of the road triangle, was filled by a battalion from 8 Brit Inf Bde occupying the area of the brickworks East of TOUFFREVILLE. Otherwise, dispositions remained the same.

During the day, counter attacks by the enemy were made against both 185 Inf Bde and 9 Inf Bde, the latter suffering heavy casualties from enemy shelling during the evening. All these attacks were successfully repelled.

185 Inf Bde reported the discovery of several enemy Tiger tanks in its area, which had been knocked out by the bombing prior to the start of the operation.

The situation on the front of 1 Corps at 2359 hours 20 July is shown on Map No. 12.

C. 2 CDN CORPS

The area held by 4 Cdn Inf Bde was duly taken over by 129 Inf Bde (43 Div, 12 Corps) and by 1200 hours, the brigade was concentrated West of CAEN. The Essex Scottish (ESSEX SCOT) were put under command 6 Cdn Inf Bde. R REGT C was relieved in the LOUVIGNY area by 0 Cdn Recce Regt.

During the whole day, 5 Cdn Inf Bde remained in the positions which were occupied as a result of the previous day's fighting, RHC in IFS, R DE MAIS in FLEURY SUR ORNE, and CALG HIGHRS on the high ground Point 67. During the morning, BASSE was reported clear of enemy.

Some confusion arose over the area of VERRIERES. 8 Corps had ordered one armoured regiment of 22 Armd Bde, after the capture of BRAS and HUBERT FOLIE had been completed by 29 Armd Bde, to push forward during the night 19/20 July, and attack VERRIERES during the morning of 20 July. This attack was commenced and by 1000 hours one squadron 4 CLY (22 Armd Bde) had reached BEAUVOIR FERME and Point 67. The question was then raised as to who was going to continue the thrust on VERRIERES, as 2 Cdn Corps had issued orders to 2 Cdn Div to carry out this task. It was therefore agreed between BGS 8 Corps and BGS 2 Cdn Corps that 2 Cdn Div would carry out the operation as planned, and that 4 CLY would withdraw to the East of the road CAEN-FALAISE, but would remain in positions of observation. At 1340 hours, therefore, all tanks of 4 CLY were withdrawn East of the FALAISE road.

6 Cdn Inf Bde with ESSEX SCOT (4 Cdn Inf Bde) under command, assembled in the area about 2,000 yards West of CORMELLES, and behind the positions held by 5 Cdn Inf Bde at FLEURY SUR ORNE, Point 67 and IFS. Air support was given for this operation, by 24 Typhoons dropping 24,000 lbs of bombs on FONTENAY LE MARMION at H-90 minutes, and by fighter bombers attacking enemy gun positions in the area 2,000 yards South-East of GARCELLES SECQUEVILLE.

The attack of 6 Cdn Inf Bde began at 1500 hours, with heavy artillery support, and the advance went well. On the Right, The Queen's Own Cameron Highlanders of Canada (CAMERONS OF C) were in ST ANDRE SUR ORNE by 1650 hours, and spent the next forty minutes consolidating. By 1700 hours, The South Saskatchewan Regiment (S SASK R) in the centre had crossed the road ST MARTIN DE FONTENAY-VERRIERES, and on the Left, Les Fusiliers Mont Royal (FUS MR) had reached TROTEVAL FERME, having been given support in their attack on the farm by tanks of 4 CLY (7 Armd Div) from positions East of the FALAISE road. ESSEX SCOT were in reserve behind S SASK R moving down the railway IFS-FONTENAY LE MARMION. Each of the three leading battalions was supported by a troop of tanks from 27 Cdn Armd Regt.

Just before 1800 hours, a strong counter-attack was put in by the enemy against CAMERONS OF C and S SASK R, supported by about ten Mk IVs. A great deal of very confused fighting then took place, particularly in the centre where S SASK R was forced to give ground. Eventually, the counter attack was beaten off, and by 2100 hours the position was stabilized, with CAMERONS OF C firmly established in ST ANDRE, S SASK R digging in astride the cross roads 2,000 yards East, and FUS MR dug in round TROTEVAL FERME.

S SASK R which had suffered fairly heavily during the counter-attack, was relieved by ESSEX SCOT, and by midnight, had been withdrawn to reorganize in the area West of IFS.

8 Cdn Inf Bde (3 Cdn Div) withdrew QOR OF C from GIBERVILLE to BELLEMAIS during the morning. Late that night a warning order was received that on 21 July, 8 Cdn Inf Bde would relieve 131 Inf Bde (7 Armd Div), which was at present holding the villages of SOLIERS, BOURGUEBUS and FOUR.

During the morning, 9 Cdn Inf Bde took over the area occupied by 159 Inf Bde (11 Armd Div) and by midday was firmly established, with SD & G HIGHRS in BRAS, and NTH NS HIGHRS in HUBERT FOLIE. HLI OF C moved up to a reserve position in the same area during the night 20/21 July.

At 2140 hours, 7 Armd Div was placed under command 2 Cdn Corps and orders were issued for the division to concentrate in the area CORMELLES-GRENTHEVILLE-BRAS during the morning 21 July. 8 AGRA was also placed under command 2 Cdn Corps.

The situation on the front of 2 Cdn Corps at 2359 hours 20 July is shown on Map No, 12.

SECTION VI

OPERATIONS DURING 21 JULY

A. 8 CORPS

11 Armd Div

4 Armd Bde came under command 11 Armd Div but remained in its present location in 12 Corps area.

At 1000 hours, 159 Inf Bde reverted from under command 7 Armd Div to 11 Armd Div, and remained in the area LE MESNIL FREMENTEL–GRENTHEVILLE.

Owing to the appalling state of the tracks in the area, as a result of the torrential rainfall, the move of 11 Armd Div West of the River ORNE was postponed until 22 July.

Gds Armd Div

Again owing to the rain, at about 0930 hours, it was proposed that the relief of Gds Armd Div by 51 (H) Div should be postponed 24 hours until the morning of 22 July.

At 1000 hours, 32 Gds Bde with under command Divisional Artillery, 2 Armd Recce WG and 2 HCR, passed under command 1 Corps, and continued to hold the area LE POIRIER–FRENOUVILLE. By midday, 5 Gds Armd Bde had withdrawn to areas immediately South-West of GIBERVILLE and DEMOUVILLE. Some enemy anti-tank mines were encountered and the concentration of the brigade was held up while these were cleared. During the day, Div Tac HQ was hit and suffered several casualties, the Divisional Commander himself being slightly wounded.

During the afternoon, 148 RAC (under command 51 (H) Div) moved down into 32 Gds Bde area ready to support 153 Inf Bde when it moved in. In the evening, there were reports of a threatened counter attack from EMIEVILLE but these turned out to be false and enemy activity and mortar fire during the day was nothing abnormal.

7 Armd Div

At 0100 hours 21 July, orders were received that 7 Armd Div would come under command 2 Cdn Corps at 1000 hours 21 July, and that 131 Inf Bde would be relieved in the area BOURGUEBUS–SOLIERS–FOUR by 8 Cdn Inf Bde during the day.

The future intention was to assist the Canadians with further operations down the road CAEN–FALAISE. The whole day was spent in reorganisation and maintenance.

By 2000 hours the hand over to 8 Cdn Inf Bde had commenced and 131 Inf Bde then concentrated North of GIBERVILLE.

8 Corps

At 1000 hours, 8 Corps ceased to have responsibility for any section of the front, and had only a reserve commitment, and Operation GOODWOOD was terminated.

The locations of troops under command of 8 Corps at 2359 hours 21 July is shown on Map No. 13.

22 JULY

11 Armd Div

On 22 July, 29 Armd Bde moved across the ORNE to the area of AUTHIE, while Main HQ 11 Armd Div moved to LASSON.

One battalion of 153 Inf Bde (51 (H) Div) had been ordered to take over from 159 Inf Bde in LE MESNIL FREMENTEL by 1300 hours, while the other two battalions relieved 32 Gds Bde in the area of FRENOUVILLE.

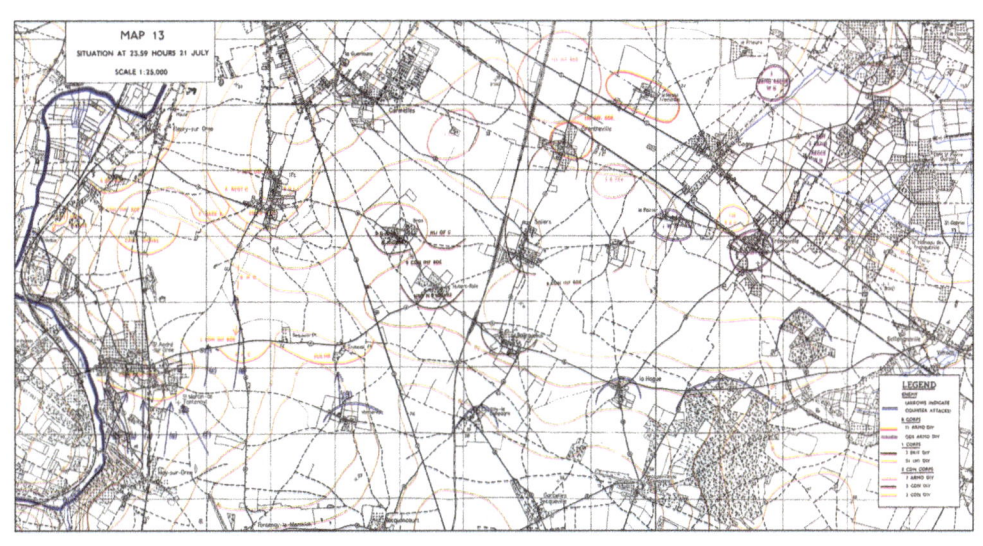

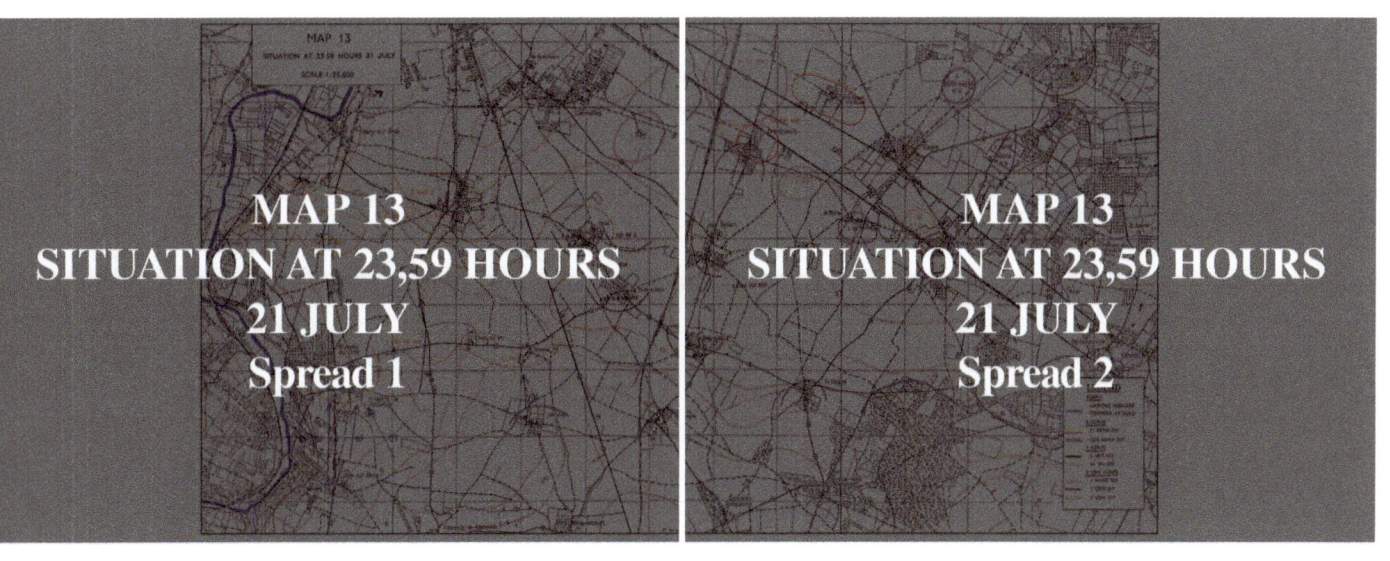

MAP 13 SITUATION AT 23,59 HOURS 21 JULY Spread 1

MAP 13 SITUATION AT 23,59 HOURS 21 JULY Spread 2

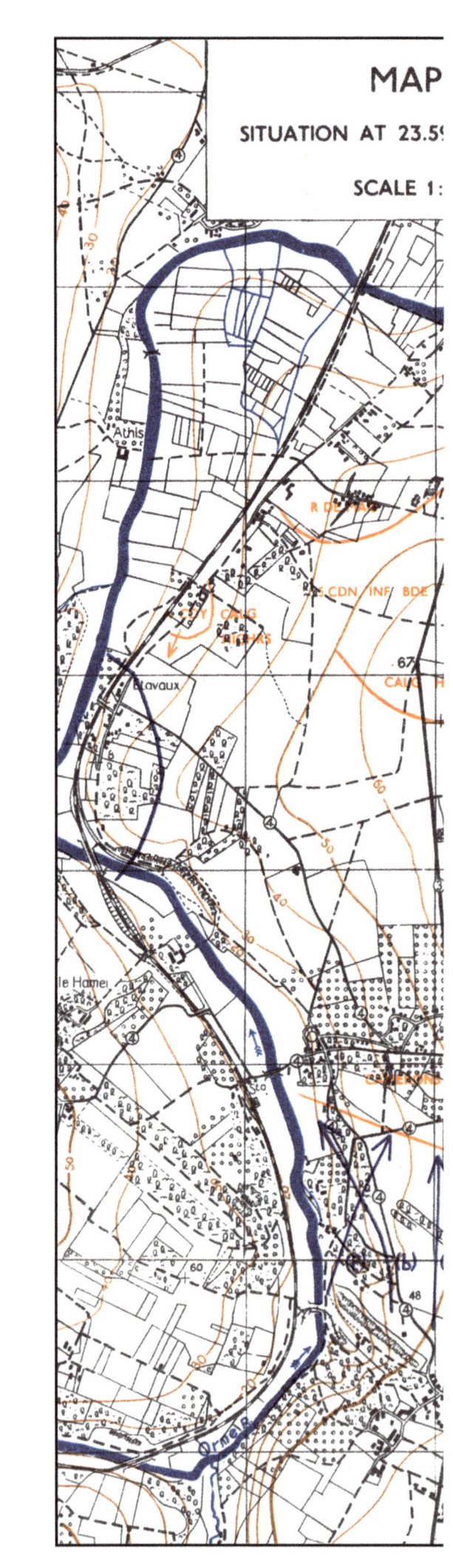

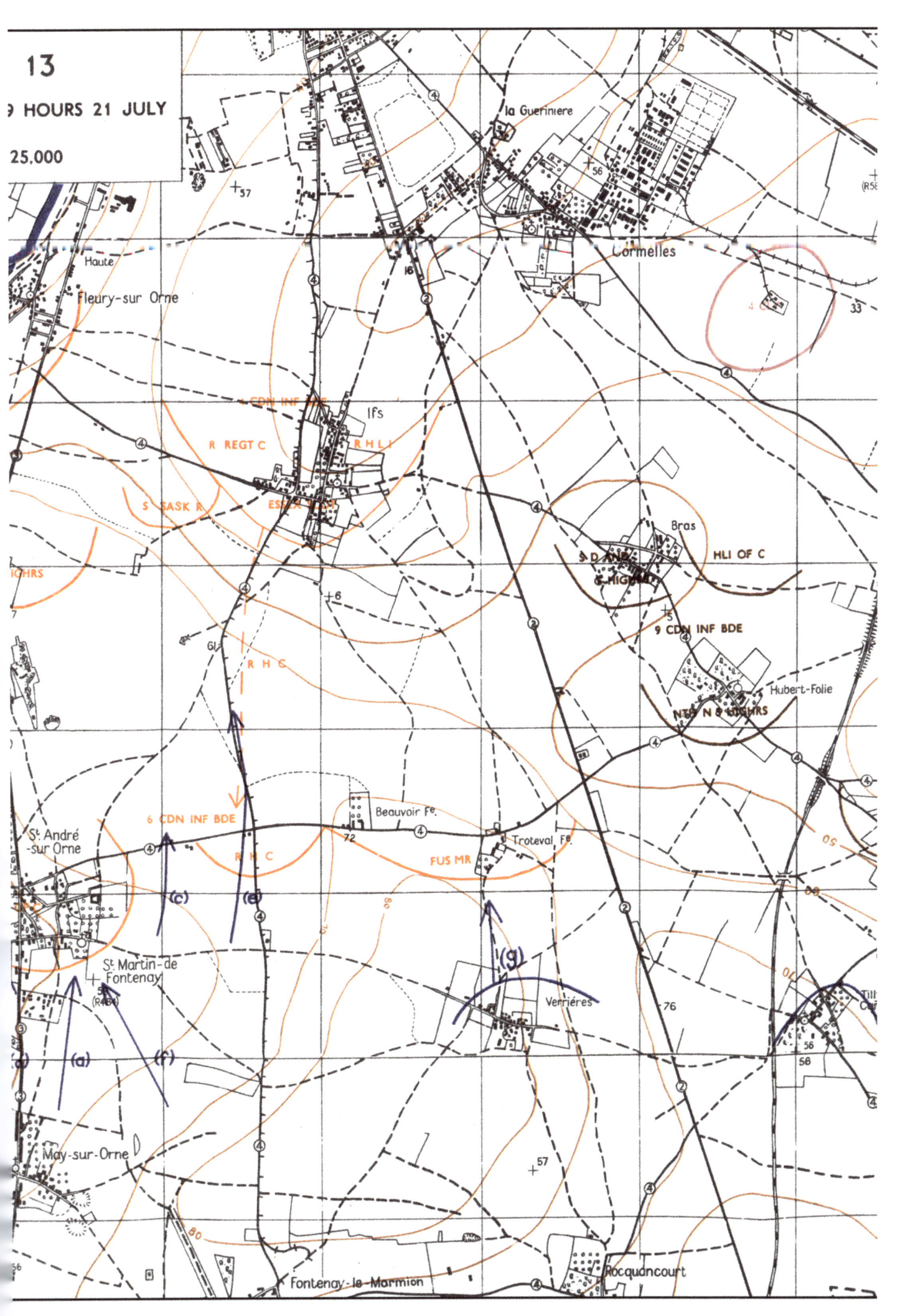

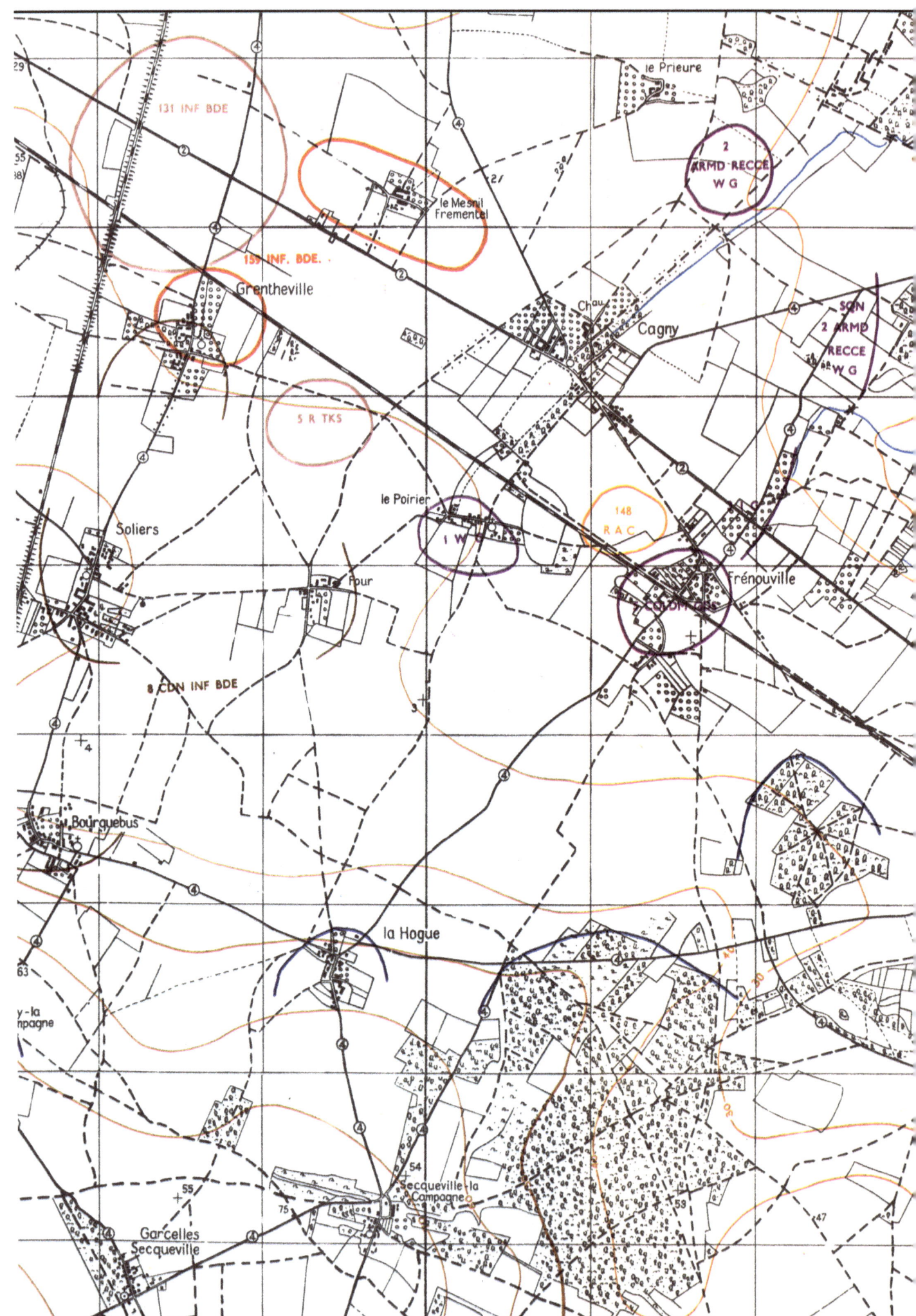

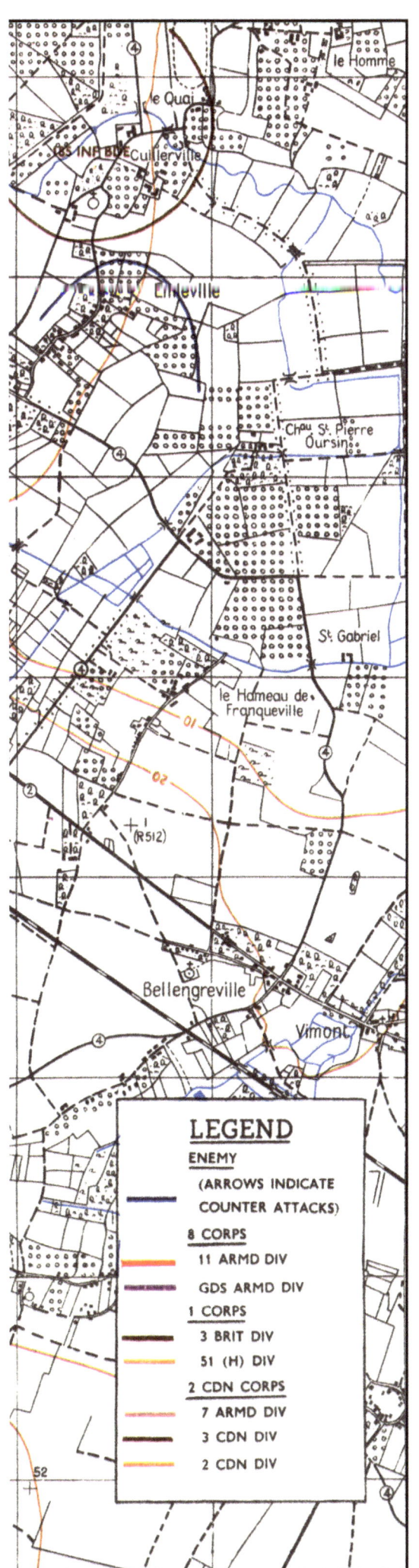

Owing to the state of the tracks however, 159 Inf Bde did not complete handing over to 1 GORDONS (153 Inf Bde) until 1800 hours. The brigade then moved over the ORNE bridges, and concentrated in the area of BURON, just North of 29 Armd Bde.

B. 1 CORPS

3 Brit Div

There was no change in the situation during 21 July. Enemy infantry forming up in EMIEVILLE during the evening for a counter attack on 185 Inf Bde were effectively dispersed by artillery fire.

51 (H) Div

As the result of the heavy thunderstorm at about 1600 hours 20 July, and very heavy rain almost all night, all tracks became impassable and by 1200 hours 21 July, no movement in the area was possible except on tarmac roads. As a result, the relief of Gds Armd Div by 51 (H) Div was postponed until 22 July, except for 148 RAC, which moved into 32 Gds Bde area during the afternoon.

The situation on the front of 1 Corps at 2359 hours on 21 July is shown on Map No. 13.

D. 2 CDN CORPS

21 July was almost entirely a day of enemy counter attacks, mostly on 6 Cdn Inf Bde front. Shortly after midnight, CAMERONS OF C, in ST ANDRE SUR ORNE, was counter attacked by about ten enemy tanks. The attack came in on ST MARTIN DE FONTENAY church, and was successfully repulsed. The enemy tanks drew off about 1,500 yards and at 0130 hours made another attack towards the ORNE bridge West of ST MARTIN. This was also repulsed.

At first light six enemy tanks attempted to infiltrate between CAMERONS OF C and ESSEX SCOT holding the area of the cross roads 1,500 yards East of ST ANDRE, but these were engaged by medium artillery and withdrew. There was considerable enemy shelling and mortaring in the brigade area during the night.

The positions held by 5 Cdn Inf Bde were, RHC in IFS, R DE MAIS in FLEURY SUR ORNE, with one company to the South in BASSE, and CALG HIGHRS holding Point 67 with A Coy 200 yards East of the railway and halfway between BASSE and ETAVAUX preparing to attack the latter. This company was subjected to heavy mortar and machine gun fire at about 0230 hours, and there was considerable enemy shelling and mortaring during the night in the whole brigade area. R DE MAIS reported that the ground to the West of the railway between FLEURY and BASSE down as far as the river was clear of the enemy.

The attack on ETAVAUX started at 0800 hours, but by 1115 hours, A Coy CALG HIGHRS was still held up in the orchard and wood immediately South-West of the railway between BASSE and ETAVAUX. It reported that enemy appeared to be infiltrating from MALTOT across the river into ETAVAUX, and artillery fire was therefore put down on the river bend just South of the village. A Coy CALG HIGHRS was told to hang on in its present position, if possible.

At about 1030 hours, CAMERONS OF C was again counter attacked by some infantry supported by a few tanks, and again the attack was beaten off. During the morning, some enemy were seen just North of VERRIERES forming up for a counter attack on FUS MR which was holding BEAUVOIR FERME and TROTEVAL FERME, and they were successfully dispersed by artillery fire. During these counter attacks, 6 Cdn Armd Regt was in support of FUS MR and 27 Armd Regt was in support of CAMERONS OF C.

At 1515 hours, a very strong counter attack was put in on ESSEX SCOT which achieved partial success. The forward companies were overrun, the battalion was pushed back to Point 61, and enemy Panther tanks established themselves on the spur just South of Point 61, overlooking IFS, and behind the positions held by the other two battalions.

Commander 2 Cdn Div therefore laid on a counter attack by RHC (5 Cdn Inf Bde), which was in IFS, and supported by both 27 Cdn Armd Regt from the Right and 6 Cdn Armd Regt from the Left. This attack started at 1800 hours and was extremely successful, and 45 minutes later the original positions of ESSEX SCOT were occupied by RHC, which continued to hold the position under command of 6 Cdn Inf Bde. ESSEX SCOT was withdrawn to IFS to reorganise.

Meanwhile, at 1715 hours, CAMERONS OF C was again strongly counter attacked from both the South-West and South-East, by infantry supported by Panther tanks, and some very stiff fighting ensued, but by 1830 hours the situation was well in hand, and half an hour later the enemy had withdrawn.

At about this time, 4 Cdn Inf Bde was ordered forward, and concentrated round IFS, with ESSEX SCOT, which reverted to command, in the village, R REGT C to the West and RHLI to the East.

During the morning, 8 Cdn Inf Bde (3 Cdn Inf Div) took over the area from 131 Inf Bde (7 Armd Div) as planned, with one battalion in BOURGUEBUS, one battalion in SOLIERS with a company in FOUR, and the third battalion in GRENTHEVILLE. A patrol sent out from FOUR got to the cross roads 500 yards North-East of LA HOGUE.

At 2100 hours, another strong counter attack was put in on FUS MR by about one company of infantry supported by eight Tiger tanks. The forward companies of FUS MR were forced to give ground, but the battalion remained firm on the line of the two farms, BEAUVOIR FERME and TROTEVAL FERME, and succeeded in knocking out two of the Tigers, and the rest finally withdrew.

During all these counter attacks, excellent support was given by the two Canadian armoured regiments, which succeeded in knocking out thirteen enemy Panthers during the day, 27 Armd Regt claiming eleven on CAMERONS OF C front, and 6 Armd Regt two in front of FUS MR.

All attempts to take ETAVAUX by CALG HIGHRS during the day failed. A joint plan was therefore made during the evening for simultaneous attacks on 22 July on ETAVAUX by 2 Cdn Div and on MALTOT by 43 Div.

The situation on the front of 2 Cdn Corps at 2359 hours on 21 July is shown on Map No. 13.

SECTION VII

SUMMARY OF OPERATION GOODWOOD

(Extracts from Notes written after the Operation by Commander 8 Corps)

(NB: a certain number of the factors, such as the objects of the operation, security, movement and concentration, the air plan, forming up, etc., have been dealt with in detail in Part I and are not, therefore, referred to again here.)

Delay in deployment of the reserve armoured division

The outline Corps plan was for 11 Armd Div to lead through the gap between DEMOUVILLE and SANNERVILLE, then to advance South-West on to the high ground North of BRETTEVILLE-SUR-LAIZE; Gds Armd Div were to follow closely behind 11 Armd Div through the same gap, and swing South and slightly East directed on VIMONT; and for 7 Armd Div to move forward to the area LE MESNIL FREMENTEL so that they would be in a position to fill the gap between Gds Armd Div and 11 Armd Div, and move to the support of either division as circumstances required. Although the leading regiment of 22 Armd Bde had reached the area CUVERVILLE at approximately 1045 hours, it did not start to deploy in the gap between Gds Armd Div and 11 Armd Div until approximately 1900 hours. This delay was attributed to the congestion of traffic between CUVERVILLE and DEMOUVILLE.

The Left flank of the attack

The air programme included the bombardment of the village of CAGNY, and although the village was hit by the bombardment, the defences in the village were by no means neutralised. As a result, 5 Gds Armd Bde came under heavy fire from the CAGNY defences, and were unable to swing to the South and East towards VIMONT. The result was that the Gds Armd Div spent the greater part of the first day clearing up this area, which proved to be a tough proposition, as the further they went, the more difficult the country became.

Enemy Defences

The enemy had known for a long while that the British Second Army contained a large force of tanks. He further knew that the best tank country was South of CAEN. He had therefore concentrated a large amount of anti-tank artillery in this sector. It is considered that a very material amount of surprise was achieved, but naturally the enemy was alive to the fact that sooner or later we might try an armoured break-through into the CAEN–FALAISE plain.

The shape and size of the British bridgehead East of the ORNE was such that 8 Corps was obliged to start its advance from what may well be described as a deep re-entrant, in that the enemy were positioned on both sides of the line of advance of the Corps from the very commencement. The initial air bombardment and the artillery programme succeeded in overcoming the enemy defences which were covering the southern flank of the re-entrant between SANNERVILLE and MONDEVILLE, and also the enemy gun line in this area was quickly overrun by the tanks. This penetration represents an advance of approximately 4,000 yards. As 11 Armd Div advanced beyond this line, so it came up against the enemy gun area sited to protect the southern suburbs of CAEN. This area was in the main some 3,000 yards beyond the gun positions overrun in the first stages of the assault. Whereas the air bombardment and artillery concentrations succeeded in destroying the first enemy line of defence, the second line remained intact, with the result that although 11 Armd Div reached this second area, it was never able to penetrate it.

As a result of these enemy dispositions, it was necessary for 8 Corps to advance up to 8,000 yards before anything approaching a break-through could be achieved. Had the Corps been able to advance initially from the line SANNERVILLE–MONDEVILLE, and a similar air bombardment put down on the enemy defences to the South of this line, it is probable that much better results would have been achieved.

Air Co-operation

In a combined air and ground attack, it must be decided at an early stage whether the ground attack is entirely dependent on the air, or whether the attack will proceed even if the RAF do not appear on the scene. If the former course is decided on, then matters must be so arranged that surprise is not given away if the attack is postponed.

The best results will be obtained if the air attack can be sustained throughout the day. This is not always possible, but it is submitted that it is important there should be not less than two air attacks when the operations in hand are directed against a strong enemy defended position.

The withdrawal of our infantry to a safety area had many disadvantages. This difficulty is not so acute in the case of tanks, who can remain nearer to the bomb line. The all-important factor is to introduce the infantry on to the enemy positions at the earliest possible moment after the bombardment has finished. This can much more readily be achieved if the infantry can be carried there in an armoured vehicle. This policy would have two advantages—firstly, that the infantry could start from a position much closer to the area of bombardment, and secondly, they would get there much more rapidly, and less tired than if they proceeded on their feet.

It is considered that in any air bombardment the enemy FDLs should be included in the target area. Against a determined infantry equipped with modern weapons the FDLs might delay the attack, in which event all the aerial bombardment to the rear might prove to be wasted effort. A possible objection to the bombardment of the FDLs is the necessity to order our own forward troops to withdraw, but this difficulty, it is considered, should be faced as being the lesser of two evils.

During the early stages of the present campaign, the planning of air support, from the point of view of Corps HQ, has been difficult, owing to the fact that the planning staffs of the RAF have been in England, and in consequence have had no direct contact with Commanders on the ground. It is considered most important that in the mounting of a big operation such as GOODWOOD MEETING, there should be the closest liaison between ground and air commanders.

General Tactics

Operation GOODWOOD MEETING was an interesting operation from many points of view. In the first phase of the battle up to approximately the CAGNY area, it was hoped to rush the armour through at the highest possible speed whilst the enemy were still under the influence of the air and artillery bombardments.

Subsequently, as the distances increased, it was realised that divisions would have to become more dependent on their own weapons, and each tactical situation would have to be dealt with individually as it arose.

Although excellent work was done by divisions in this second phase, it is considered that there was a tendency to solve all tactical problems in the same way, rather than treat each problem on its merits.

Results

At the end of two days' fighting, 8 Corps had advanced over 10,000 yards to the South, thereby enabling 2 Cdn Corps to capture the large built-up area of FAUBOURG DE VAUCELLES, and to exploit South to FLEURY SUR ORNE and IFS. 3 Brit Div of 1 Corps, who attacked at the same time as 8 Corps, were assisted in the capture of the villages of TOUFFREVILLE, SANNERVILLE and CUILLERVILLE.

2,000 prisoners were captured by 8 Corps, and the enemy suffered a severe setback in the area in which he was most sensitive to attack, as his whole defensive position hinged on CAEN.

Another important result of this operation was that sufficient elbow-room was gained for the Canadian Army to mount the operations which finally succeeded in driving the enemy out of the CAEN–FALAISE plain, which in turn, materially affected the whole campaign.

In view of the general difficulties connected with the mounting of the attack, it is considered that these very material results were achieved with comparatively light casualties in personnel, although the loss in tanks was considerable.

However, the third object of the operation, namely to draw the maximum amount of enemy armour in the CAEN sector, was also achieved. The enemy reacted strongly and quickly to the thrust of 8 Corps, and was forced to concentrate his armour on the Corps front, which, in turn, prevented him from mounting any large-scale operation in any other sector of the Allied line.

The fact that 8 Corps did not succeed in achieving an even deeper penetration into this area was mainly due to the following reasons :—

(a) The smallness of the bridgehead East of the ORNE, which in turn limited the number of troops which could be brought across before the operation commenced, and forced the divisions to enter the battle one after the other instead of simultaneously.

(b) The narrowness of the gap through which the armour was obliged to pass, which affected the formation adopted.

(c) The fact that 8 Corps started its advance out of a deep re-entrant into the enemy defences, thereby necessitating the reduction of two enemy gun lines.

(d) The difficulty experienced by the infantry in keeping up with the tanks, which was due to the lack of a suitable armoured vehicle in which they could be carried forward. The introduction of some such vehicle, it is felt, is of the utmost importance..

APPENDICES

A. Order of Battle. (8 Corps)

B. 8 Corps Operation Instruction No. 4 (less Appendices).

C. 11 Armd Div Operation Order No. 3 (less Appendices).

D. RA 8 Corps Operation Order No. 2 (including Appendix showing RA Order of Battle).

Appendix 'A'

ORDER OF BATTLE

8 CORPS

(Lieut General Sir Richard N. O'Connor, KCB, DSO, MC)

GDS ARMD DIV (Major General A.H.S. Adair, CB, DSO, MC)

    5 *GDS ARMD BDE* (Brigadier N.W. Gwatkin, DSO, MVO)
        2 Armd GREN GDS
        1 Armd COLDM GDS
        2 Armd IG
        1 Mot GREN GDS

    32 *GDS BDE* (Brigadier G. F. Johnson, DSO)
        5 COLDM GDS
        3 IG
        1 WG
        1 Indep MG Coy NF

    2 Armd Recce WG

    RA (CRA—Brigadier H. C. Phipps, DSO)
        153 Fd Regt (Leicester Yeo) (SP)
        55 Fd Regt (West Somerset Yeo)
        21 A Tk Regt
        94 LAA Regt

    RE
        14 Fd Sqn
        615 Fd Sqn
        148 Fd Pk Sqn

    Under Comd GDS ARMD DIV
        2 HCR (Armd C Regt)
        79 Aslt Sqn (AVsRE)

7 ARMD DIV (Major General I. D. Erskine, DSO)

    22 *ARMD BDE* (Brigadier W. R. N. Hinde, DSO)
        1 R Tks
        5 R Tks
        4 CLY (Sharpshooters)
        1 RB

    131 *INF BDE* (Brigadier E. C. Pepper, CBE, DSO)
        1/5 QUEENS
        1/6 QUEENS
        1/7 QUEENS
        3 Indep MG Coy NF

    8 H (Armd Recce Regt)

    RA (CRA—Brigadier T. Lyon Smith, CBE, DSO)
        3 RHA
        5 RHA (SP)
        65 A Tk Regt (Norfolk Yeo)
        15 LAA Regt

    RE
        4 Fd Sqn
        621 Fd Sqn
        143 Fd Pk Sqn

Under Comd 7 *ARMD DIV*
    11 H (Armd C Regt)
    One tp 26 Aslt Sqn (AVsRE)

11 **ARMD DIV** (Major General G. P. B. Roberts, CB, DSO, MC)

    29 *ARMD BDE* (Brigadier C. B. C. Harvey, DSO)
        23 H
        3 R Tks
        2 FF YEO
        8 RB

    159 *INF BDE* (Brigadier J. B. Churcher, DSO)
        3 MON
        4 KSLI
        1 HEREFORD
        2 Indep MG Coy NF

    2 N YEO (Armd Recce Regt)

    RA (CRA—Brigadier B. J. Fowler, DSO, MC)
        13 RHA (HAC) (SP)
        151 Fd Regt (Ayrshire Yeo)
        75 A Tk Regt
        58 LAA Regt

    RE
        612 Fd Sqn
        13 Fd Sqn
        147 Fd Pk Sqn

    Under Comd 11 *ARMD DIV*
        One sqn 22 DGNS (Flails)
        INNS OF COURT (Armd C Regt)
        26 Aslt Sqn less one tp (AVsRE)

NB.—1. For RA Order of Battle see Appendix to RA 8 Corps Operation Order No. 2 (reproduced at Appendix 'D').

    2. Commanders are shown in the ranks they held at the time of this operation. Decorations are given in full.

Appendix 'B'

ORGANISATION and EQUIPMENT

(Allied and German)

Appendix 'B'

(Note—Appendices to this Operation Instruction are not reproduced)

8 CORPS OP INSTR No 4
OP GOODWOOD

TOP SECRET
Copy No.
16 Jul 44

Ref Maps 1/25,000 : 37/14 NE
37/16 SE
40/14 NE & NW
40/16 SE & SW
37/18 SE
40/18 SW

INFORMATION

1. **Army Plan**

    (a) *12 Corps*

    On 16 Jul, 12 Corps is continuing the attack SW on a one-Div front to seize the high ground SOUTH of EVRECY.

    (b) *30 Corps*

    On 16 Jul, 30 Corps is attacking SOUTH on a one-Div front on the axis FONTENAY LE PESNEL 8767–NOYERS 8862.

2. **Grouping**

1 *Corps*	8 *Corps*	12 *Corps*
3 Br Div	Gds Armd Div	15 (S) Div
51 (H) Div	7 Armd Div	43 Div
6 A/B Div	11 Armd Div	53 (W) Div
27 Armd Bde	8 AGRA	4 Armd Bde
One Regt 33 Armd Bde	11 H	31 Tk Bde
	INNS OF COURT	34 Tk Bde
	2 HCR	

30 *Corps*	2 *Cdn Corps*
49 Div	2 Cdn Div
50 Div	3 Cdn Div
59 Div	2 Cdn Armd Bde
8 Armd Bde	
33 Armd Bde	
56 Inf Bde	

3. **Enemy**

    As per latest Int Notes.

INTENTION

4. On 18 Jul, 8 Corps will debouch from the existing bridge head EAST of the R ORNE with a view to

    (a) Dominating the area BOURGUEBUS 0761–VIMONT 1461–BRETTEVILLE SUR LAIZE 0553.

    (b) Destroying any enemy armour or other forces encountered en route to and in this area.

    (c) If conditions are favourable, subsequently exploiting to the SOUTH.

METHOD

5. Ops of 2 Cdn Corps

On 18 Jul, 2 Cdn Corps is to

(a) Capture the town of FAUBOURG DE VAUCELLES 0466 and the village of GIBERVILLE 0868, and subsequently exploit to the area ST ANDRE SUR ORNE 1261.

(b) Hold CAEN as a firm base for 8 Corps.

(c) Est a bridge over the ORNE between CAEN and FAUBOURG DE VAUCELLES by 2359 hours 18 Jul.

(d) Provide arty sp for 8 Corps.

6. Ops of 1 Corps

On 18 Jul, 1 Corps is to

(a) Maint a firm base for 8 Corps in present area

(b) Simultaneously with the adv of 8 Corps, occupy gen area
TOUFFREVILLE 1368–SANNERVILLE 1368–BANNEVILLE LA CAMPAGNE 1367 –EMIEVILLE 1364, to protect the left flank of 8 Corps.

(c) Assist 8 Corps in their passage through 1 Corps area.

(d) Provide arty sp for 8 Corps.

7. Allotment of Tps

(a) Gds Armd Div with under comd
Two Sqns 2 HCR
One Sqn 22 DGNS

(b) 7 Armd Div with under comd
11 H

(c) 11 Armd Div with under comd
INNS OF COURT
One Sqn 22 DGNS

(d) In Corps res
2 HCR less two sqns.

8. Order of March

8 Corps will adv one up :—
11 Armd Div
Gds Armd Div
7 Armd Div.

9. Tasks of 11 Armd Div

(a) 11 Armd Div with tps under comd will
  (i) At H hr (see approx timings below), break out to the SOUTH between the bdys of 8 Corps, occupying the villages of CUVERVILLE 1069 and DEMOUVILLE 1067.
  (ii) Continue the adv, crossing the rly in the area GRENTHEVILLE 0864–CAGNY 1164. One armd regt will be left in this area until relieved by Gds Armd Div. The task of this armd regt is to prevent any interference by the enemy from the direction of VIMONT.
  (iii) Continue the adv and est itself firmly in the area incl BRAS 0663–incl ROCQUANCOURT 0558–excl FONTENAY LE MARMION 0358–incl BEAUVOIR FERME 0461.

(b) The main task of the Div is to destroy any enemy forces that may be encountered.

(c) *Patrolling*

Patrolling tasks of the Div will incl. :—

(i) ST ANDRE SUR ORNE

(ii) BRETTEVILLE SUR LAIZE

(iii) Main rd ST ANDRE SUR ORNE–br 0157–along rd towards THURY HARCOURT.

Patrols will gain contact with 7 Armd Div and Gds Armd Div and also with 2 Cdn Div to the NORTH when opportunity offers.

10. Tasks of Gds Armd Div

(a) Gds Armd Div with tps under comd will move in rear of 11 Armd Div, and will

(i) Move to the area CAGNY, where it will relieve the armd regt of 11 Armd Div

(ii) Continue the adv and est a firm base in the area VIMONT.

(b) The main task of the Div is to destroy any enemy forces encountered and to protect the left flank of 8 Corps.

(c) *Patrolling*

Patrolling tasks of the Div will incl :—

(i) Rd ARGENCES 1761–ST PIERRE DU JONQUET 2066

(ii) Along the rd towards MEZIDON 2556

(iii) EMIEVILLE 1364.
The Div will contact 7 Armd Div.

11. Tasks of 7 Armd Div

(a) 7 Armd Div with tps under comd will follow Gds Armd Div and will be prepared to :—

(i) Cross the rly WEST of CAGNY.

(ii) Move in sp of 11 Armd Div if required.

(iii) Subsequently move to the area all incl LA HOGUE 0960–wooded area NE of SECQUEVILLE LA CAMPAGNE 0959–ST AIGNAN DE CRAMESNIL 0956–high ground 0756–GARCELLES SECQUEVILLE 0858.

(b) *Patrolling*

Patrolling tasks of the Div will incl :

(i) High ground 1657–QUATRE PUITS 1955

(ii) ST SYLVAIN 1354

(iii) Towards LANGANNERIE 0949.

12. Inter-Corps Bdys

(a) *Between 2 Cdn Corps and 8 Corps*

Buildings and copses 090696–GIBERVILLE 0868–level crossing 093672 (all incl 2 Cdn Corps)–BRAS 0663 (excl 2 Cdn Corps)–church 026607–buildings 023603 (incl 2 Cdn Corps).

(b) *Between 8 Corps and 1 Corps*

ESCOVILLE and church 1271–thence track SOUTH to level crossing 118673 (all incl 1 Corps)–X tracks 119664 (incl 8 Corps)–building 125657 (incl 1 Corps)–wood 135652 (excl 1 Corps)–river at 156652–thence line of river to JAUVILLE 1865 (all incl 1 Corps).

13. Start Line

Start line common to all three Corps :—

R ORNE at 097733–rd and track junc 104728–FERME DE LIEU HARAS 118723–rd junc 118721–corner of wood 126718–SOUTH edge of wood 129717.

14. **Forecast of Timings**

   (a) The start of the op is dependent on the air programme, which is not yet fixed. The following times are given as a guide only :—

   0630–0730 : Attack by heavies of Bomber Command
   0730–0815 : Attack by medium bombers dropping fragmentation bombs
   0830–0930 : Attack by Fortresses on gun areas.

   (b) Zero hr is the time when the last fragmentation bomb is dropped by the medium bombers : if these times hold, H hr will therefore be 0815 hrs.

   (c) In view of the attack by the Fortresses on hostile btys in the area BOURGUEBUS between 0830 and 0930, 11 Armd Div will NOT cross the rly before 0930 hrs.

   (d) It is hoped that the actual time of H hr will be known by the evening of 16 Jul.

15. **Corps Report Line**

   Rd ARGENCES–VIMONT–LA HOGUE–BOURGUEBUS–BEAUVOIR FERME–ST ANDRE SUR ORNE

   Code Name : NEWMARKET.

16. **RA**

   (a) *Fire Plan*

   (i) 1 Corps are being made responsible for CB.
   (ii) The Fire Plan for the sp of the armd divs will be the responsibility of the CCRA.

   (b) *8 AGRA*

   (i) 8 AGRA will sp 8 Corps.
   (ii) 8 AGRA will come out of action after 1200 hrs 17 Jul and lie up in the area ST CROIX GRAND TONNE 8874.
   (iii) 8 AGRA will move after 1900 hrs by arrangements to be made with 2 Cdn Corps by Q(Mov) into action in the area FRANQUEVILLE 9770–AUTHIE 9871–GALMANCHE 0073–ST CONTEST 0072. Move to be completed by 2300 hrs 17 Jul.
   (iv) A minimum number of vehs will be taken except for 63 and 77 Med Regts who may later be required to go fwd with Gds and 11 Armd Divs respectively.

   (c) *91 A tk Regt*

   91 A tk Regt will remain in Corps res and move into the area 0877–0977.

   (d) *10 Svy Regt*

   (i) Before the attack 10 Svy Regt will co-operate with Svy Regt 1 Corps and arrange for all guns to be put on the Army Grid.
   (ii) During the attack det 10 Svy Regt (one half track) will be in sp each armd div. 10 Svy Regt, less dets, will remain in Corps res in present location. CO and IO will remain at Corps HQ.

   (e) *121 LAA Regt*

   121 LAA Regt (less one bty) under comd 8 AGRA wef 1200 hrs 17 Jul.

   (f) *Air OP*

   (i) C Flt 658 Air OP Sqn remains under comd 8 AGRA.
   (ii) Flts of 659 Air OP Sqn are placed in sp of Divs as follows :—

   A Flt : 11 Armd Div
   B Flt : Gds Armd Div
   C Flt : 7 Armd Div.

17. **RE**

   (a) *Tps under Comd*

   26 Sqn ARE less one tp
   79 Sqn ARE
   25 Mech Eqpt Sec
   130 Pnr Coy
   Adv HQ 212 Coy RASC
   B Pl 212 Coy RASC
   D Pl 212 Coy RASC
   Det 35 Coy RASC (Tippers)
   One Pl (Tippers) RASC
   HQ 128 Br Coy RASC
   1631 Bailey Pl 128 Br Coy RASC
   1632 Bailey Pl 128 Br Coy RASC
   1623 Bailey Pl 106 Br Coy RASC
   Det FBE Pl 128 Coy RASC
   (4 LSUs 2 LSUCPs)

   (b) *ARE*

   (i) 79 Sqn less one tp (6 AVsRE) under comd Gds Armd Div (with 4 fascines).

   (ii) 26 Sqn less one tp (10 AVsRE) under comd 11 Armd Div.

   (iii) One tp 26 Sqn (6 AVsRE) under comd 7 Armd Div.

   (iv) Fascines : 6 will be carried on wheels to be mounted later–tpt provided by CE.

   (c) Development of routes fwd for wheels and tracks must depend on course of ops and will be carried out by Div RE as required. CRE Corps Tps, under instrs to be given by CE, will take over maint of routes beyond present area held by 1 Corps. These routes to be Cl 40 except rd CAEN–FALAISE which will eventually be Cl 70, all brs being two-may. Initially this route to be developed as Cl 40 one-way.

   (d) *Mech Eqpt*

   Under comd each Gds, 7 and 11 Armd Divs: one armd D.7 (Bulldozer).

   (e) *Stores*

   Mobile res of 30 lorries to be held under control CE. Details will be issued separately.

   (f) *Bridging*

   All bridging, as shown above, will be held initially under control CE.

   (g) 101 and 224 Fd Coys (8 Corps Tps RE) will be under comd Gds Armd Div for movement across R ORNE.

18. **Air**

   The adv of 8 Corps is receiving maximum air sp, which is based on an Army plan. The main features of the air-attack will be :—

   (a) An attack by heavy bombers on

   (i) Factory area 0769.

   (ii) Area GIBERVILLE.

   (iii) Area TOUFFREVILLE–SANNERVILLE–BANNEVILLE–EMIEVILLE.

   (b) The neutralisation by fragmentation bombs of the villages of CUVERVILLE and DEMOUVILLE.

   (c) The neutralisation of enemy posns and killing by fragmentation bombs of enemy personnel in the path of the tk run through which 8 Corps debouches.

   (d) The destruction of the village of CAGNY.

   (e) The neutralisation and damaging of enemy guns in the area BOURGUEBUS and TROARN.

ADM

19. **Gen**

   Detailed Adm Instr will be issued separately.

20. **Movement**

See Appx "A" and Trace (Trace to limited distribution only).

21. **Medical**

   (a) Cas in the initial phase will be evacuated to med installations already est in the br head EAST of the R ORNE and thence to the LA DELIVRANDE (0381) Gp of CCS and Gen Hosp.

   (b) 24 FDS and 1 FDS with att FSU and FTUs will be phased fwd as early as possible to est an Adv Surgical Centre in area DEMOUVILLE–CAGNY, but not South of this, as soon as the tactical situation permits.

   (c) 34 CCS will remain on wheels prepared to move fwd as early as possible to est a Med Area in conjunction with the Adv Surgical Centre.

   (d) *Med Installations*

   (i) WEST OF THE ORNE

   LA DELIVRANDE Gp

16 CCS	026807
32 CCS	026807
86 Gen Hosp (200 beds)	030808
88 Gen Hosp (200 beds)	030808

   (ii) EAST OF THE ORNE

195 Air Landing Fd Amb	LE MARIQUET	115733
225 Para Fd Amb	115749	
152 Fd Amb	105735	

22. **Civil Affairs**

   Basic dets will be under comd Divs as follows :—

Gds Armd Div :	224 Det
7 Armd Div :	218 Det
11 Armd Div :	217 Det

   The tasks of these dets is to deal with CA problems in Div areas.

INTERCOMN

23. **Wireless Silence**

   (a) HQ 8 Corps and 8 Corps Tps will continue to observe Wireless Silence until H—30 minutes. Any 8 Corps Tps at present under comd 12 Corps, and using wireless, will observe silence from time of returning to comd 8 Corps.

   (b) 7 Armd Div will continue to observe wireless silence until H—30 mins. Rear Links to HQ 8 Corps will open listening watch at H—30 mins but will NOT transmit until called by HQ 8 Corps control sets.

   (c) 11 Armd Div will continue to observe Wireless Silence until H—30 mins.

   (d) Gds Armd Div will observe Wireless Silence from 2359 hrs 15 Jul until H—30 mins.

24. **Locations of HQ at the Commencement of the Op**

Main HQ 8 Corps	9980
Gds Armd Div	0878
7 Armd Div	In area of Main 8 Corps : actual location later
11 Armd Div	124746

25. **Axis of Adv**

   Divs will mark their axis of adv as they proceed SOUTH of the Start Line.

26. LOs

Fmns will keep close liaison with flanking fmns by the interchange of LOs. This is particularly important where the flanking fmn belongs to another Corps.

27. Traffic Control

Line and wireless comns will be provided. Separate instrs will be issued.

ACK

Time of Signature : 0300 hrs.   *H Floyd*   B.G.S.

By Tel and Sign   A Corps

NB.—In para 14 (*b*) H Hour is forecast as 0815 hours. It was subsequently advanced to 0745 hours.

Appendix "C"

(Note:— Appendices to this Operation Order are not reproduced)

SECRET

11 ARMD DIV OO NO. 3

Copy No.

16 Jul 44

Ref Maps : 1/25,000. Sheets : 37/16 NE, SE, 40/16 NW SW, 37/14 NE SE, 40/14 NW SW.
1/50,000. Sheets : 7F/1, 7F/2, 7F/3, 7F/4.

INFM

1. Enemy

The only enemy fmns known to be facing 1 Corps between the BOIS DE BAVENT and R ORNE are 16 GAF Div and 25 SS PGR (12 SS Pz Div).

16 GAF is thought to be disposed with two regts (32 and 46 LJR) up with the remnants of 31 LJR which were withdrawn from NORTH of CAEN in res. The str of 25 SS PGR is uncertain but it is known that this regt was withdrawn across the R ORNE at the expense of 31 LJR and should be up to str.

At present unlocated but considered to be held in res are 1 SS Pz Div (less one PGR) 12 SS Pz Div (less one PGR) and 21 Pz Div.

Of these Pz Divs 1 SS and 12 SS are likely to be harbouring in the area BRETTEVILLE-SUR-LAIZE 0553, or possibly even WEST of the R LAIZE, whereas 21 Pz is thought to be in the area of ARGENCES 1761.

The extent to which 9 and 10 SS Pz Divs can be released for ops EAST of the R ORNE will depend on their commitments WEST of the river and the state of the main brs which are reported destroyed from SOUTH of CAEN to incl PONT DU COUDRAY 983578. The rly br at 013597 is still standing and the river is reported as fordable at several places. Due to lack of contact it is not possible to give an accurate estimate of enemy tk str. Incl 9 and 10 SS Pz Divs it is considered to be not less then 300 tks, of which 200 are thought to be EAST of the R ORNE. A more detailed estimate will be given in later Int summaries.

2. Own Tps.

Second Army are starting an offensive consisting of :—

(a) Attack by 12 Corps in which 15 (S) Div attack night 15/16 Jul with final objective of line BOUGY 9160–EVRECY 9259–MAIZET 9457 and subsequent adv to AUNAY–SUR–ODON or THURY–HARCOURT.

(b) Attack by 30 Corps in which 59 Div attacks at first light 16 Jul with final objective gen line ETREGY 8464–LANDELLE 8662–NOYERS 8862–MISSY 8961.

(c) Attack by 2 Cdn Corps in the area COLOMBELLES 0770–GIBERVILLE and subsequently the area of CAEN SOUTH of the ORNE. At the same time 1 Corps on the LEFT with 3 Brit Div are attacking area TOUFFREVILLE 1368–LES CARRIERES 1367 and exploiting towards TROARN 1667.

(d) Simultaneously with (c) above 8 Corps with under comd Gds Armd Div, 7 Armd Div and 11 Armd Div are est themselves in the area of BRAS–VERRIERES–high ground NORTH of CRAMESNIL 0857–VIMONT 1561.

11 Armd Div on RIGHT, 7 Armd Div CENTRE, Gds Armd Div LEFT.

Order of March :   (i) 11 Armd Div
(ii) Gds Armd Div
(iii) 7 Armd Div.

(e) **Air**

Before 8 Corps op considerable preparation will take place for details of which see Appx "A".

3. Intention

11 Armd Div will est itself in the area BRAS 0663–VERRIERES 0560–ROQUANCOURT 0558–BOURGUEBUS 0761.

4. Method

Phases.

Phase 1. The move of Div EAST of the ORNE into the area at present occupied by 51 (H) Div.

Phase 2. (a) The establishment of the Armd Bde in the area immediately SOUTH of the rly CAEN–TROARN and

(b) The clearing of the area CUVERVILLE–DEMOUVILLE by 159 Inf Bde.

Phase 3. Move fwd of the Armd Bde to est itself in the area VERRIERES–CRAMESNIL.

Phase 4. The moving fwd of the Inf Bde to form a firm base in the area VERRIERES–CRAMESNIL in order to release the Armd Bde for further exploitation SOUTHWARDS.

4. Grouping

(a) 29 *Armd Bde* with under comd :—

13 RHA
One Sqn and one tp 22 DGNS
119 A Tk Bty
One tp 612 Fd Sqn RE with one tp AVREs.
One sec Pro.

(b) 159 *Inf Bde* with under comd :—

75 A Tk Regt less two btys
One tp 612 Fd Sqn RE
One Sec Pro.

(c) *Div Tps*

2 N YEO
INNS OF COURT (Armd Cs).
RA   151 Fd Regt.
     117 Bty 75 A Tk Regt.
RE   13 Fd Sqn
     612 Fd Sqn less two tps
     147 Fd Pk Sqn.

6. Tasks

(a) *Phase* 1. Details of Routes, mov tables and assembly areas EAST of R ORNE are shown in Appces "B", "C", "D" respectively.

(b) *Phase* 2. 29 *Armd Bde*. As soon as air attack starts 29 Armd Bde will form up ready to move fwd with their head on the 71 Northing Grid line between 11 and 12 Eastings grid lines. Move to this SL on PALM wheel and track route.

At H hr they will be moved fwd between the above mentioned Easting grid lines covered by an arty barrage, details of which will be arranged by CRA, and est themselves in the area LE MESNIL FREMENTEL 1065. If during this phase any delays should occur and it is desired to halt the barrage this can be done either on the opening line, the 678 Northing grid line or the 665 Northing grid line, but once halted it will take a ¼ hr to restart. Requests for this and also requests for the second phase of the barrage to commence will be made direct to RA over the Div Comd net. 29 Armd Bde have no responsibility regarding the LEFT flank towards ARGENCES except of course as far as their own LEFT flank protection is concerned, but if CAGNY 1164 is occupied and of nuisance value it will be watched and neutralised until taken over by Gds Armd Div.

159 Inf Bde. As soon as the air attack starts 159 Inf Bde will form up with their head on the rd ST HONORINE 0971–HEROUVILLETTE 1272 between 10 and 11 Easting grid lines via HOLLYWHEELS route. At H hr this Bde will adv and capture and clear the area CUVERVILLE-DEMOUVILLE both incl. For this task they will have the sp of 2 N YEO but this regt is likely to be withdrawn from this sp when the first village is cleared and the second village entered in order that it can assist 29 Armd Bde in Phase 3. Details of arty sp to be issued by CRA.

2 N YEO. During this Phase 2 N YEO will sp 159 Inf Bde.

INNS OF COURT. As soon as they have crossed R ORNE INNS of COURT less two sqns will move fwd in rear of 29 Armd Bde but immediately on conclusion of Phase 2 i.e. when the Armd Bde reaches the area LE MESNIL –FREMENTEL, INNS of COURT will infiltrate fwd in order to carry out the following tasks :—

(a) Recce and report on enemy str and mov from the river valley between ST ANDRE SUR–ORNE 0161 and BRETTEVILLE SUR LAIZE both incl.

(b) Report on enemy strs and mov between BRETTEVILLE SUR LAIZE and ST SYLVAIN. On arrival of 7 Armd Div these patrols will be withdrawn and the recce bdy between 7 and 11 Armd Divs will be CAEN–FALAISE rd incl to 7 Armd Div.

(c) As a priority task, but only for a limited period as soon as reaching the area LE MESNIL-FREMENTEL patrols should be pushed out SE in order to report on enemy mov from the area VIMONT 1561. These patrols to be withdrawn as soon as the Gds Armd Div passes through.

117 A Tk Bty will remain in Div res and move fwd in rear of INNS OF COURT and halt in the area immediately NORTH of CUVERVILLE to await further orders.

(c) *Phase 3.* 29 Armd Bde will endeavour to est itself on the final objective BRAS-VERRIERES–ROQUANCOURT and until relieved by 7 Armd Div will occupy high ground NORTH of CRAMESNIL continuing if necessary to leave a containing force opposite CAGNY. If it is possible to relieve 2 N YEO from the sp of 159 Inf Bde they will be moved fwd and will come under cmd 29 Armd Bde.

159 Inf Bde will complete the clearing of CUVERVILLE and DEMOUVILLE. As soon as CUVERVILLE is cleared it need not be held but DEMOUVILLE if cleared must still be held until the whole GIBERVILLE area is taken by Cdn Corps.

RA. 151 Fd Regt will be moved fwd across the R ORNE under orders of CRA by "C" route and LONDON BR.

RE. CRE will construct route either through or round CUVERVILLE-DEMOUVILLE. For this purpose 13 Fd Sqn with Det Pro attached will move closely behind 159 Inf Bde Gp. The tp AVREs will be returned under orders of CRE as soon as 29 Armd Bde have crossed the line of the second rly CAEN-VIMONT.

Pro. APM will arrange to make Div CL from LONDON BR thence approx line of HOLLY route–CUVERVILLE-DEMOUVILLE and thence onwards in rear of 29 Armd Bde.

APM will est TP at 060746 on "C" route. This will open as soon as air attack starts, and will control tfc on "C" route as long as units of 11 Armd Div are passing.

ADM

7. Adm Orders will be issued separately.

INTERCOMN.

8. LOs. The following LOs will report by 1800 hrs 17 Jul :—

    From 3 Brit Div to 11 Armd Div.

    From 7 Armd Div to 11 Armd Div.

    From 11 Armd Div to Gds Armd Div.

    From 29 Armd Bde to 27 Armd Bde (only until 29 Armd Bde reach rly CAEN—TROARN).

9. **Code Words.** List of Place Code Names and report lines are issued as Appx "E".

10. **HQ.** Main HQ 11 Armd Div closes present location 1900 hrs 16 Jul, opens at 123745 at 0600 hrs 17 Jul.

    GSO I will be at rear 11 Armd Div until 1200 hrs 17 Jul.

    Rear 11 Armd Div remains present location.

    Tac 11 Armd Div will be established from H Hour at 133743 and will later move fwd to join Tac HQ 29 Armd Bde.

11. **H Hr** is the time at which the last bomb drops (this may be about 0815 hrs).

12. **WT.** Wrls silence until H—30.

13. **Line** from Main Div HQ to Main 8 Corps
    to HQ 29 Armd Bde
    to HQ 159 Inf Bde.

    ACK.

    Time of Signature : 1000 hrs.

    Lt col,
GS,
11 Armd Div.

Amendments issued as Amendment No. 1 to the above Operation Order dated 16 Jul 44.
1. Para 6(*b*). 29 Armd Bde will form up at H—2¼ hours.
2. Para 6(*c*). 151 Fd Regt will cross LONDON BR in rear of 22 Armd Bde. They will join "C" route at 081731.
3. Para 8. Delete "from 11 Armd Div to Gds Armd Div".

Appendix 'D'

(Note: Appendix "A" is the only Appendix to this Operation Order which has been reproduced.)

TOP SECRET

RA 8 CORPS OP ORDER No. 2

Copy No.

16 Jul 44

Op GOODWOOD

Ref Maps 1/25,000. Sheets 37/14 NE
37/16 SE
37/18 SE
40/14 NE & NW
40/16 SE & SW
40/16 NE & NW
40/18 SW

INFM

1. **Enemy**

    See latest int summaries.

2. **Army Plan**

    (a) Second Army is attacking in a southerly direction from the br hd EAST of CAEN with

    rt 2 Cdn Corps
    centre 8 Corps
    lt 1 Corps.

    (b) 2 Cdn Corps is attacking with 3 Cdn Div with the following object.

    (i) To clear the WEST bank of the R ORNE in the area FAUBOURG DE VAUCELLES 0466 and the village of GIBERVILLE 0868 and subsequently to exploit to the area ST ANDRE SUR ORNE 0261.

    (ii) To hold CAEN as a firm base for 8 Corps.

    (iii) To est a br over the ORNE at CAEN by 2359 hrs 18 Jul.

    (c) 1 Corps is attacking with 3 Br Div with the following object

    (i) To maintain a firm base for 8 Corps.

    (ii) To occupy the gen area TOUFFREVILLE 1368, SANNERVILLE 1368, BANNEVILLE LA CAMPAGNE 1367, EMIEVILLE 1369, to protect the lt flank of 8 Corps.

3. **8 Corps Plan**

    8 Corps consisting of Gds Armd Div

    7 Armd Div
    11 Armd Div
    8 AGRA
    11 H
    INNS OF COURT
    2 HCR.

is debouching from existing br bd EAST of R ORNE with a view to.

(a) Dominating the area BOURGUEBUS 0761, VIMONT 1461, BRETTEVILLE SUR LAIZE 0553.

(b) Destroying any enemy armour or other forces encountered en route to and in this area.

(c) If conditions are favourable subsequently exploiting to the SOUTH.

8 Corps is adv one up :—

> 11 Armd Div
> Gds Armd Div
> 7 Armd Div.

4. 11 Armd Div Plan

11 Armd Div is going

(a) At H hour to break out to the SOUTH between the boundaries of 8 Corps occupying the villages of CUVERVILLE 1069 and DEMOUVILLE 1067.

(b) To continue the adv crossing the rly in the area GRENTHEVILLE 0864–CAGNY 1164 and leaving one armd regt in this area until relieved by Gds Armd Div.

(c) To continue the adv and est itself firmly in the area incl BRAS 0663–incl ROCQUANCOURT 0558–excl FONTENAY LE MARMION 0358–incl BEAUVOIR FERME 0461.

5. Task of Gds Armd Div

Gds Armd Div is

(a) Moving to the area CAGNY where it will relieve the armd regt of 11 Armd Div.

(b) Continuing the adv and est a firm base in the area of VIMONT to protect lt flank of 8 Corps.

6. Task of 7 Armd Div

7 Armd Div is following Gds Armd Div with the object of

(a) Crossing the rly WEST of CAGNY.

(b) Moving in sp of 11 Armd Div if required.

(c) Subsequently moving to the area all incl LA HOGUE 0960–wooded area NORTH-EAST of SEQUEVILLE LA CAMPAGNE 0959–ST AIGNAN DE CRAMESNIL 0956–high ground 0756–GARCELLES SEQUEVILLE 0858.

7. Inter Corps Boundary

(a) *Between 2 Cdn Corps and 8 Corps*

Buildings and copses 090696–GIBERVILLE 0868–level crossing 093672 (all incl 2 Cdn Corps)–BRAS 0663 (excl 2 Cdn Corps)–church 026607–buildings 023603 (incl 2 Cdn 2 Corps).

(b) *Between 8 Corps and 1 Corps*

ESCOVILLE and church 1271–thence track SOUTH to level crossing 118673 (all incl 1 Corps)–X tracks 119664 (incl 8 Corps)–building 125657 (incl 1 Corps)–wood 135652 (excl 1 Corps)–river at 156652–thence line of river to JAUVILLE 1865 (all incl 1 Corps).

8. Start Line

Start line common to all three Corps :—

R ORNE at 097733–rd and track junc 104728–FERME DE LIEU HARAS 118723–rd junc 118721–corner of wood 126718–SOUTH edge of wood 129717.

9. Air

The adv of 8 Corps is receiving maximum air sp. The main features are as follows :—

(a) Attack by bombers on

  (i) Factory Area 0769.

  (ii) Area GIBERVILLE.

  (iii) Area TOUFFREVILLE–SANNERVILLE–BANNEVILLE–EMIEVILLE.

(b) The neutralisation by fragmentation bombs of the villages of CUVERVILLE and DEMOUVILLE.

(c) The neutralisation of enemy posns and killing by fragmentation bombs of enemy personnel in the path of the tk run through which 8 Corps debouches.

(d) The destruction of the village CAGNY.

(e) The neutralisation and damaging of enemy guns in the area BOURGUEBUS and TROARN.

10. **Additional Tps under Comd**

(a) The following additional tps will be under comd :
Two med regts 9 AGRA placed under comd 8 AGRA.

(b) For RA Order of Battle see Appendix A att.

11. **Additional Fire Support**

(a) The Corps Arty of 1 Corps and 2 Cdn Corps are co-operating in RA 8 Corps Fire Plan.

(b) The RN is co-operating in the Fire Plan under arrangements being made by RA 1 Corps.

(c) For Air sp see para 9 above.

12. **Forecast of Timings**

(a) The start of the op is dependent on the air programme.

The following times are given as a guide only :—

0630—0730 : Attack by heavies of Bomber Command.

0730—0815 : Attack by med bombers dropping fragmentation bombs.

0830—0930 : Attack by Fortresses on gun areas.

(b) Zero hr is the time when the last fragmentation bomb is dropped by the med bombers: if these times hold, H hr will therefore be 0815 hrs.

(c) In view of the attack by the Fortresses on hostile btys in the area BOURGUEBUS between 0830 and 0930, 11 Armd Div will NOT cross the rly before 0930 hrs.

(d) It is hoped that the actual time of H hr will be known by the evening of 16 Jul.

INTENTION

13. 8 Corps Arty will sp the attack of 8 Corps.

METHOD

14. **Allotment and Control**

The sp for the attack will be in 5 Phases for each of which the allotment of arty will be different.

The allotment will be as follows :—

(a) *Phase I*

Before H-100 depending on the time when hy bombing begins such available arty as is required will fire CB anti flak (APPLEPIE) on a programme to be prepared by RA 1 Corps.

(b) *Phase II*

H—100 TO H—10

(i) CB on a programme to be prepared by 1 Corps to be fired by RN and the following regts controlled by 4 AGRA :—

1 Corps	2 Cdn Corps	8 Corps
3 Br Div Arty Gp	3 Cdn Div	Gds Armd Div
7 Fd Regt	12 Cdn Fd Regt	55 Fd Regt
33 Fd Regt	13 Cdn Fd Regt	7 Armd Div
76 Fd Regt	14 Cdn Fd Regt	3 RHA
128 Fd Regt	19 Cdn Fd Regt	

1 Corps	2 Cdn Corps	8 Corps
51 Div Arty Gp	2 Cdn AGRA	8 AGRA
126 Fd Regt	3 Cdn Med Regt	25 Fd Regt
127 Fd Regt	4 Cdn Med Regt	61 Med Regt
150 Fd Regt	7 Cdn Med Regt	63 Med Regt
191 Fd Regt	15 Med Regt	77 Med Regt
4 AGRA	1 Hy Regt	107 Med Regt
53 Med Regt		146 Med Regt
65 Med Regt		53 Hy Regt
68 Med Regt		165 HAA Regt
79 Med Regt		
51 Hy Regt		
107 HAA Regt		

(c) *Phase III*

H TO H+80

11 Armd Div adv from SL to line of rly CAEN–CAGNY–VIMONT.

(i) Under comd 11 Armd Div 13 RHA
                                 151 Fd Regt.

(ii) CB continued on a programme being prepared by 1 Corps to be fired by RN, RAF fighter bombers and the following regts grouped under 4 AGRA :—

1 Corps	8 Corps
4 AGRA	8 AGRA
68 Med Regt	146 Med Regt
107 HAA Regt	

(iii) Barrage and concs in sp of 11 Armd Div

1 Corps	2 Cdn Corps	8 Corps
51 Div Arty Gp	2 Cdn AGRA	Gds Armd Div
126 Fd Regt *	Two med regts	153 Fd Regt **
127 Fd Regt	1 Hy Regt	55 Fd Regt **
150 Fd Regt *		7 Armd Div
191 Fd Regt *		3 RHA **
4 AGRA		5 RHA **
Two 155 Btys		11 Armd Div
(51 Hy Regt)		151 Fd Regt
		8 AGRA
		25 Fd Regt **
		61 Med Regt
		63 Med Regt
		77 Med Regt
		107 Med Regt
		53 Hy Regt
		165 HAA Regt

All regts mentioned above not firing on barrages will fire timed concs controlled by 8 AGRA.

Note :—All regts marked ** will be firing on barrages and will be grouped under RA 7 Armd Div.

All regts marked * above will be firing on barrages and will be grouped under RA 51 Div.

(iv) Regts in sp 3 Cdn Div

    2 Cdn Corps

  3 Cdn Div
    12 Cdn Fd Regt
    13 Cdn Fd Regt
    14 Cdn Fd Regt
    19 Cdn Fd Regt
  2 Cdn AGRA
    Two med regts.

(v) Regts in sp 3 Br Div

    1 Corps

3 Br Div Arty Gp
  7 Fd Regt
  33 Fd Regt
  76 Fd Regt
  128 Fd Regt
4 AGRA
  53 Med Regt
  65 Med Regt
  79 Med Regt
  Two 7.2 btys 51 Hy Regt

    3 Br Div are being made responsible for engaging tgts on the lt flank of 11 Armd Div attack from excl lt hand lane of 11 Armd Div first barrage.

(d) *Phase IV*

    H+80 TO H+200

    Adv of 11 Armd Div from line of rly CAEN–VIMONT to BOURGUEBUS 0761 and adv of Gds Armd Div in rear of 11 Armd Div :—

(i) Under comd 11 Armd Div :   13 RHA
                               151 Fd Regt

Under comd Gds Armd Div : 153 Fd Regt
                               55 Fd Regt

(ii) CB continued on a programme being prepared by 1 Corps to be fired by the RN and by regts grouped under 4 AGRA as follows :—

1 Corps	*2 Cdn Corps*	*8 Corps*
51 Div Arty Gp	2 Cdn AGRA	7 Armd Div
126 Fd Regt	Two Med Regts *	3 RHA
127 Fd Regt	1 Hy Regt	5 RHA
150 Fd Regt		8 AGRA
191 Fd Regt		107 Med Regt
4 AGRA		165 HAA Regt
68 Med Regt		
79 Med Regt		
107 HAA Regt		

    * These two med regts will also be available for observed shooting in the area SOUTH of CAEN.

(iii) Concs in sp of the armour—all regts grouped under 8 AGRA on call from 11 Armd Div.

    8 Corps

8 AGRA
  25 Fd Regt
  61 Med Regt
  63 Med Regt **
  77 Med Regt **
  146 Med Regt
  53 Hy Regt

    ** 63 and 77 Med Regts will be superimposed and at call for Gds Armd and 11 Armd Divs respectively.

(iv) Regts in sp of 3 Cdn Div

    2 Cdn Corps
   3 Cdn Div
    12 Cdn Fd Regt
    13 Cdn Fd Regt
    14 Cdn Fd Regt
    19 Cdn Fd Regt
   2 Cdn AGRA
    Two med regts

(v) Regts in sp of 3 Br Div

   1 Corps
  3 Br Div Arty Gp
   7 Fd Regt
   33 Fd Regt
   76 Fd Regt
   128 Fd Regt
  4 AGRA
   53 Med Regt
   65 Med Regt
   Two 7.2 btys 51 Hy Regt

(e) *Phase V*

 H + 200 ONWARDS

 Adv to objective of Gds and 11 Armd Divs.

(i) Under comd 11 Armd Div :   13 RHA
            151 Fd Regt
Under comd Gds Armd Div : 153 Fd Regt
            55 Fd Regt
In sp of Gds Armd Div   Two 155 btys 51 Hy Regt
Under comd 7 Armd Div :   3 RHA
            5 RHA

(ii) CB continued on a programme being prepared by 1 Corps to be fired by RN and the following Regts grouped under 4 AGRA :—

1 Corps	*2 Cdn corps*	*8 Corps*
51 Div Arty Gp	2 Cdn AGRA	8 AGRA
126 Fd Regt	Three Med Regts *	165 HAA Regt
127 Fd Regt	1 Hy Regt	
150 Fd Regt		
191 Fd Regt		
4 AGRA		
68 Med Regt		
79 Med Regt		
107 HAA Regt		

 * Two med regts will be available for observed shooting in the area SOUTH of CAEN.

(iii) Concs in sp of the armour :   All regts grouped under 8 AGRA on call from 11 Armd and Gds Armd Divs.

                   8 Corps
                   8 AGRA
                   25 Fd Regt

**61, 63 and 77 Med Regts to be superimposed   61 Med Regt **
and at direct call for 7 Armd, Gds Armd and   63 Med Regt **
11 Armd Divs respectively.   77 Med Regt **
                   107 Med Regt
                   146 Med Regt
                   53 Hy Regt

(iv) Regts in sp of 3 Cdn Div

2 Cdn Corps

3 Cdn Div
  12 Cdn Fd Regt
  13 Cdn Fd Regt
  14 Cdn Fd Regt
  19 Cdn Fd Regt
2 Cdn AGRA
  One med regt

(v) Regts in sp 3 Br Div

1 Corps

3 Br Div Arty Gp
  7 Fd Regt
  33 Fd Regt
  76 Fd Regt
  128 Fd Regt
4 AGRA
  53 Med Regt
  65 Med Regt
  Two 7.2 btys 51 Hy Regt

15. Preliminary Moves

(a) Regts of div artys will move into action in the areas already recced under orders of divs.

(b) 8 AGRA will come out of action after 1200 hrs 17 Jul and lie up in the area ST CROIX GRANDE TONNE 8874. It will move again after 1900 hrs into action in the area FRANQUEVILLE 9770–GALMANCHE 0073–ST CONTEST 0072 in the posns already recced under orders Q(Mov) 8 Corps. Move to be completed by 2300 hrs 17 Jul.

A minimum number of vehs will be taken except for 63 and 77 Med Regts who may later be required to go fwd with Gds and 11 Armd Divs respectively.

16. OPs and Reps

(a) 2 Cdn Corps are being made responsible for observed shooting SOUTH of CAEN.

(b) Arrangements for reps to and from divs and 8 AGRA will be made by comd 8 AGRA.

17. Gun Areas

Regts will occupy gun areas as already allotted by 1 Corps and 2 Cdn Corps.

18. Registration

There will be no registration except by regts of 1 Corps and 2 Cdn Corps which are already in posn and then registration is to be reduced to an absolute minimum and is to be made to represent HF.

19. Occupation of Posns

Gun posns EAST of the R ORNE and those in view of the enemy will be only occupied by night.

20. Svy

(a) 10 Svy Regt will co-operate with 9 Svy Regt and arrange for all guns to be put on the Army Grid.

(b) 9 Svy Regt report centres

  (i) For regts WEST of R ORNE : BEUVILLE CHURCH 061749.

  (ii) For regts EAST of R ORNE   X rds LE MARIQUET 121732.

(c) During the attack det 10 Svy Regt (1 half track) will be in sp each armd div.

(d) 10 Svy Regt less dets will remain in Corps res in present location. CO, IO and one Svy Tp Comd will remain at Corps HQ.

21. Tasks

(a) *Fire Plan*

    (i) The Fire Plan for the sp of 3 Br Div is being made and issued by RA 1 Corps to the regts allotted in para 14 above.

    (ii) The Fire Plan for the sp of 3 Cdn Div is being made and issued by RA 2 Cdn Corps to the regts allotted in para 14 above.

    (iii) The Fire Plan for the sp of 8 Corps will be issued separately as a trace. This trace will also incl the outline fire plan of 3 Br and 3 Cdn Divs for infm.

(b) *CB*

    (i) 1 Corps is being made responsible for CB.

    (ii) CB task tables are being issued as follows :—

        By RA 1 Corps to RA Gds Armd Div RA 7 Armd Div and 8 AGRA.

        By RA 2 Cdn Corps to 8 AGRA.

    (iii) LOs from the above fmns will report to RA 1 Corps and RA 2 Cdn Corps at 1000 hrs 17 Jul to collect task tables.

22. Fwd Moves

When armd divs have reached their objective the positioning of 8 AGRA in the area CAGNY 1164 and NORTH of the rly CAEN–VIMONT would suit the Corps plan with rt 77 Med centre 61 Med and lt 63 Med Regts. The exact siting of these med regts will be decided by CRAs of armd divs.

As soon as possible after the southern half of CAEN has been cleared of the enemy it is the intention to move fwd the remainder of 8 AGRA as far SOUTH as possible but NW of the R ORNE. Fwd posns should be recced as soon as possible and arrangements made with 2 Cdn Corps for those posns to be reserved.

23. A Tk

91 A Tk Regt will remain in Corps res and move into the area 0877–0977. Detailed orders for the move will be issued later.

24. LAA

121 LAA Regt is placed under comd 8 AGRA wef 1200 hrs 17 Jul.

25. Air OP

(a) C Flt 658 Air OP Sqn will revert to under comd 659 Air OP Sqn wef 1200 hrs 17 Jul.

(b) Flts of 659 Air OP Sqn are placed in sp of fmns as follows :—

    A Flt   11 Armd Div

    B Flt   Gds Armd Div

    C Flt   7 Armd Div

    C Flt 658 Air CP Sqn 8 AGRA

26. CBO

CBO will remain in res in the area of Corps HQ.

27. Met

8 Corps Met Sec will issue a meteor for the opening stages of 8 Corps attack to fmns of 8 Corps only. Div and AGRA met secs will issue meteors for all subsequent periods.

ADM

28. Amn

(a) *Allotment*

    The following amounts of amn have been allotted :—

        Fd   500 rpg

        Med   300 rpg

        Hy   150 rpg

(b) *Dumping*

The following amounts are being dumped :—

11 Armd and Gds Armd Divs	350 rpg Fd
7 Armd Div and 8 AGRA	400 rpg Fd
8 AGRA	250 rpg med & 150 rpg hy

INTERCOMN

29. **Locations**

RA 8 Corps	992803
HQ 8 AGRA	978736
RA Sig Centre	023752
HQ RA Gds Armd Div	089761
HQ RA 11 Armd Div	114745
HQ RA 7 Armd Div	022792
RA 1 Corps	015804
RA 3 Br Div	100736
HQ 4 AGRA	036770
RA 2 Cdn Corps	966743
HQ RA 3 Cdn Div	VILLONS LES BUISSONS 0075
HQ 2 Cdn AGRA	975738

30. **Wireless Silence**

HQ 8 Corps and 8 Corps Tps will continue to observe wireless silence until H—30 minutes.

31. **Code Names**

See appendix "B" to 8 Corps Op Instr No. 4 att.

32. **Synchronisation**

BBC time.

33. Ack.

Major. GS.

Time of Signature : 2145 hrs.

NB. Ref para 12(b). H Hour is forecast as 0815 hrs. This was subsequently advanced to 0745 hrs.

Appendix "A" to RA 8 Corps
Op Order No. 2

GOODWOOD MEETING

RA ORDER OF BATTLE

	25 pr SP	25 pr	105 mm	5.5	7.2	155 mm	3.7
8 Corps							
Gds Armd Div							
153 Fd Regt	24						
55 Fd Regt		24					
7 Armd Div							
3 RHA		24					
5 RHA	24						
11 Armd Div							
13 RHA	24						
151 Fd Regt		24					
8 AGRA							
25 Fd Regt		24					
61 Med Regt				16			
63 Med Regt				16			
77 Med Regt				16			
107 Med Regt				16			
146 Med Regt				16			
53 Hy Regt					8	8	
165 HAA Regt							24
1 Corps							
3 Br Div							
7 Fd Regt			24				
33 Fd Regt			24				
76 Fd Regt			24				
51 Div							
126 Fd Regt		24					
127 Fd Regt		24					
128 Fd Regt		24					
4 AGRA							
150 Fd Regt		24					
191 Fd Regt		24					
53 Med Regt				16			
65 Med Regt				16			
68 Med Regt				16			
79 Med Regt				16			
51 Hy Regt					8	8	
107 HAA Regt							24

	25 pr SP	25 pr	105 mm	5.5	7.2	155 mm	3.7
2 Cdn Corps							
3 Cdn Div							
12 Cdn Fd Regt			24				
13 Cdn Fd Regt			24				
14 Cdn Fd Regt			24				
19 Cdn Fd Regt			24				
2 Cdn AGRA							
3 Cdn Med Regt				16			
4 Cdn Med Regt				16			
7 Cdn Med Regt				16			
15 Br Med Regt				16			
1 Hy Regt					8	8	
TOTAL	72	216	168	208	24	24	48

TOTAL

19 Fd Regts	=	456 guns
13 Med Regts	=	208 guns
2 HAA Regts	=	48 guns
3 Hy Regts	=	48 guns
Total	=	760 guns

OPERATION GOODWOOD
18-21 JULY 1944

OPERATION GOODWOOD
18-21 JULY 1944
OPERATION GOODWOOD
18-21 JULY 1944
Spread 1
OPERATION GOODWOOD
18-21 JULY 1944
Spread 2
OPERATION GOODWOOD
18-21 JULY 1944
Spread 3
OPERATION GOODWOOD
18-21 JULY 1944
Spread 4

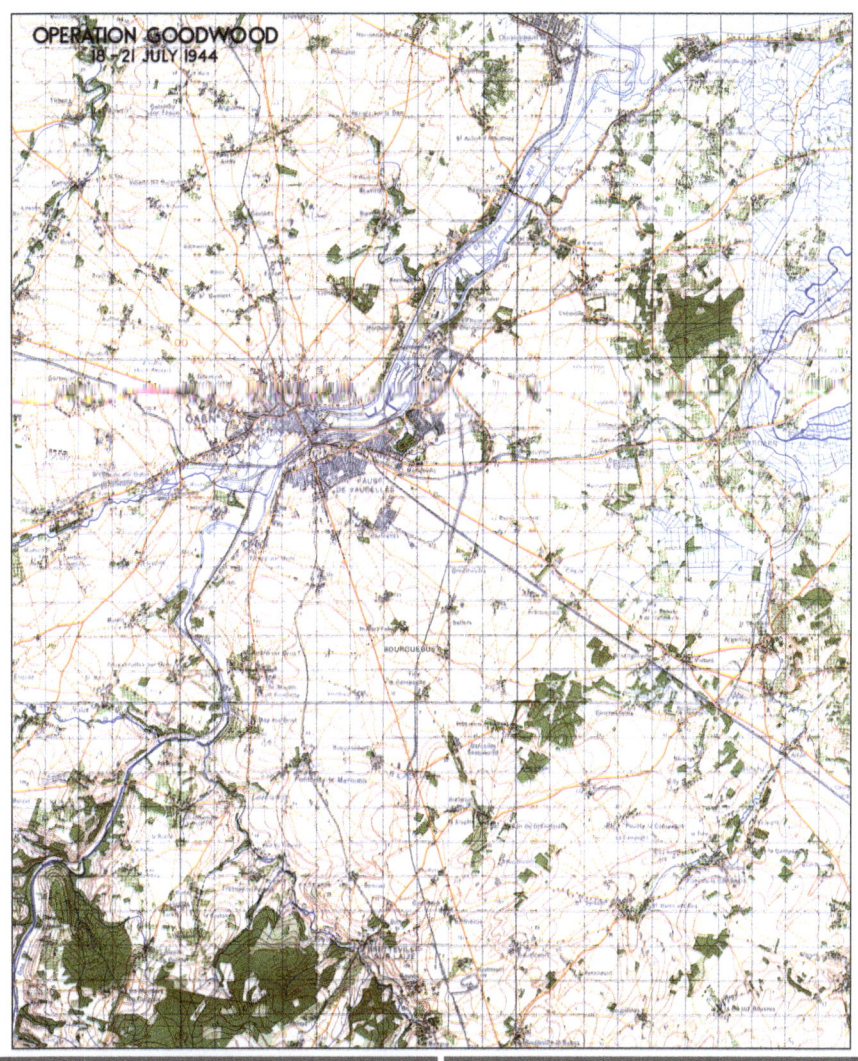

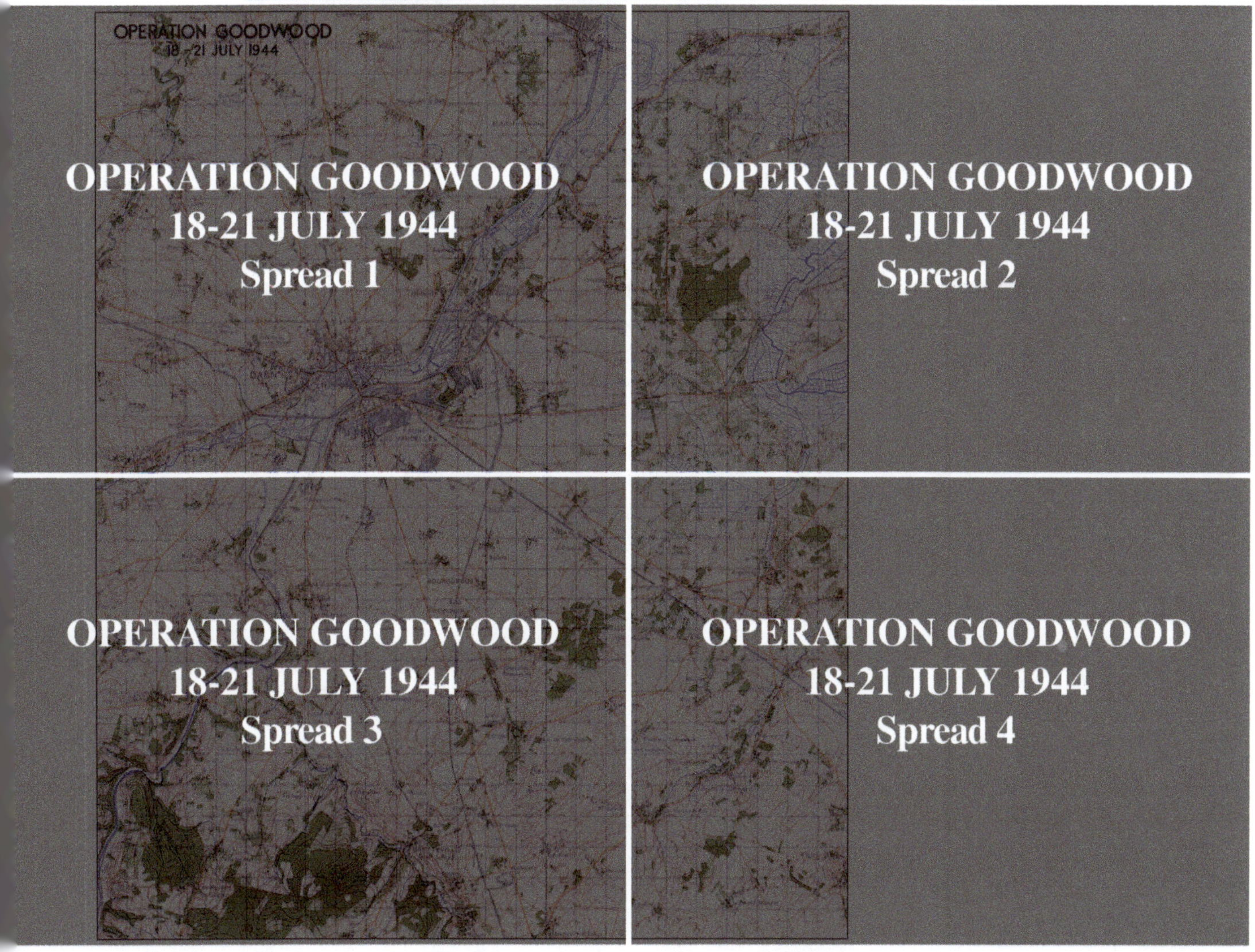

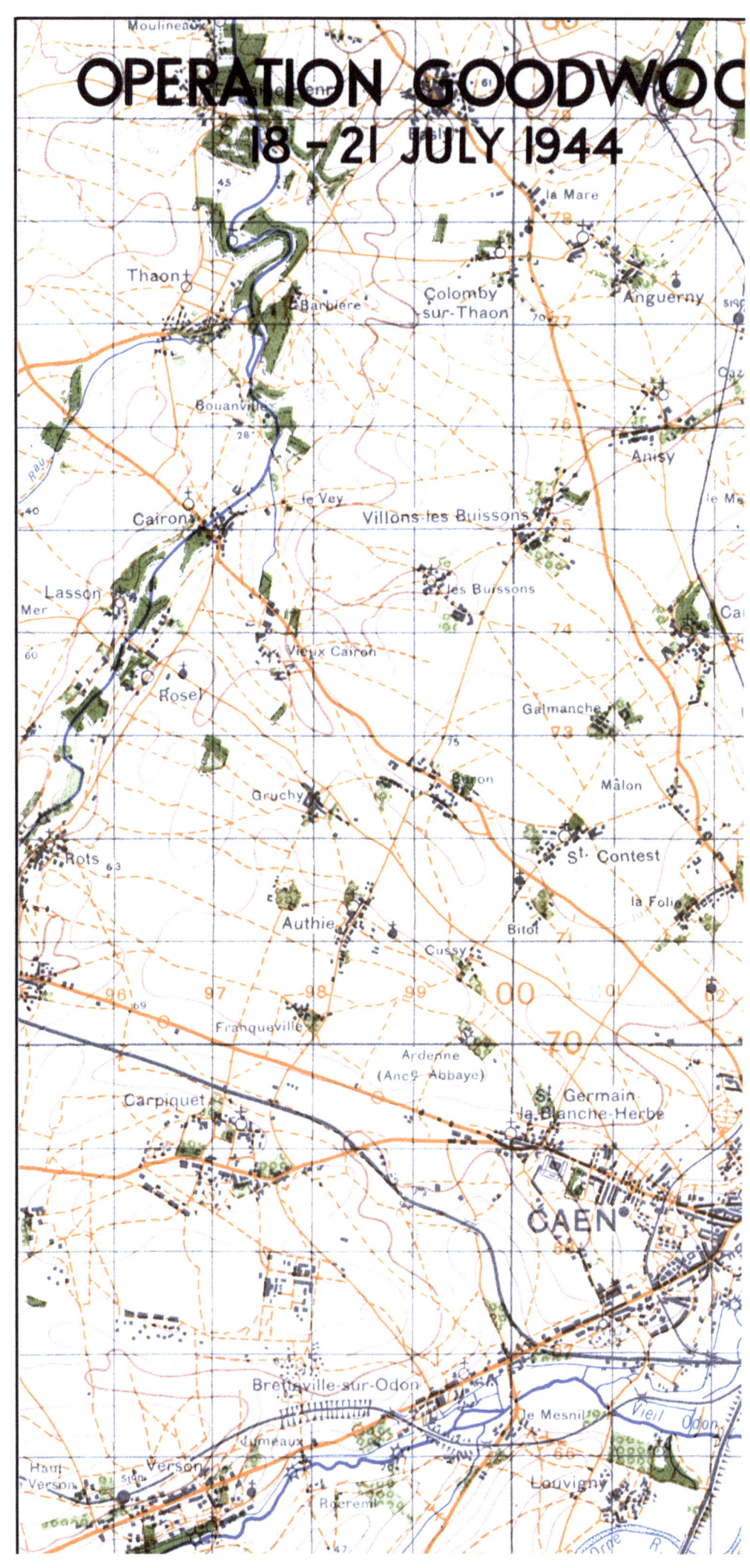

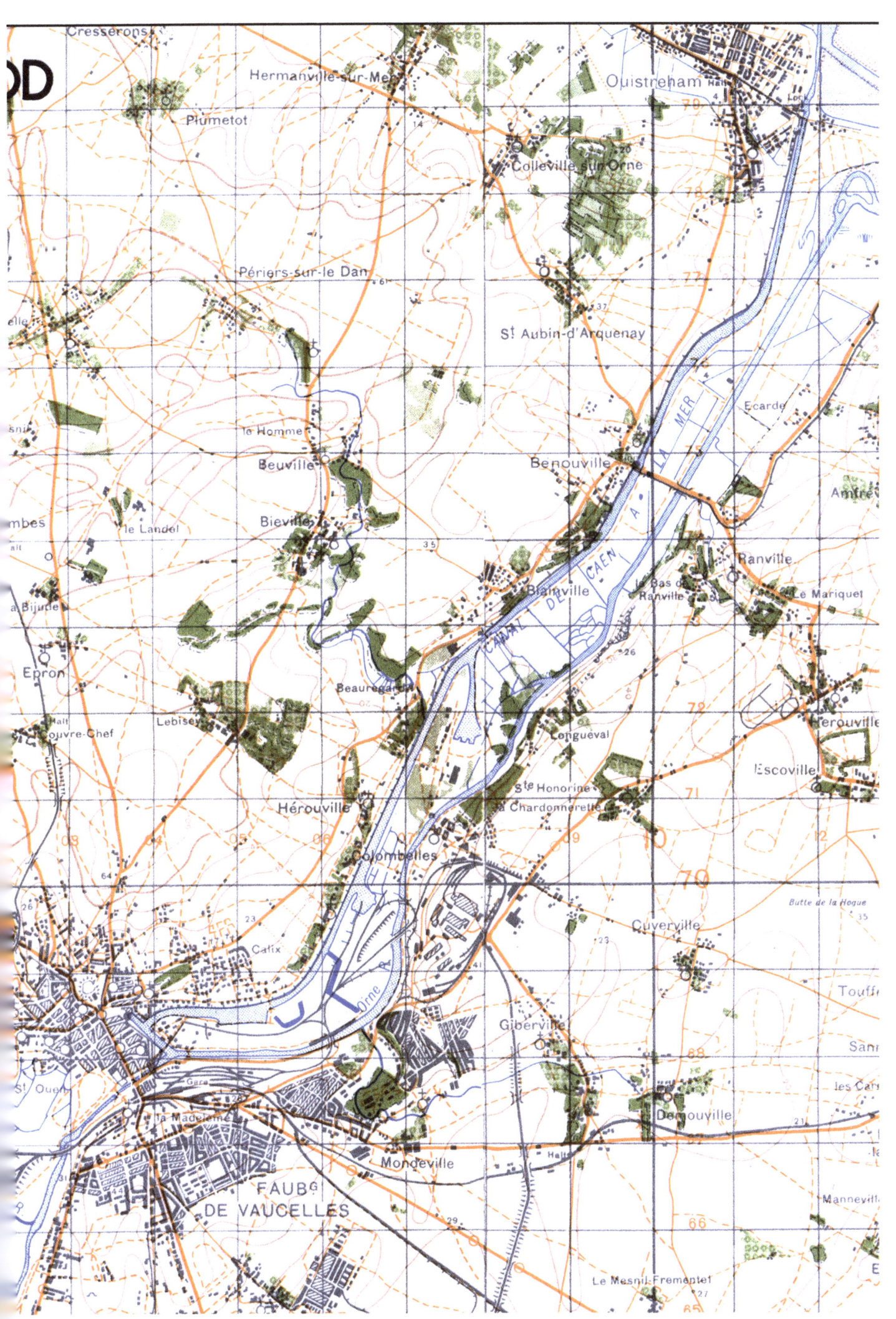

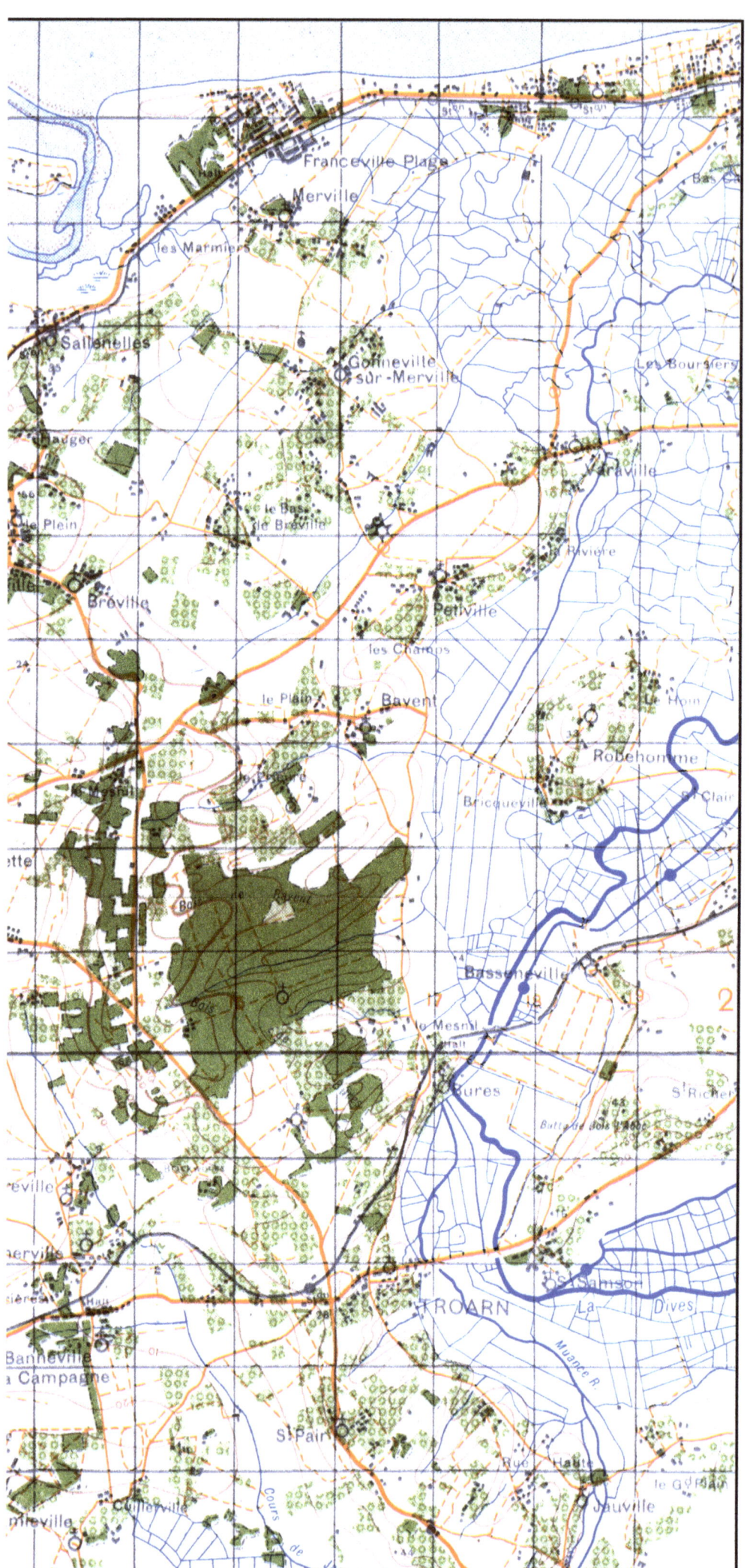

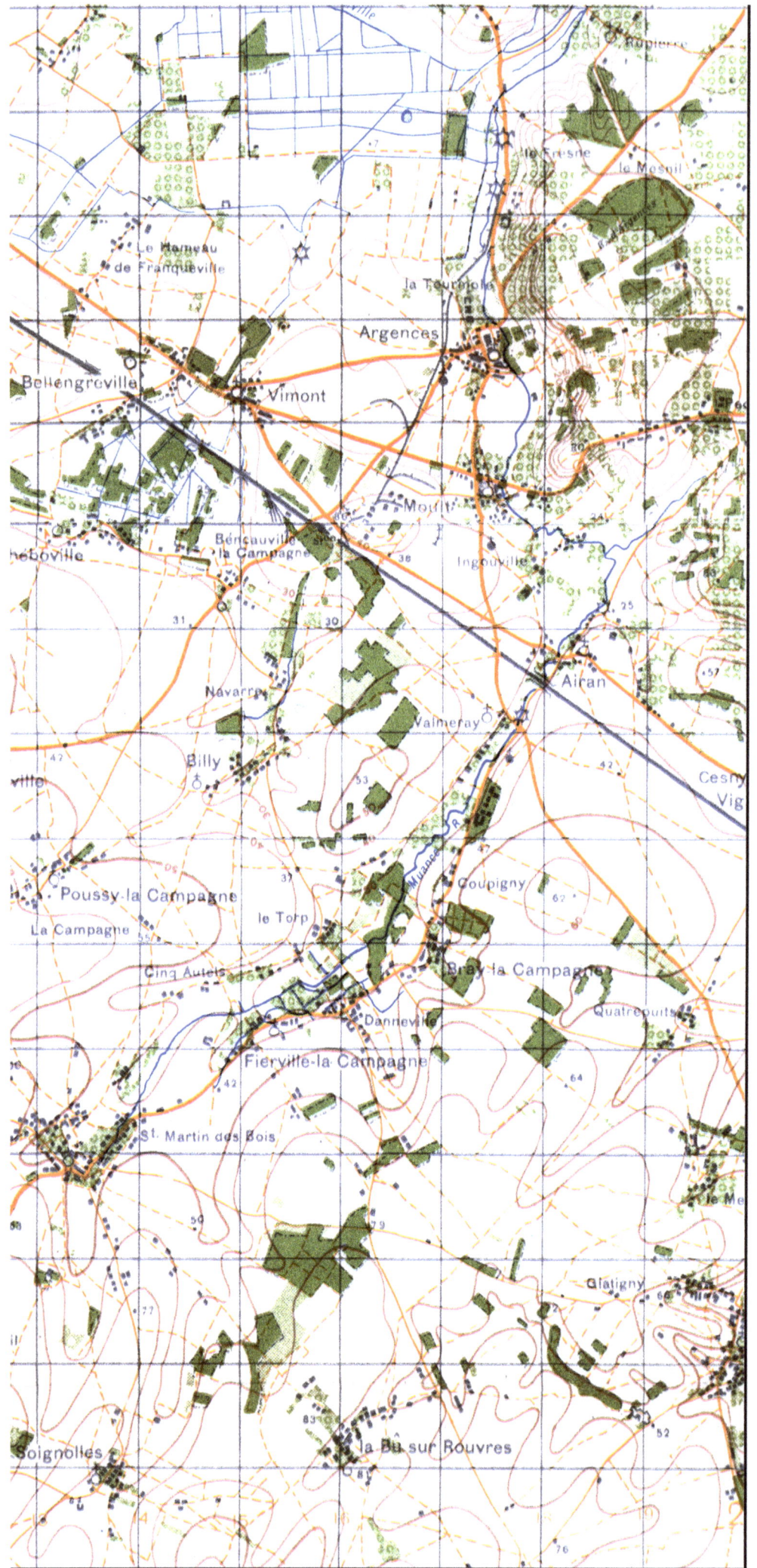

BAOR
BATTLEFIELD TOUR GUIDES

You don't get much better than this for first-hand information from the officers who commanded the formations and units carrying out these operations, these collected before time had blurred their memories of events

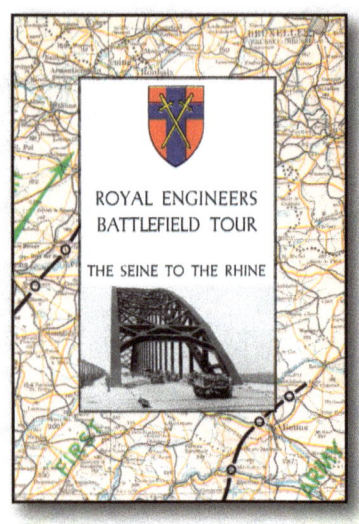

BAOR ROYAL ENGINEERS BATTLEFIELD TOUR
THE SEINE TO THE RHINE

Vol. 1 – An account of the operations included in the tour
Vol. 2 – A guide to the conduct of the tour

SB: 9781783316717
HB: 9781783317714

BAOR ROYAL ENGINEERS BATTLEFIELD TOUR
NORMANDY TO THE SEINE

SB: 9781783317516
HB: 9781783317813

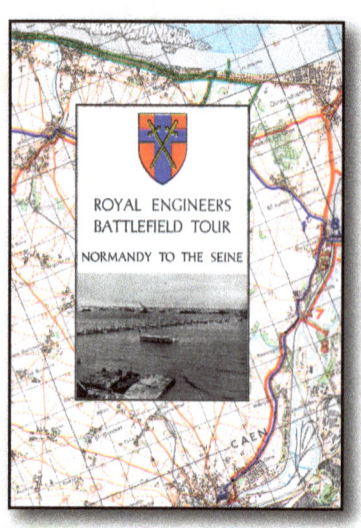

BAOR BATTLEFIELD TOUR
OPERATION BLUECOAT
– Directing Staff Edition

SB: 9781783318124
HB: 9781783318438

BAOR BATTLEFIELD TOUR
OPERATION VERITABLE
– Directing Staff Edition

SB: 9781783318131
HB: 9781783318421

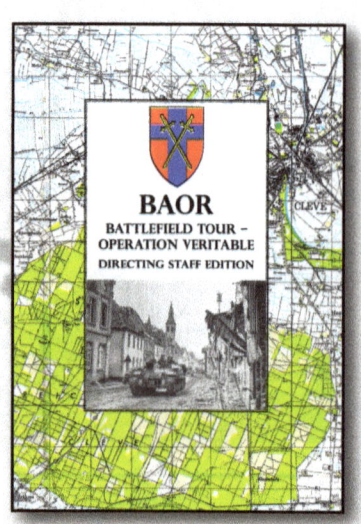